FEMINIST INTERPRETATIONS OF MARY ASTELL

RE-READING THE CANON

NANCY TUANA, GENERAL EDITOR

This series consists of edited collections of essays, some original and some previously published, offering feminist re-interpretations of the writings of major figures in the Western philosophical tradition. Devoted to the work of a single philosopher, each volume contains essays covering the full range of the philosopher's thought and representing the diversity of approaches now being used by feminist critics.

Already published:

Nancy Tuana, ed., *Feminist Interpretations of Plato* (1994)

Margaret Simons, ed., *Feminist Interpretations of Simone de Beauvoir* (1995)

Bonnie Honig, ed., *Feminist Interpretations of Hannah Arendt* (1995)

Patricia Jagentowicz Mills, ed., *Feminist Interpretations of G. W. F. Hegel* (1996)

Maria J. Falco, ed., *Feminist Interpretations of Mary Wollstonecraft* (1996)

Susan Hekman, ed., *Feminist Interpretations of Michel Foucault* (1996)

Nancy Holland, ed., *Feminist Interpretations of Jacques Derrida* (1997)

Robin May Schott, ed., *Feminist Interpretations of Immanuel Kant* (1997)

Céline Léon and Sylvia Walsh, eds., *Feminist Interpretations of Soren Kierkegaard* (1997)

Cynthia Freeland, ed., *Feminist Interpretations of Aristotle* (1998)

Kelly Oliver and Marilyn Pearsall, eds., *Feminist Interpretations of Friedrich Nietzsche* (1998)

Mimi Reisel Gladstein and Chris Matthew Sciabarra, eds., *Feminist Interpretations of Ayn Rand* (1999)

Susan Bordo, ed., *Feminist Interpretations of René Descartes* (1999)

Julien S. Murphy, ed., *Feminist Interpretations of Jean-Paul Sartre* (1999)

Anne Jaap Jacobson, ed., *Feminist Interpretations of David Hume* (2000)

Sarah Lucia Hoagland and Marilyn Frye, eds., *Feminist Interpretations of Mary Daly* (2000)

Tina Chanter, ed., *Feminist Interpretations of Emmanuel Levinas* (2001)

Nancy J. Holland and Patricia Huntington, eds., *Feminist Interpretations of Martin Heidegger* (2001)

Charlene Haddock Seigfried, ed., *Feminist Interpretations of John Dewey* (2001)

Naomi Scheman and Peg O'Connor, eds., *Feminist Interpretations of Ludwig Wittgenstein* (2002)

Lynda Lange, ed., *Feminist Interpretations of Jean-Jacques Rousseau* (2002)

Lorraine Code, ed., *Feminist Interpretations of Hans-Georg Gadamer* (2002)

Lynn Hankinson Nelson and Jack Nelson, eds., *Feminist Interpretations of W. V. Quine* (2003)

Maria J. Falco, ed., *Feminist Interpretations of Niccolò Machiavelli* (2004)

Renée J. Heberle, ed., *Feminist Interpretations of Theodor Adorno* (2006)

Dorothea Olkowski and Gail Weiss, eds., *Feminist Interpretations of Maurice Merleau-Ponty* (2006)

Nancy J. Hirschmann and Kirstie M. McClure, eds., *Feminist Interpretations of John Locke* (2007)

Penny A. Weiss and Loretta Kensinger, eds., *Feminist Interpretations of Emma Goldman* (2007)

Judith Chelius Stark, ed., *Feminist Interpretations of Augustine* (2007)

Jill Locke and Eileen Hunt Botting, eds., *Feminist Interpretations of Alexis de Tocqueville* (2008)

Moira Gatens, ed., *Feminist Interpretations of Benedict Spinoza* (2009)

Marianne Janack, ed., *Feminist Interpretations of Richard Rorty* (2010)

Maurice Hamington, ed., *Feminist Interpretations of Jane Addams* (2010)

Nancy J. Hirschmann and Joanne Wright, eds., *Feminist Interpretations of Thomas Hobbes* (2012)

Erin C. Tarver and Shannon Sullivan, eds., *Feminist Interpretations of William James* (2015)

FEMINIST INTERPRETATIONS OF MARY ASTELL

EDITED BY
ALICE SOWAAL
AND
PENNY A. WEISS

THE PENNSYLVANIA STATE UNIVERSITY PRESS
UNIVERSITY PARK, PENNSYLVANIA

Library of Congress Cataloging-in-Publication Data

Names: Sowaal, Alice, 1969– , editor. | Weiss, Penny A., editor.
Title: Feminist interpretations of Mary Astell / edited by Alice Sowaal and
    Penny A. Weiss ; preface, Nancy Tuana.
Other titles: Re-reading the canon.
Description: University Park, Pennsylvania : The Pennsylvania State University Press,
    [2016] | Series: Re-reading the canon | Includes bibliographical references and index.
Summary: "A collection of essays on the early modern English writer, proto-feminist,
    and rhetorician Mary Astell. Includes discussions on human nature, equality, rationality,
    power, freedom, friendship, marriage, and education"—Provided by publisher.
Identifiers: LCCN 2016008738| ISBN 9780271071244 (cloth : alk. paper) |
    ISBN 9780271071251 (pbk. : alk. paper)
Subjects: LCSH: Astell, Mary, 1668–1731. | Feminist theory.
Classification: LCC HQ1595.A7 F46 2016 | DDC 305.4201—dc23
LC record available at http://lccn.loc.gov/2016008738

Copyright © 2016 The Pennsylvania State University
All rights reserved
Printed in the United States of America
Published by The Pennsylvania State University Press,
University Park, PA 16802–1003

The Pennsylvania State University Press is a member of the Association of
American University Presses.

It is the policy of The Pennsylvania State University Press to use acid-free paper.
Publications on uncoated stock satisfy the minimum requirements of American National
Standard for Information Sciences—Permanence of Paper for Printed Library Material,
ANSI Z39.48–1992.

From Alice:
To women philosophers of the past, present, and future.

From Penny:
To the Weiswerdas, always.

Contents

Preface   vii
  Nancy Tuana

Acknowledgments   xi

1   Locations and Legacies: Reading Mary Astell and
Re-Reading the Canon   1
  Penny A. Weiss

2   Mary Astell and the Virtues   16
  Jacqueline Broad

3   Mary Astell's Account of Feminine Self-Esteem   35
  Kathleen A. Ahearn

4   Mary Astell and the Development of Vice: Pride,
Courtship, and the Woman's Human Nature Question   57
  Alice Sowaal

5   Custom, Freedom, and Equality: Mary Astell on Marriage
and Women's Education   74
  Karen Detlefsen

6   Further Reflections upon Marriage: Mary Astell and
Sarah Chapone   93
  Susan Paterson Glover

7   Mary Astell: Some Reflections upon Trauma   111
  Elisabeth Hedrick Moser

viii   Contents

8 "From the Throne to Every Private Family":
   Mary Astell as Analyst of Power   128
   Penny A. Weiss

9 Mary Astell's Feminism: A Rhetorical Perspective   153
   Christine Mason Sutherland

10 Mary Astell on the Existence and Nature of God   168
   Marcy P. Lascano

11 The Emerging Picture of Mary Astell's Views   188
   Alice Sowaal

   References   207

   List of Contributors   219

   Index   221

Preface

Nancy Tuana

Take into your hands any history of philosophy text. You will find compiled therein the "classics" of modern philosophy. Since these texts are often designed for use in undergraduate classes, the editor is likely to offer an introduction in which the reader is informed that these selections represent the perennial questions of philosophy. The student is to assume that she or he is about to explore the timeless wisdom of the greatest minds of Western philosophy. No one calls attention to the fact that the philosophers are all men.

Though women are omitted from the canons of philosophy, these texts inscribe the nature of woman. Sometimes the philosopher speaks directly about woman, delineating her proper role, her abilities and inabilities, her desires. Other times the message is indirect—a passing remark hinting at women's emotionality, irrationality, unreliability.

This process of definition occurs in far more subtle ways when the central concepts of philosophy—reason and justice, those characteristics that are taken to define us as human—are associated with traits historically identified with masculinity. If the "man" of reason must learn to control or overcome traits identified as feminine—the body, the emotions, the passions—then the realm of rationality will be one reserved primarily for men,[1] with grudging entrance to those few women who are capable of transcending their femininity.

Feminist philosophers have begun to look critically at the canonized texts of philosophy and have concluded that the discourses of philosophy are not gender-neutral. Philosophical narratives do not offer a universal perspective, but rather privilege some experiences and beliefs over others. These experiences and beliefs permeate all philosophical theories whether they be aesthetic or epistemological, moral or metaphysical. Yet this fact has often been neglected by those studying the traditions of philosophy.

x   Preface

Given the history of canon formation in Western philosophy, the perspective most likely to be privileged is that of upper-class white males. Thus, to be fully aware of the impact of gender biases, it is imperative that we reread the canon with attention to the ways in which philosophers' assumptions concerning gender are embedded within their theories.

This series, Re-Reading the Canon, is designed to foster this process of reevaluation. Each volume will offer feminist analyses of the theories of a selected philosopher. Since feminist philosophy is not monolithic in method or content, the essays are also selected to illustrate the variety of perspectives within feminist criticism and highlight some of the controversies within feminist scholarship.

In this series, feminist lenses focus on the canonical texts of Western philosophy, both those authors who have been part of the traditional canon, and those philosophers whose writings have more recently gained attention within the philosophical community. A glance at the list of volumes in the series reveals an immediate gender bias of the canon: Arendt, Aristotle, Beauvoir, Derrida, Descartes, Foucault, Hegel, Hume, Kant, Locke, Marx, Mill, Nietzsche, Plato, Rousseau, Wittgenstein, Wollstonecraft. There are all too few women included, and those few who do appear have been added only recently. In creating this series, it is not my intention to rectify the current canon of philosophical thought. What is and is not included within the canon during a particular historical period is a result of many factors. Although no canonization of texts will include all philosophers, no canonization of texts that excludes all but a few women can offer an accurate representation of the history of the discipline, as women have been philosophers since the ancient period.[2]

I share with many feminist philosophers and other philosophers writing from the margins of philosophy the concern that the current canonization of philosophy be transformed. Although I do not accept the position that the current canon has been formed exclusively by power relations, I do believe that this canon represents only a selective history of the tradition. I share the view of Michael Bérubé that "canons are at once the location, the index, and the record of the struggle for cultural representation; like any other hegemonic formation, they must be continually reproduced anew and are continually contested."[3]

The process of canon transformation will require the recovery of "lost" texts and a careful examination of the reasons such voices have been silenced. Along with the process of uncovering women's philosophical history, we must also begin to analyze the impact of gender ideologies upon the process of canonization. This process of recovery and examination

Preface   xi

must occur in conjunction with careful attention to the concept of a canon of authorized texts. Are we to dispense with the notion of a tradition of excellence embodied in a canon of authorized texts? Or, rather than abandon the whole idea of a canon, do we instead encourage a reconstruction of a canon of those texts that inform a common culture?

This series is designed to contribute to this process of canon transformation by offering a re-reading of the current philosophical canon. Such a re-reading shifts our attention to the ways in which woman and the role of the feminine are constructed within the texts of philosophy. A question we must keep in front of us during this process of re-reading is whether a philosopher's socially inherited prejudices concerning woman's nature and role are independent of her or his larger philosophical framework. In asking this question attention must be paid to the ways in which the definitions of central philosophical concepts implicitly include or exclude gendered traits.

This type of reading strategy is not limited to the canon, but can be applied to all texts. It is my desire that this series reveal the importance of this type of critical reading. Paying attention to the workings of gender within the texts of philosophy will make visible the complexities of the inscription of gender ideologies.

Notes

1. More properly, it is a realm reserved for a group of privileged males, since the texts also inscribe race and class biases that thereby omit certain males from participation.

2. Mary Ellen Waithe's multivolume series, *A History of Women Philosophers* (Boston: M. Nijhoff, 1987), attests to this presence of women.

3. Michael Bérubé, *Marginal Forces/Cultural Centers: Tolson, Pynchon, and the Politics of the Canon* (Ithaca: Cornell University Press, 1992), 4–5.

Acknowledgments

From Alice: I am extremely grateful to San Francisco State University for providing me with release time and financial assistance by way of several awards that made research and editorial work on this project possible—the Sabbatical Award (2012), Presidential Award (2008), Summer Stipend (2008), and Faculty Affirmative Action Award (2007)—and to the Department of Philosophy and its faculty and students for being tireless supporters of diversity in the discipline. I wish to thank several students who either contributed to conversations about the initial composition of the volume, did editorial work during its completion, or both—Rachel Buddeberg, Elizabeth Hedrick Moser, Syl Kocięda, Helen Sakkaris, and Allison Sherman. I am deeply indebted to Nancy Tuana, who paved the way for this volume with her vision for the series and who enthusiastically supported this volume from its inception to its completion. For their careful eyes in preparing this manuscript, I wish to extend my thanks to Laura Anne Reed-Morrisson, managing editor, Hannah Hebert, editorial assistant, and Kathryn Gucer, copyeditor, at the Pennsylvania State University Press. Two anonymous referees from the press provided many valuable suggestions for improvement, and for this I am grateful. Finally, many thanks to Penny for her work on and enthusiasm for this volume.

From Penny: Thanks to Berenice Carroll and Hilda Smith, with whom I first read Astell, and to my many students who read her with me, in turn. Many thanks to Alice for carrying this book across the finish line.

1

Locations and Legacies

Reading Mary Astell and Re-Reading the Canon

Penny A. Weiss

In the critically important Re-Reading the Canon series, the Pennsylvania State University Press has provided audiences with new, feminist perspectives on well-recognized canonical works. Of the thirty-four current volumes, seven, surprisingly, focus on female theorists overwhelmingly excluded from that same canon: Mary Wollstonecraft, Hannah Arendt, Simone de Beauvoir, Ayn Rand, Mary Daly, Emma Goldman, and Jane Addams. Perhaps these "other" collections reflect the exciting, ever-evolving, and ultimately more radical sense of what it can mean to "re-read a canon." With this volume on Mary Astell, we bring significant and intellectually stimulating attention to another understudied (though newly and increasingly popular) female philosopher, the first in the series from the late seventeenth century. This anthology, composed entirely of original essays, places

2   Feminist Interpretations of Mary Astell

Astell in historical and philosophical contexts and examines her nuanced and sometimes also contentious relationships to both historical and contemporary feminisms.

Twenty years ago, this volume on Astell was almost inconceivable—witness the paucity of references in this collection to secondary works before then. Those writing on early modern philosophy had barely begun to talk about women thinkers from the period. Some feminists were particularly circumspect toward philosophers who, like Astell, identified with rationalism and Cartesian theories. Both (sometimes overlapping) groups were generally uninterested in historical feminist thinkers, whose very existence was frequently contested. This volume, then, is testimony to considerable changes in the academy and beyond.

We had two broad goals in compiling this collection: to continue to fill in the large gaps in the secondary literature on Astell's philosophical views, and to further the debate about the nature of her feminism. Regarding the former, contributors offer philosophical and political readings of Astell's writings, drawing on both historical and contemporary perspectives. The focus is often on such matters as how Astell stands in relation to Descartes and other rationalist philosophers, or how she works with Aristotle's ethics, but also considers how she compares to other historical female and feminist theorists. Regarding the latter, the most basic issue is this: while many contemporary feminists recognize Astell's adamant claims—and powerful theorizing in defense of these claims—that women deserve respect and education, they tend to see these positions as being in tension with her devotion to God, her Tory allegiances, and her defense of conventional marriage. In addressing these issues and tensions, the essays here explore what it means to be an early modern feminist, what the relationship is between modern philosophy and modern feminism, how contemporary feminist theory can help us understand earlier feminisms, and, reversing the roles, what we today can learn from thinkers like Astell. The authors accomplish both goals with sensitivity to the social and historical background against which Astell wrote, with the acumen necessary to raise and to deal with the philosophical puzzles in her texts, and with admirable mastery of both primary texts and secondary literature.

Excitingly, what all of this means is that in at least some cases we are moving beyond the early phases of recovering women philosophers to integrating some, including Astell, into the whole of philosophy, now even understood to include feminist philosophy. Whether our readers are academic philosophers, scholars of the modern period, or historians of feminist thought, their knowledge of Mary Astell will be enriched, we are convinced,

Reading Astell and Re-Reading the Canon   3

in ways that encourage them to rethink her, modern philosophy, and feminist theory.

In what follows I use the words "locations" and "legacies" to introduce some background to this volume as well as to set the stage for possible new lines of inquiry. By "locations" I mean two things: first, how the questions and perspectives of our authors compare with those of their predecessors—"locating" Astell in a stream or even tradition of interpretations; and, second, into what philosophical conversations our contributors place, or "locate," Astell. Studying the evolution of commentary about her allows us to see and build upon what others have said, as both changing times and more sophisticated readings make different aspects of her thought visible or important. Developing connections between Astell and other thinkers and schools of thought offers evidence of Astell's breadth and of her significant engagement with consequential figures and core ideas. These connections contribute to her ultimate fate, as well: "Feminists know perhaps as well as anyone that making of a theorist an anomaly—as if he or she came from nowhere and touched no one—is often a philosophical kiss of death" (Weiss and Kensinger 2007, 10). In this volume, then, we expand on existing links and begin work on new ones, hoping for an ever-fuller understanding and appreciation of Mary Astell.

My use of "legacies" is perhaps more singular. The term usually refers to a widely recognized past accomplishment; philosophically, it is not unusual to speak of the "legacy" of ancient thinkers, or of a particular school of thought—by which is meant their influence and impact. By and large, however, women theorists have not been permitted legacies, since their diverse writings, their varied political and artistic accomplishments, and even the profound, unambiguous lines of their influence have been erased. I do not use the term, then, to denote Astell's agreed-upon heritage that generations following her have built upon; instead, using only the arguments of our authors, I focus on what they say we *might* or even *should* read as her gifts to us—her legacies, were we to claim and use them.

Locating Astell: Traditions and Conversations

From the earliest research on Mary Astell, scholars have been intrigued by the links they could make between her and other figures and traditions. Some historical ties are relatively apparent, given that an exchange of letters between Astell and Reverend John Norris was published, for example, and that her debates with Lady Damaris Masham and with

4   Feminist Interpretations of Mary Astell

Anthony Ashley Cooper, the third Earl of Shaftesbury, were then well known. What scholars note in such cases of actual historical connections are primarily positions on particular political, epistemological, social, and religious issues; the nature, tone, and outcomes of the debates; and, to a lesser extent, any personal relationships between these figures. For example, Florence Smith's 1916 dissertation, *Mary Astell*, the first book-length analysis of Astell, develops numerous such relationships: "From 1704–1705 she was engaged in political and religious controversy. She attacked Defoe in *A Fair Way with the Dissenters and Their Patrons*; she opposed Shaftesbury, in *Bart'lemy Fair or an Enquiry After Wit*" ([1916] 1966, 20), and *Moderation Truly Stated* was "a direct reply to [Reverend James] Owen's *Moderation a Virtue*" (147). The lines of influence go both directions, Smith notes. For example, "Lady Damaris Masham in 1696 published *A Discourse Concerning the Love of God*, intended as a reply to John Norris and Mary Astell" (109). Of central significance in this strain of commentary is the critical acknowledgment that "she was engaged" in the political, epistemological, religious, and philosophical debates of the day (Smith [1916] 1966, 20).

Still, even the quest to make evident actual historical links is not so easy. As Springborg summarizes the problem, "For every George Wheeler who gave unqualified acknowledgment to Astell's influence in *A Protestant Monastery* of 1698, there were ten who stole her ideas without acknowledgment and then satirized her to cover their tracks" (2002, 14). But the search can help encourage us to read Astell carefully and alongside other understudied and overstudied works with overlapping themes, and to reestablish actual lines of influence and philosophical and political connections perhaps even deeper and more revealing than temporal ones.

A second set of links and locations focuses more specifically on Astell's relationships with her "female contemporaries," in order to develop "an important context for understanding a woman like Mary Astell" (Perry 1986, 4). The emphasis here is on networks, audience, influence, and, given the unconventional lives most female theorists led (and Astell's independence and philosophical community certainly fits this description), links between lived experience and positions advocated in writing. What enabled this woman, at this time, to survive and flourish in that political, social, economic, philosophical, religious, and philosophical environment? In this vein, Ruth Perry's *The Celebrated Mary Astell*, the only biography of Astell, explores her relationships with Lady Elizabeth Hastings, Lady Catherine Jones, Elizabeth Elstob, and Lady Mary Wortley Montagu, among others. In general, research on other female thinkers has also investigated the female networks that supported them and their work in ways crucial to their intellectual survival (Cook 1977).

Moving beyond the period and circumstances in which she lived and wrote, a third set of conversations and "locations" can be detected in Astell's relations to the individuals and traditions she cited or wrestled with in her writings. Included in this category are figures who died before Astell's birth in 1666 (René Descartes, 1596–1650) or shortly thereafter (Thomas Hobbes, 1588–1679; Sir William D'Avenant, 1606–1688; John Locke, 1632–1704; Anthony Ashley Cooper, 1621–1683), as well as those whose lives overlapped with hers (she died in 1731) for at least a few decades (Daniel Defoe, 1660–1731; Antoine Arnauld, 1616–1698); and, beyond individuals, Tories, the Church of England, and the Dissenters. Scholarly attention here is especially on the comparative philosophies, politics, and theologies of these people and schools of thought, and on their influence—that is, how Astell understood and used them in her work, accepting, rejecting, and/or modifying their ideas, and how she impacted others. For example, Patricia Springborg's *Mary Astell: Theorist of Freedom from Domination* (2005) pays special attention to the philosophical contexts of Astell's ideas, examining figures from Judith Drake to Nicholas Malebranche, with special emphasis on John Locke, as well as larger political ideas and movements such as republicanism and contractarianism. Making Astell more a contending voice in these debates than a mere commentator upon them is, again, critical to reclaiming her true philosophical and political importance.

A final set of links and "connections" frequently made (clearly these categories overlap) is with Astell's predecessors and contemporaries who were explicitly feminist advocates and authors. Here, too, the scholarly emphasis is on continuities and discontinuities, as well as possible "traditions" in which feminists critique certain practices and institutions, especially regarding women's education and the institution of marriage, which were central topics in Astell's writings. For example, Bridget Hill's 1986 introduction to the first collection of Astell's writings, erroneously but tantalizingly titled *The First English Feminist*, links Astell's essay on women's education with other analyses and critiques of education, including Clement Barksdale's *A Letter Touching a Colledge of Maids, or a Virgin Society*, Anna Maria Schurman's *The Learned Maid, or Whether a Maid May Be a Scholar*, and Daniel Defoe's *An Essay upon Projects*. Astell's critique of marriage is likewise placed among other appraisals of the institution, including Lord Halifax's *The Lady's New Year Gift; or, Advice to a Daughter*, and Hannah Woolley's *The Gentlewoman's Guide to the Female Sex*.

6   Feminist Interpretations of Mary Astell

These last two kinds of links are of the greatest interest and utility to our contributors. They have been the focus of more recent literature on Astell that moves the discussion beyond the early publications referred to thus far. While the earliest pieces helped frame subsequent scholarship, publications from more recent decades have made ever-broader connections. Astell has been examined with respect to Descartes on the topic of reason by Margaret Atherton (1993) and on the topic of sensation by Eileen O'Neill, who also reads Astell against the backdrop of Aristotelian natural philosophers and theologians (2007). Other connections between Astell and early modern philosophers are made by Jane Duran, who sees in Astell "a forerunner of Hume" (2000, 150); Sarah Ellenzweig, who discusses Astell's entanglement with anti-Spinozism in the late seventeenth and early eighteenth centuries (2003); and Penny Weiss, who uses Thomas Hobbes as "a useful backdrop for introducing Astell" (2004, 66), concluding that her incorporation of women into political theory is much more thorough and consequential than Hobbes's. Astell has also been discussed in light of many more theoretical frameworks, including utopianism (Johns 1996), possessive individualism (Perry 1990), and, of course, feminism (about which more in a moment).

In discussing philosophical frameworks and thinkers with whom Astell was in conversation, actual or theoretical, the authors in this volume, like those they followed, make clear that "influence" does not mean mere "imitation" or simple "adoption." Instead, these scholars show what she accepted, what she rejected, what she added, and what she modified, making their work especially important contributions to the literature. The commonalities are as essential to marking Astell's general political and philosophical locations as the differences are to marking her philosophical and political originality and distinction. It requires rigorous scholarship to clarify and understand both the overlap and the deviations.

"Locations" in This Volume

In "Mary Astell's Feminism: A Rhetorical Perspective," Christine Mason Sutherland places Astell in "the rhetorical tradition" dating back to Plato, and sees Astell's role in it as "attempt[ing] to upgrade, theorize, and recommend to her audience of women" the "kind of rhetoric" called "sermo" (154–55). Sutherland also shows the use Astell makes of Descartes's rules of logic and, as important, how Astell adds to his rules as she "accommodates his directions to her primary audience of women" (157). Similarly,

Sutherland shows the strong similarities between Cicero and Astell on the characteristics of sermo, but also how, despite "her debt to Cicero," Astell adds a Christian perspective, "melding . . . classical advice with the precepts of Christian morality," and drawing on Bernard Lamy, whom she also "adapts . . . to her own purpose and her own audience of women" (160). These are novel and exciting contributions.

As Sutherland puts Astell in the rhetorical tradition, Jacqueline Broad, in "Mary Astell and the Virtues," argues for seeing Astell as a moral philosopher. In particular, while Astell is not a virtue theorist in the strictest sense, Broad locates Astell in "the ancient virtue tradition that originated with Plato . . . and Aristotle . . . , and was later adapted by Stoic and Christian thinkers" (20). According to the virtue tradition, the character of the moral agent is of prime importance in evaluating ethical behavior, and Broad shows how Astell explores themes central to this tradition: virtue, moral education, moral judgment, character, friendship, and the role of the passions in moral action. Specifically, according to Broad, Astell explains how passions can be transformed into virtues when they are redirected such that the mind turns from objects of little worth to those of greater worth. Especially, but not exclusively, for women, "if we train ourselves to love the right objects, then the other passions will follow suit" (24). Friendship, including women's friendships, proper marriages, and communities such as the Religious Retirement for women that Astell advocates, are sources of moral improvement, inasmuch as they involve the Aristotelian notion of "character friendship," rooted in the love of benevolence, familiarity with each other's character, and "the mutual desire to promote another's well-being for her own sake" (27). Broad also develops Astell's links with Aristotle, Malebranche, Norris, Henry More, and Descartes, on subjects from freedom and friendship, on the one hand, to prudence and generosity, on the other. Given the growing interest today in virtue epistemology, looking at Astell as offering an early version of it can mean making greater use of her as the theory continues to develop, especially given the centrality of her attention to women, something still often missing.

In "Mary Astell and the Development of Vice: Pride, Courtship, and the Woman's Human Nature Question," Alice Sowaal focuses on how Astell addresses the "collection of questions" surrounding the issue of whether human nature is basically good or bad. She compares Astell's relatively optimistic view with those of Hobbes and the Calvinists. Sowaal is most interested in the social circumstances that Astell perceives as giving rise to vices that are sometimes thought to be more common in women, and she does that, interestingly, by reconstructing Astell's account

8   Feminist Interpretations of Mary Astell

of generosity. Generosity in this account is "a desire to perfect," which is itself related to a "generous Temper" (65). One of the important links Sowaal makes is to show how Astell's women have less access to Descartes's method of doubt than do men. Among other attributes, this piece is a significant addition to literature addressing the relationship between Astell and Descartes.

In "Mary Astell on the Existence and Nature of God," Marcy Lascano carefully analyzes the intricacies of Astell's arguments for the existence of God, and connects them to the history of similar arguments and philosophical issues presented by Plato, Aristotle, Aquinas, Descartes, Malebranche, Leibniz, and Locke. She shows how, for Astell, *all* created beings have the duty and obligation "to achieve the greatest perfection of which it is capable in order to glorify God," and to attain happiness, avoid evil, resist the sway of custom, and contribute to the overall moral perfection of the world (180). Lascano, like Sowaal above, especially notes how Astell was in conversation with Descartes, as seen in Astell's use of Descartes's definition of the term "self-existence," and in Astell's ideas about the mind-body distinction. Lascano also mentions Norris's influence on Astell, as well as the possibility of Malebranche's indirect influence via Norris.

In "Further Reflections upon Marriage: Mary Astell and Sarah Chapone," Susan Glover looks at Astell as the influencer more than the influenced. Glover links Astell with another understudied—maybe even virtually unknown—female figure, Sarah Chapone. Chapone stands in for "the men and women of England who read her [Astell's] arguments about religion, education, and marriage," rather than the more famous people who were influenced by Astell (95). Through her reading of Chapone's correspondence and a pamphlet she published anonymously, Glover claims that "we can observe Chapone's reception and revision of Astell's arguments refracted through her own hermeneutical engagement with a range of textual authorities; legal, doctrinal, and fictional" (96). Chapone takes Astell's ideas a step further and in directions Astell herself may not have supported. For example, according to Glover, Chapone maintains that a woman in a bad marriage does not need to "school her mind to the consolation of the soul," but "suggests that it is the law, rather than the mind, that must adjust" (100). While there is not yet enough scholarship to fully understand how Astell's views on marriage were received at the time, Glover's research on Chapone's reception of her ideas reveals that Astell's work was read closely and evaluated by other women of the period. Glover's piece is a novel and important contribution.

Karen Detlefsen's essay, "Custom, Freedom, and Equality: Mary Astell on Marriage and Women's Education," tackles an ongoing controversy—the seeming incompatibility between Astell's Cartesian belief in the "unsexed rational soul" and her advocacy of wives' subordination to their husbands. Detlefsen, too, "show[s] the points of overlap and divergence with Descartes's thought," but here the purpose is more "to draw out the feminist character of her Cartesianism" (76). In her re-rereading, Detlefsen concludes that Astell is firmly Cartesian in her views of both natural equality and how to improve marital injustices. Wrestling with the precise nature of Astell's feminism, Detlefsen concludes that Astell offers "a recognizably feminist account of freedom," linking it to recent feminist theory on autonomy (86). Detlefsen's contributions, then, are numerous and stimulating.

Kathleen Ahearn argues for the importance of women's self-esteem in Astell. She links and compares Astell to a range of figures in "Mary Astell's Account of Feminine Self-Esteem," including Henry More, Descartes, Aristotle, and Norris. She clarifies Astell's critique of Norris's theory of love, shows how Astell works with the Cartesian theory of self-regulation, and argues that she uses and expands upon Aristotle's ideas of *phronesis* and friendship. Like Detlefsen, Ahearn connects Astell to contemporary problems and practices not limited to or identified only with individual thinkers, including care relationships, virtue ethics, and "the problem of embodiment." Like Broad, Ahearn discusses the regulation of the passions, noting the role of proper self-esteem, which emerges when women align their true selves with God, through what Astell calls "that particle of Divinity" within us (51). The vexing and consequential problem of women's low self-esteem remains with us today around the world, so an account of its importance and how to raise it can be especially valuable. Again, we see that philosophical issues have more of a feminist history than has been presumed or acknowledged.

Ahearn and Broad both discuss love as the leading passion for Astell. Ahearn explains that love for Astell is not self-sacrificial but self-preserving, even though being long-suffering, and obedient are popularly defined as feminine virtues. Broad writes that, for Astell, "if we train ourselves to love the right objects, then the other passions will follow suit" (24). She argues that Astell's "paradigmatic feminist claim about *custom versus nature*" in *Serious Proposal* is in fact a claim about women's capacity for Aristotelian prudence, which requires a reformation in moral education, and allows happiness, freedom, and the other virtues to develop (27).

10   Feminist Interpretations of Mary Astell

Several authors begin to introduce readers to more contemporary ideas that Astell can be linked with (among them care ethics, virtue ethics, self-esteem, embodiment, and justice in marriage). In other chapters, authors focus more closely on such connections. For instance, in "Mary Astell: Some Reflections upon Trauma," Elisabeth Hedrick Moser uses recent "trauma theory as a lens through which to read Astell" in order to make "visible the more insidious layers of the consequences of abusive power" in Astell's thought (112). Hedrick Moser also uses recent developments in feminist epistemology, especially Amanda Fricker's concept of testimonial injustice, to make the unjust situation Astell confronts and criticizes more visible and urgent.

In "'From the Throne to Every Private Family': Mary Astell as Analyst of Power," Penny Weiss continues this more political analysis, linking Astell with major issues treated by theorists of power. She begins with "Foucault fatigue," noting that "those who read political theory today, even including feminist political theory, might understandably reach the erroneous conclusion that Foucault's writing on power was without precedent (especially without female precedent)" (130). She argues that feminists, including Astell, "have been urging us for several centuries down many of the paths Foucault has more recently and much more famously traveled regarding power" (130). Again and again the essays here raise the question of how our understanding of certain ideas and traditions would be enriched were we to consider Astell's contributions to them. What would it mean to footnote Astell's intricate and insightful theory of power just half as often as Foucault's ideas are cited? Hope springs eternal.

The variety of approaches and "locations" visible in this volume is its strength rather than its weakness. Using multiple lenses and connections is part of what it means to take a philosopher seriously. Granting any woman this degree of credibility is still relatively new. To assume Astell's writings have such richness and complexity that they can both enlighten and be enlightened by other theories and theorists is to grant authority where it has not generally been recognized before. And what fruit this diverse method bears! Interestingly, many of the authors in this volume argue with Astell themselves even as they argue about her "objectively," In doing so, these authors contend that a number of ideas, schools of thought, and disciplines that they find worthy would be elevated by a more serious engagement with Astell's thought. Such will no doubt be the task for a good while to come, as we truly engage in a re-reading of the canon.

Reading Astell and Re-Reading the Canon   11

Legacies

Across the board, women thinkers, Astell included, have generated very little scholarship. For many women, we have more biographies than monographs—meaning that we take the lives of women more seriously than their ideas. There are more arguments about why women should not be considered philosophers, or original, or influential, than there are inquiries into what women actually said, how what they said fits into and/or disrupts various traditions or theories, and who read, used, stole, built upon, and reworked their ideas. Naming "legacies" marks someone as worth reading, and certainly every scholar in this volume, all of whom are familiar with numerous figures, theories, and eras besides Astell and her milieu, advances our understanding of her influence, impact, and importance. They thus illuminate why she intrigues and impresses readers across academic disciplines. A "legacy," after all, is by definition a "gift," bestowed by a predecessor; accordingly, Astell without question has left us a bounty. So, were we to take Astell even more seriously, what, according to some of our authors, would be among her legacies?

Returning to the earliest literature, Smith says that Astell's "contribution to the history of education lies . . . in her practical application of her ideas and in her clear view of the social possibilities lying back of the education of women and of the economic changes necessary to bring about new ends" (1966, 61). Smith adds that it is "her attempt to show the relation between woman's education and her economic position in marriage that calls attention to her to-day" (1966, 166). By contrast, among contemporary scholars, Patricia Springborg sees Astell's legacy in her offering of "not only the first but perhaps also the most sustained contemporary critique of Locke's *Two Treatises* (1995, 629), and she reads Astell's *Reflections upon Marriage* as "perhaps the first articulated critique of the analogue between the marriage contract and the social contract on which early modern natural rights theories so heavily depend" (Astell 1996b, 4). Even more recently, in her monograph on Astell's political theory, Springborg concludes that Astell's "contribution to the print debate that surrounded the constitutional battle over toleration and dissent in Britain, one of the most vigorous and democratic of early modern political debates[,] . . . was among Astell's signal public achievements. . . . Her contribution to the critique of morals and mores surrounding women's education and marriage was another. Her role in the reception of Descartes and the Platonist philosophical debate . . . is [also] of great importance" (2005, 237). Smith, like Springborg, delineates a legacy for Astell that is broad and weighty;

12   Feminist Interpretations of Mary Astell

nonetheless, the payoff from increasing, and increasingly serious, attention to Astell over time is obvious in the range and specificity of claims made by the two scholars.

"Legacies" in This Volume

In this volume, authors continue to explore the nature of Astell's contributions to diverse disciplines and schools of thought. Like Springborg, Lascano makes a bold claim for Astell's significance within a number of particular debates, and shows how she challenges the very terms of those debates (an amazing accomplishment, really, named by several of our contributors). For example, "Astell actively engages in the debates regarding God's existence and nature. In doing so, she provides unique arguments for the existence of God" (186).

The legacy that Sutherland focuses on has the added benefit of challenging those who contend that the relatively "conservative" Astell was essentially uninterested in social change. She argues that Astell's advice on rhetoric amounts to "training" that could "alleviate the troubles" of many women (153). Like any feminist, Astell attempts to enable women to resist "immoral gentlemen," and "to improve the lot of the ladies . . . [and] enable them to be useful in their world"—that is, to "make a contribution to the public good" (155, 162). In enlarging women's possibilities through speech, "Astell is an important figure in both the history of rhetoric and the history of feminism" (167).

Detlefsen finds in Astell a precursor to the recent feminist argument for "relational autonomy." Significantly, "Astell imagines that her prototheory of relational autonomy could hold not only among women in the religious retreat but also between a woman and a man in the marriage bond" (88). Many things are interesting in this argument, but as far as legacy goes, one idea may be dominant: despite her debt to Descartes's epistemology, Astell, unlike Descartes, understands how this idea can lead to "acknowledg[ing] the importance of good communal relations, relations which are anything but the highly individualistic" ones found in Descartes (89). "So, ultimately, Astell's feminism is based upon an acknowledgment of our essential, communal inter-relatedness," a topic of continuing interest to communitarian-minded feminists today, as well as scholars of Astell and Descartes (89).

Broad, like Detlefsen, works to "uncover" in Astell "something of philosophical interest to modern feminist ethicists" and to clarify her distinctive feminism (19). That version of feminism, Broad argues, "is grounded on promoting *excellence of character* in women rather than the consistent application of political concepts and principles, such as the principles of equality and justice, to women in the public sphere" (19). While Broad finds some weakness in this approach, she nonetheless concludes that Astell's "emphasis on excellence of character might be considered a strength . . . of her feminist philosophy," one that in fact some feminist ethicists today can use as a precedent (30). An important and even inspiring part of Astell's legacy is how she "reconceives the classical virtues of courage, friendship, and generosity as essential tools in the service of female emancipation" (31). This "reconceiving" of patriarchal concepts and practices is a project many contemporary feminists are drawn to, but too often without the benefit of feminist predecessors such as Astell.

In "Mary Astell and the Development of Vice: Pride, Courtship, and the Woman's Human Nature Question," Sowaal, too, looks at questions of character. She sees Astell's legacy as an argument for the goodness of human nature that was original at the time, primarily because Astell wrestled with a "version of the question . . . that specifically addresses woman's nature" (59). Astell was able to move away from then well-known arguments for both the goodness and badness of human nature and offer a novel social, moral, and epistemological account of how women "degenerate into vice" (64). Again, according to Sowaal, Astell shifts the debate a bit through her attention to how issues of gender underlie the questions we ask and where we look for answers.

For Weiss, Astell's legacy is a profound seventeenth-century critique of patriarchy. It includes her important condemnation of women's deep and constructed dependence and vulnerability; her understanding of how "[p]atriarchy infiltrates and organizes the supposedly separate public and private, the male and the female, attitudes as well as institutions" (138); her recognition of "the hatred of all things female that is (part of) patriarchy, and the practices it leads to and requires" (139); and the ways she models and encourages forms of resistance. Overall, Weiss imagines those who wrestle today with power and authority would do well to use Astell as a resource and a model.

Ahearn also finds in Astell a worthy feminist foremother, whose theorizing is intended "to emancipate women from inner and outer forms of oppression." Ahearn shows how Astell makes use of a theory of "sensible Congruity" to understand how women are particularly prone to loving incorrectly because they are beholden to male desires (37, 40). More practically,

14   Feminist Interpretations of Mary Astell

Ahearn finds in Astell's social account of feminine self-esteem a combination of respect for the worth of self and others, practical care for the
self, and negotiation with others, including in love relationships. In a
twenty-first-century world where sacrificing the self for others is still connected to femininity, and self-injurious and self-destructive practices from
cutting to anorexia occur primarily among women, this self-preserving
account may be a depressingly contemporary legacy, complete with due
recognition for the particular hurdles patriarchy erects to such self-
esteem.

Concluding Thoughts

My claims here, and the claims of the volume overall, are that new, more
rigorous and open-minded readings of Astell are necessary, and that
through such novel interpretations we will come to understand Astell,
modern philosophy, and feminism in important, useful, and unprecedented
ways. These are not modest claims, especially as they revolve around a
thinker still unread by most philosophers and feminists.

We also hope that readers will see the essays in this volume as being in
conversation with one another, even if not explicitly so. There are multiple
discussions of "human essences" and "human nature," especially as these
relate to equality. Many essays focus on the moral, epistemological, and
political consequences of "patriarchy." Readers will find several accounts of
Astell's views on how to enact change, from moral education and coming-
to-voice to spiritual development and political resistance. The interaction
between Astell's theology and ethics is central to several pieces. A number
of links are made with Descartes, especially regarding the mind-body relationship and, related to it, the passions. In fact, several contributors give
accounts of Astell's views of particular passions: love, prudence, generosity,
self-esteem, courage, and vanity among them. There is a conversation
between the chapters on communities and friendships, especially which
kinds are beneficial and lead to moral and intellectual improvement, on
the one hand, and which kinds are destructive and lead to vice, on the
other. Knowledge is compared to faith and linked with freedom, healthy
relationships, and gender. Finally, and perhaps least surprisingly, there is
repeated attention to marriage: what type of institution it is, what kinds of
relationships are possible and beneficial between spouses, the impact on
marriage of courtship and social customs, and the character of the real and
potential harms of what we now often call patriarchal marriage. A system-

atic philosopher, Astell addresses abstract issues of God, the soul, and bodies; structural issues of patriarchy, marriage, and custom; and personal issues of care, friendship, and love.

In her own day, Mary Astell was known (and ridiculed) as one of the "philosophical ladies" (Smith 1966, 27), widely read and influential in political, philosophical, and theological debates and circles. Would that it could be so again! For as we can see from the entries in this collection, re-reading the canon with Astell in the conversation has the potential to lead to understanding early modern versions of virtue ethics and communitarian feminism; to develop a fuller understanding of rhetorical, political, and theological traditions; and to reckon with broader understandings of oppressive power and the conditions that might sustain respectful relations and inclusive practices. May we continue to find ways to read and connect Astell's thoughts and writings such that we, and the next generations of philosophers and feminists, will gain a richer picture of our intellectual past and move toward an expansive vision of our future.

2

Mary Astell and the Virtues

Jacqueline Broad

In 1694, Mary Astell published her first work, a short treatise titled *A Serious Proposal to the Ladies, for the Advancement of Their True and Greatest Interest*. Her proposal was a call for a women's college or "a Retreat from the World" in which young English women might be given a thorough

I would like to acknowledge the generous financial assistance of the Australian Research Council (ARC): this essay was completed during my tenure as an ARC Future Fellow in the School of Philosophical, Historical, and International Studies at Monash University, Melbourne, Australia. An earlier version of this essay was presented in the Philosophy Department staff seminar series at Monash in 2010. I am very grateful for the comments and questions of participants at that seminar, including Linda Barclay, John Bigelow, Karen Green, Justin Oakley, and Rob Sparrow. I am also extremely grateful for the tremendous advice and assistance of the editors of this volume, Alice Sowaal and Penny Weiss.

academic training in reason and religion (*SP I*, 18). In one key passage of the work, Astell writes,

> Altho' it has been said by Men of more Wit than Wisdom, and perhaps of more malice than either, that Women are naturally incapable of acting Prudently, or that they are necessarily determined to folly, I must by no means grant it; that Hypothesis would render my endeavours impertinent, for then it would be in vain to advise the one, or endeavour the Reformation of the other. Besides, there are Examples in all Ages, which sufficiently confute the Ignorance and Malice of this Assertion.
>
> The Incapacity, if there be any, is acquired not natural; and none of their Follies are so necessary, but that they might avoid them if they pleas'd themselves. (*SP I*, 9–10)

Recent scholars have highlighted the modern feminist sentiment in these words. In her annotations to the *Proposal*, Patricia Springborg observes that here "Astell seriously engages the question of the relation between gender and custom, arguing throughout that women's subordination is customary, not natural," and that Astell subscribes to "nurture over nature as formative of character" (*SP I*, 50n25). Astell suggests that women are disadvantaged compared to men—or that they have a certain "incapacity" by virtue of their womanhood—but that their incapacity is a social construct rather than the product of nature or biology. The primary blame for women's defects lies with "the mistakes of our Education; which like an Error in the first Concoction, spreads its ill Influence through all our Lives" (*SP I*, 10). For Astell, the proper intellectual education of women is the key to rectifying their disadvantage.

If we look closely at the passage, however, when Astell says that women's incapacity "is acquired not natural" (*SP I*, 10), she targets a specific incapacity. Her comment comes on the heels of an earlier observation that some men believe that "Women are naturally incapable of *acting Prudently*, or that they are necessarily determined to folly" (*SP I*, 9; my emphasis).[1] In response to these men, Astell alludes to "Examples in all Ages" (*SP I*, 10) or to counterexamples that refute their generalizations about women's lack of prudence. (In a later work, her *Reflections upon Marriage* of 1706, Astell would name several exemplary women, such as Samson's mother, who "so prudently answer'd" the vulgar fears of her husband, and the wise woman of Abel, who "by her Prudence deliver'd the City and appeas'd a dangerous Rebellion" [*RM*, 24].) Placed in its proper context, then, Astell's paradigmatic

18   Feminist Interpretations of Mary Astell

feminist claim about *custom versus nature* is in fact a claim about women's capacity for prudent conduct. In the second part of her *Proposal* (first published in 1697), Astell develops this point by saying,

> Rational Creatures shou'd endeavour to have right Ideas of every thing that comes under their Cognizance, but yet our Ideas of Morality, our thoughts about Religion are those which we shou'd with greatest speed and diligence rectifie, because they are of most importance, the Life to come, as well as all the Occurences of This, depending on them. We shou'd search for Truth in our most abstracted Speculations, but it concerns us nearly to follow her close in what relates to the Conduct of our Lives. For the main thing we are to drive at in all our Studies, and that which is the greatest Improvement of our Understandings is *the Art of Prudence*, the being all of a Piece, managing all our Words and Actions as it becomes Wise Persons and Good Christians. (*SP II*, 120; my emphasis)

In this chapter, I interpret Astell's *Proposal* in light of these remarks and in light of Astell's explicit design to bring about a reformation in women's *moral* education.

At first glance, it might be odd to think that "the Art of Prudence" plays such a central role in Astell's work. To our modern way of thinking, prudence is typically an ability to avoid undesirable consequences, or to be circumspect and discreet in one's actions. More specifically, prudence is a way to bring about good to one's self, or to promote one's rational self-interest. A woman might be considered prudent when she marries a man of equal social standing even though he is lacking in virtue; or she might be regarded as prudent when she fails to admonish a friend's wickedness for the sake of retaining the friendship. It is difficult to reconcile such "prudence" with Astell's opinion that "our Ideas of Morality, our thoughts about Religion are those which we shou'd with greatest speed and diligence rectifie, because they are of most importance" (*SP II*, 120). If Astell's goal is to bring about a moral reformation for women, then why does she describe prudence as "the *main thing* we are to drive at in all our Studies"?

In what follows, I offer an explanation for why the art of prudence is a vital part of Astell's educational program. But before I do so, it will be necessary to broaden my focus to Astell's wider ethical project in both parts of the *Proposal*, and in her later work, *The Christian Religion, as Profess'd by a Daughter of the Church of England* (1705). In particular, I propose to offer an interpretation of Astell's feminist philosophy from the point of view of her *theory of virtue*. This ethical interpretation of Astell's writings might be useful and instructive for at least two reasons. First, by highlighting Astell's indebtedness to the virtue approach, it is possible to identify different meanings or resonances in her feminist terminology—in this case, not only the term *prudence* but also *happiness, freedom, love, admiration, generosity, courage,* and *friendship*. These are important concepts in Astell's feminist thought, and they are sometimes misunderstood or simply overlooked. Part of the problem is that Astell's words do not always carry the same meanings now that they did then. In some cases, they stand for ethical and religious concepts that have long passed out of usage. But by highlighting such forgotten meanings, I think it might be possible to uncover something of philosophical interest to modern feminist ethicists. Second, an interpretation of Astell as a moral philosopher can help us to recognize why she is so different from her present-day feminist counterparts. As we will see, Astell's feminism is grounded on promoting *excellence of character* in women rather than the consistent application of political concepts and principles, such as the principles of equality and justice, to women in the public sphere. Again, while Astell's emphasis on virtuous character might make her feminism sound rather strange to modern ears, it can nonetheless be interpreted as a strength and not a weakness.

Virtue, Happiness, and Freedom

In the past few decades, commentators have identified the various philosophical commitments underlying Astell's feminism. Some scholars highlight her promotion of an egalitarian concept of reason and rationality (Atherton 1993; Smith 1982b); some point to her use of Cartesian method in the pursuit of truth and knowledge (Kinnaird 1979; Perry 1985, 1986; Springborg 1997, xxiii–xxvii; 2005, chap. 2); and others examine her theory of mind (Bryson 1998; Sowaal 2007), and the Malebranchean aspects of her theory of causation (Taylor 2001; Broad 2002, 90–113; Ellenzweig 2003; O'Neill 2007). But we are yet to see any systematic treatment of the *moral* philosophy behind Astell's feminism. This is surprising given that Astell consistently reminds her readers that "it is to little purpose to Think well and speak well, unless we *Live well*, this is our Great Affair and truest Excellency" (*SP II*, 147). While Astell embraces certain tenets of Cartesian rationalism and Malebranchean metaphysics, she always makes her philosophy serve a moral or moral-theological purpose. "Truths merely

20   Feminist Interpretations of Mary Astell

Speculative and which have no influence upon Practice, which neither contribute to the good of Soul or Body," she says, "are but idle Amusements, an impertinent and criminal wast of Time" (SP II, 97). In Astell's view, the overriding purpose of philosophy is to provide guidance on "the Art of Well-Living" (SP II, 97).

Perhaps one reason that Astell is not typically seen as a moral philosopher is that her approach predates the two dominant moral traditions, Kantian deontology and utilitarianism. In the past few decades, however, there has been a significant revival of interest in a third tradition: the ancient virtue approach to ethics. Generally speaking, virtue ethics is concerned with the virtues or with those admirable character traits ("moral excellences") that are seen as requisite for leading a good life or attaining lasting happiness and well-being. In the classical tradition, and in the later thought of the Roman philosopher Cicero (143–106 B.C.E.), the primary or cardinal virtues are prudence (wisdom), justice, temperance, and courage. In the early modern period, this list of virtues is typically supplemented with the theological or Christian virtues of faith, hope, and charity or love (1 Corinthians 13:13), as well as humility and meekness.[2]

At first glance, Astell would not appear to be a virtue theorist. As a sincere and devout Christian,[3] she frequently uses the language of an ethics of duty in her writings. Her longest and most mature work, The Christian Religion,[4] is divided into five sections, three of which are devoted to "our Duty to GOD more immediately" (CR, 122–95), "our Duty to our Neighbour" (CR, 196–244), and "our Duty to our Selves" (CR, 245–390). At the start of this text, she poses a fundamental moral question to her readers: "what Obligations am I under?" (CR, 10). And in the second Proposal, Astell warns that "it cannot be thought sufficient that Women shou'd but just know whats Commanded and what Forbid, without being inform'd of the Reasons why, since this is not like to secure them in their Duty" (SP II, 148; my emphasis). In light of these comments, Astell appears to subscribe to the view that the most important moral question is a deontic one, such as "what are my duties?" or "what is it right or obligatory to do?" Because she does not support the virtue-ethical principle that "goodness is prior to rightness," we must hesitate to call her a virtue ethicist in the strictest sense.[5]

Notwithstanding this fact, Astell's moral approach still shares many features in common with the ancient virtue tradition that originated with Plato (ca. 428–348 B.C.E.) and Aristotle (384–322 B.C.E.), and was later adapted by Stoic and Christian thinkers. For Astell, the primary virtues (or the virtues that she highlights above all others) are love, prudence, courage, generosity, and friendship. As we will see, in both the *Proposals* and *The Christian Religion*, Astell highlights the importance of moral character and moral education, she presents guidelines for attaining happiness, she gives advice on perfecting one's capacity for practical judgment, she defines the vital role of the passions (or emotions) in moral action, and she highlights the moral significance of friendship. These topics are now considered to be the typical subject matter of virtue ethics.[6]

Above all, Astell teaches women that virtue and a virtuous character are things that ought to be pursued for the sake of attaining true and lasting happiness: "'tis Virtue only," she says, "which can make you truly happy in the world as well as in the next" (*SP I*, 46). She maintains that our souls are naturally inclined toward happiness or toward the good in general. It is in fact impossible to will something that we think is not good: for "why do we Prefer a thing but because we Judge it Best?" she asks, "and why do we Chuse it but because it Seems Good for us?" (*SP II*, 153). Our irresistible inclination toward happiness provides a vital clue to how we should live: natural reason informs us that we must endeavor to be *"as happy as possibly we may"* (*SP II*, 82–83). The only problem is that we do not have a clear and distinct idea of happiness. Most people blindly follow the path that their parents, teachers, neighbors, and church leaders have recommended. They come to think that happiness can be found in sensual pleasures or material goods, and other mutable things of this world. Both men and women are susceptible to the influence of custom, but in the case of women the problem is compounded by the fact that they are poorly educated. Men have "all the advantages of Nature, and without controversy have, or may have all the assistance of Art" (*RM*, 63). But a woman is taught that "'tis enough for her to believe," and that "to examine why, and wherefore, belongs not to her" (*SP I*, 16). She is given so little training in reason and argument that she is incapable of rectifying the mistakes of her upbringing and unable to use her reason to determine the true source of happiness. Yet this matter—wherein her happiness consists—is "the most important concern" of a woman's life (*SP II*, 83). The purpose of Astell's seminary is to give women a serious training in religion and philosophy so that they might gain knowledge of true happiness and the good in general. Here they will learn that lasting happiness can only ever consist in spiritual union with an immutable, infinite, perfectly wise, and perfectly benevolent being—that is, with God himself.

On this subject, Astell's thought closely resembles that of the French philosopher Nicolas Malebranche (1638–1715) and his English disciple John Norris (1657–1711). The similarities are not surprising given that Astell's

22   Feminist Interpretations of Mary Astell

first foray into philosophical debate was an exchange of letters with Norris concerning the love of God.[7] In their correspondence, the two writers discuss the moral and metaphysical opinions of Norris's "Discourse Concerning the Measure of Divine Love," a long essay in the third volume of his *Practical Discourses* (1693). In the "Discourse," Norris maintains that God has designed human beings such that the natural or irresistible inclination of the will is toward the good in general, or God himself. But as a result of the Fall, human inclinations have become corrupted and individuals stray from the path to truth and happiness. To return to the path, Norris teaches that the individual must methodically exercise *freedom of the will* in the search for wisdom and happiness. This emphasis on human freedom is also a key feature of Malebranche's *Search After Truth* ([1674–75] 1980).[8]

Like Norris and Malebranche, Astell emphasizes that the proper exercise of freedom is vital to the attainment of happiness. In the *Proposal*, she points out that every woman is free to question her moral upbringing and "break the enchanted Circle that custom has plac'd" her in (*SP I*, 7). "Why shou'd not we assert our Liberty," she asks, "and not suffer every Trifler to impose a Yoke of Impertinent Customs on us?" (*SP II*, 73). In *The Christian Religion*, Astell provides a definition of freedom or "true Liberty": it consists, she says, "in making a right use of our Reason, in preserving our Judgments free, and our Integrity unspotted, (which sets us out of the reach of the most Absolute Tyrant) not in a bare power to do what we Will" (*CR*, 278). Freedom consists to some degree in the power "to do what we will" (i.e., in acting upon our inclinations), but it does not consist in this alone. More importantly, freedom also consists in the power of *refraining from doing* what we will; it consists in "pulling on the reins," so to speak, when the will has a strong inclination to assent to particular goods, but is not properly guided by reason.

Feminist emancipation, on this view, consists in liberating the will from the "manacle" of custom (*SP II*, 93); freedom is freedom of the will rather than freedom from bodily constraint. For Astell, women are not free when they are deprived of their ability to exercise their freedom in the giving and withholding of assent—when they are taught, that is, to have a blind faith rather than examine the "whys" and "wherefores" of their beliefs. In the *Proposal*, she emphasizes that women are free to avoid sin and error by not "fixing their foot" or forming conclusions about what is good or true based upon confused and obscure ideas (*SP II*, 90, 110). Women go astray when they let customary notions of right and wrong determine their judgments. In order to avoid error and sin, they must be careful and "Judge of Nothing" but what they see clearly (*SP II*, 122). "It is in your Power to regain your Freedom," she reminds her female readers, "if you please but t'endeavour it" (*SP II*, 74).

On the basis of such comments, some scholars claim that Astell's feminism is founded on an extreme reverence for mind, on the one hand, and a denigration of the body, on the other. Cynthia Bryson asserts that, for Astell, "the body was unimportant to philosophy; for her, and other Cartesians, all that really mattered was the 'freedom' of the disembodied mind for 'self-determination'" (1998, 45). Along similar lines, Catharine Stimpson says that Astell teaches women "to repress the body in order to release the mind" (1986, xii). But if we look carefully at Astell's theory of virtue, we can see that for her the female moral agent is always an embodied subject. In her moral philosophy, she does not ignore the fact that, as whole human beings, women are intimately associated and connected with their bodies.

Admiration and Love

In particular, Astell takes into account the fact that women cannot avoid feeling the passions, those necessary by-products of the mind-body union.[9] While women cannot prevent the passions from having an impact on the mind, according to Astell, they can direct them to objects of greater worth by a process of transference or channeling, and in this way a passion might be transformed into a virtue. This is in fact the essence of a virtue for Astell: having a virtue consists in having a certain disposition to feel, choose, or act in accordance with right reason toward the right ends.

The passion of admiration provides an apt example of how a passion might become a virtue. Astell observes that our feelings of admiration fix the mind's attention (*SP II*, 144). In fact, "Admiration gives Rise to all the Passions; for unless we were Affected with the Newness of an Object, or some other remarkable Circumstance, so as to be attentively engag'd in the Contemplation of it, we shou'd not be any wise mov'd, but it wou'd pass by unregarded" (*SP II*, 165–66).[10] When our admiration is reserved for things of little merit, then it is bad or vicious. But the passion of admiration can be useful: it can help us to concentrate our attention on a previously unknown object and retain it in our memory. It is important that we train ourselves, so that we are not "struck with *little* things, or . . . busie our Minds about 'em, but . . . fix all our Attention on, and . . . keep all our Admiration for things of the greatest moment, such as are those which relate to another World" (*SP II*, 166). At this point, the proper exercising

of the free will and the art of suspending one's judgment become important. The passion of admiration becomes a virtue when it is purposely
directed to things of the greatest worth, such as everlasting happiness and
God (SP II, 166–67).

But generally speaking, for Astell, there is really only one passion that
matters: the passion of love. Love is not only "the predominant Passion in
everyone," but a "great inducement to all manner of Vertue" (SP II, 166,
159). A woman motivated by love will want to bring about good for others,
and her actions will be inspired by kindness and concern for another's
well-being. Nevertheless, if a woman acts from the passion of love alone,
this is no guarantee that she will get things right, morally speaking; after
all, she might have wrong notions about where the true good lies. To
become a virtue, the passion of love must be informed by reason, and
directed at the right objects, in the right measure. In the case of other
people, Astell says, we must cultivate a love of benevolence or charity
alone: we must wish well or will good to them, but we must not fool ourselves that they can satisfy our desire for lasting happiness. In the case of
God, we must cultivate a love of desire or concupiscence: we must love and
desire him as our good, and true happiness will be "the natural Effect as
well as the Reward" of such love (SP II, 167).

Once again, for Astell, the exercise of freedom is vital to the process of
retraining the passion of love. As a result of their upbringing, women cannot avoid feeling an inordinate love of desire for other people and material
things. But when such passions arise, Astell advises that women must suspend their "Inclinations as we both May and Ought, and restrain them
from determining our Will, till we have fairly and fully examin'd and
ballanc'd, according to the best of our Knowledge, the several degrees of
Good and Evil present and future that are in the Objects set before us" (SP
II, 155). If the object of our love is morally unworthy, then we must divert
our passion to another object, or somehow modify, redirect, or transfer it.
In Astell's view, the key passions, such as sorrow, desire, joy, admiration,
and hatred, are simply different modifications of love; so if we train ourselves to love the right objects, then the other passions will follow suit.
"The due performance of which," Astell says, "is what we call Vertue, which
consists in governing Animal Impressions, in directing our Passions to
such Objects, and keeping 'em in such a pitch, as right Reason requires"
(SP II, 161).

There are three further virtues that play an important role in Astell's
feminism: generosity, courage, and friendship.

Generosity and Courage

Astell's moral concept of generosity closely resembles that of René Descartes and Henry More.[11] In the seventeenth century, generosity does not always stand for liberality or munificence of character, as it does today. It is not (or not *simply*) a willingness to give to others. Instead this virtue has more in common with the ancient moral ideal of magnanimity or *megalopsychia*, a kind of high-mindedness or greatness of spirit.[12] Generosity is the legitimate self-esteem that comes from recognition of one's capacity for self-determination, or one's freedom to choose the good for oneself and others. Both Descartes and More highlight the importance of cultivating generosity (*generosité*) in this sense. In the *Passions of the Soul* ([1649] 1989), Descartes stipulates that the virtue has two components: it consists in knowing that one ought to be praised or blamed only insofar as one exercises one's freedom well or badly; and it consists in feeling within oneself "a firm and constant resolution" to use one's freedom to do what is best (AT XI, 446; CSM I, 384). Above all, a generous person has mastery over her passions, including not only love but also desire, jealousy, envy, hatred, and anger; she is always "courteous, gracious and obliging to everyone" (AT XI, 448; CSM I, 385). In a work that is heavily indebted to Descartes's *Passions*, the *Account of Virtue* (first published in 1690), More characterizes generosity in similar terms: it "consists in this," he says, "That a Man exercise his own freedom and liberty of Thinking in the best manner he can; that he rest contented herein; and as to Fortune, and the World's Opinion, to look on them as things of indifferency" (143).

Astell appropriates Descartes's and More's concept of generosity for feminist purposes. In her *Proposal* and *The Christian Religion*, she teaches women that once they have the virtue of generosity they need not feel anger or fear toward their persecutors. This virtue enables women to disregard "the Censures of ill People" (SP II, 95), and to have a "Generous Disdain of such things as are beneath us" (CR, 265). A "Great and *Generous* Mind without *Pride*" knows "what is Valuable and what Contemptible," and knows also "that all Men may make a due use of their Liberty as well as we, which is that which distinguishes them" (CR, 285). A virtuous woman does not strive "to pull down others"; she has "too just a Sentiment of [her] own Merit to envy or detract from others," and harbors only "a generous Resolution to repair [her own] former neglects by future diligence" (SP II, 74). To have a generous mind is to be free from meanness and petty resentment toward others, because one knows that one's dignity and esteem come are from a private struggle alone, and is not dependent on other people's good opinion. Like Descartes, Astell maintains that this virtue consists in a firm resolution to exercise one's freedom toward the best ends. In a 1714 letter to her friend Ann Coventry, Astell says, "It is indeed essential to y^e. Character of y^e. Generous y^t. they govern y^m.selves by Right Reason, & not by Example, or y^e. receiv'd Maxims & Fashions of the Age."[13] Scorn and contempt are "therefore to be submitted to, I had almost said Gloried in, by all who make a Right use of their Liberty, endeavouring to do always what is Best."[14]

Along similar lines, Astell urges women to cultivate the traditional Aristotelian virtue of courage in their search for happiness. For her, courage is not the typically masculine character trait of being bold and fearless in the face of physical danger; it does not require the pursuit of heroic deeds and honor in the public political domain. A woman as well as a man might cultivate the excellence of courage, as a private virtue rather than a civic one. She might *"put on the whole Armor of God* without degenerating into a Masculine Temper" and "without any offence to the Men" (CR, 103). This is because courage consists in "Bravery of the Mind" (SP II, 73) or "Bravery and Greatness of Soul" (SP I, 46). It is the mental capacity to stand firm and to show resolution in the face of psychological pressures—such as ridicule and criticism ("the scoffs and insignificant noises of ludicrous Wits and pert Buffoons" [SP I, 44])—as well as in the face of one's own weaknesses, such as unruliness or laziness. An enlightened woman might not necessarily risk her life on the battlefield, but she must be prepared to sacrifice her public reputation. Such women require courage in order to bear "being Censur'd as Singular and Laugh'd at for Fools, rather than comply with the evil Customs of the Age" (SP II, 172). Astell asks, "How hard is it to quit an old road?" and adds, "What courage as well as prudence does it require? How clear a Judgment to overlook the Prejudices of Education and Example and to discern what is best, and how strong a resolution, notwithstanding all the Scoffs and Noises of the world to adhere to it!" (SP I, 33). Above all, courage comes from knowing that true happiness cannot be found in the particular goods of this world, only the general good of the next. This knowledge renders us *"firm and bold* in Difficulties, and intrepid in the greatest Dangers" (CR, 284). It enables us "to throw off Sloth and to Conquer the Prejudices of Education, Authority and Custom" (SP II, 94). Once a woman acquires such firmness of character, she might "Conquer the World . . . without doing violence to any Person" (CR, 103); she might become the "greatest Hero" (CR, 104).

Friendship

In Astell's view, women can learn to acquire the virtue of courage with the assistance of another virtue—that of friendship. Rosalind Hursthouse notes that friendship is an "awkward exception" to the fact that virtues are typically character traits or "a state of one's character" (1999, 11). But we can think of "being a friend" as having a certain disposition to love other people in a certain way. In Astell's mind, friendship is "one of the brightest Vertues" (*L*, 80) and "a Vertue which comprehends all the rest; none being fit for this, who is not adorned with every other Vertue" (*SP I*, 36). In her *Proposal*, Astell says that one of the main benefits of an all-female academy is that it will encourage the cultivation of "noble Vertuous and Disteress'd" friendships between women (*SP I*, 20). Her concept of friendship thus differs from the modern notion of friendship, which some see as a potential source of moral degeneration rather than advancement.[15] For Astell, friendship consists in "the greatest usefulness, the most refin'd and disinteress'd Benevolence, a love that thinks nothing within the bounds of Power and Duty, too much to do or suffer for its Beloved; And makes no distinction betwixt its Friend and its self except that in Temporals it prefers her interest" (*SP I*, 36–37).

To conceive of friendship on Astell's terms, as a source of moral improvement rather than corruption, it is useful to consider the parallels between Astell's notion of friendship and the ancient Aristotelian conception.[16] Astell herself never refers to Aristotle, but she puts forward a concept that has much in common with his normative ideal of friendship as the mutual desire to promote another's well-being for her own sake. In book eight of the *Nicomachean Ethics* (350 B.C.), Aristotle identifies a form of friendship based upon mutual recognition of the other's moral goodness or excellence of character. Such friendship, known as "perfect" or "character" friendship, requires that two friends develop certain intentions toward each another. It consists in wanting, and actively promoting, a friend's well-being for her own sake, and not for self-interested motives. Character friends love one another for who they essentially are, and not (or not *only*) for the pleasure and utility that they bring to the relationship.[17] Such friendship does not happen overnight. It is the outcome of two persons spending a long period of time together, such that they become familiar with each other's character and develop lasting ties of love and affection.

In keeping with this view of friendship, Astell emphasizes that it is important for friends to learn to love one another for who they essentially are. In her academy, she says, close friendships will help to contribute

28   Feminist Interpretations of Mary Astell

toward a woman's moral advancement because virtuous friends will be as devoted to "bettering the beloved Person" as they are to bettering themselves (*SP I*, 37). There can be no selfishness or envy among such friends, for "how can she repine at anothers wel-fare, who reckons it the greatest part of her own?" (*SP I*, 20) Like Cicero, Astell suggests that friends have a duty "to watch over each other for Good, to advise, encourage and direct, and to observe the minutest fault in order to its amendment" (*SP I*, 37). Through kind admonition and "watching over each others Souls for their mutual Good" (*CR*, 230), friends can further each other's moral perfection. In this way, friendship is a special instance of the theological virtue of charity, or the love of benevolence, at work in promoting the good of others.

Prudence

By now, it ought to be clear that Astell does not use the term "prudence" in the modern, nonmoral, sense of rational self-interest. In the context of her work, prudence is in fact synonymous with the ancient moral concept of *phronesis* or practical wisdom.[18] In his *Politics*, Aristotle defines phronesis as the capacity to deliberate upon the correct means to bring about the right end in a situation that calls for action. In the early modern period, moral philosophers continued to uphold this ideal, and like Aristotle, they regarded it as a necessary condition of virtue. In his *Treatise Concerning Christian Prudence* (1710), John Norris advises that "there is no possibility of a Man's being Vertuous without Prudence" (*TCP*, 5). Following Aristotle (whom he cites on page 75), Norris defines prudence as "*Practical Knowledge*" (*TCP*, 67) or an ability to "judge right in the very instant of Action" (*TCP*, 34). More specifically, prudence is "the same with the last Practical Dictate of the Understanding, *judging rightly*, and directing the Will to the choice of that which is right and fit to be Chosen" (*TCP*, 69). Prudence requires that we choose the right end; and the right end, according to Norris, is that which causes, or is an object of, our lasting happiness.[19]

Once prudence is understood in this sense, as a capacity for *practical moral judgment*, it is possible to detect numerous references to the idea in the *Proposal*. Astell says that women suffer from "a want of understanding to compare and judge of things, to chuse a right End, to proportion the Means to the End, and to rate ev'ry thing according to its proper value" (*SP I*, 13). They live "at Random without any design or end," and they lack the "judgment to discern when to fix" upon a steady course of action (*SP I*, 31). As a remedy, she calls upon women to acquire a "true Practical Knowledge"

(*SP I*, 24) and a clear "Judgment to overlook the Prejudices of Education and Example and to discern what is best" (*SP I*, 33). The "Art of Prudence" is not only "the being all of a Piece, managing all our Words and Actions as it becomes Wise Persons and Good Christians" (*SP I*, 120), but is also the ability to make the most of everything that happens. It is the ability to judge which actions are "not only Fit but Necessary" in certain circumstances, even though in different times and places the same actions might be inappropriate (*SP I*, 127). Above all, prudence gives us a capacity for sound judgment in situations that call for moral action. When the passions threaten to gain mastery over our will, Astell says that

> Recollection, a sedate and sober frame of Mind, prevents this Mischief, it keeps our Reason always on her Guard and ready to exert her self; it fits us to Judge truly of all occurrences, and to draw advantage from whatever happens. This is the true Art of Prudence, for that which properly speaks us Wise, is the accommodating all the Accidents of Life to the great End of Living. And since the Passiveness of our Nature makes us liable to many Sufferings which we cou'd wish to avoid, Wisdom consists in the using those Powers, which GOD has given us the free disposal of, in such a manner, as to make those very things which befal us against our Will, an occasion of Good to us. (*SP II*, 162–63)

We can now see why Astell recommends the art of prudence as "*the main thing* we are to drive at in all our Studies" (*SP II*, 120; my emphasis). Out of all the virtues, women need prudence most of all in order to do the best thing or to get things right in the sphere of moral action. A prudent woman will choose the right end, she will choose *happiness* or the good in general. She will correctly exercise her *freedom* when making judgments about what to do, and she will direct her *love* to the right objects. She will have the correct emotional responses in practical situations: she will *admire* the right things, she will be *generous* when confronted with the moral failings of others, and *courageous* in the face of adversity and criticism. She will contract *virtuous friendships*, or friendships that promote the moral well-being of both herself and her friend. Taken as a whole, these are the most crucial factors in a woman's moral reformation. Without prudence, a woman will lose the most precious thing possible, everlasting happiness and union with God. All the core features of Astell's educational program—the proper exercising of freedom of the will, the suspension of judgment, the redirecting of the passions,

30   Feminist Interpretations of Mary Astell

and so on—are designed to help women achieve this vital moral-theological objective.

Conclusion

On the whole, then, Astell conceives of the problem of female subordination and male domination in markedly different terms from those of most modern feminists. For Astell, the problem is a moral one. The "vilest Slavery" for women is not political or social in nature, but rather moral and psychological. It involves "the Captivation of . . . Understandings" (SP II, 136) and the enslavement of souls (SP II, 94). Since the source of a woman's oppression is principally inside her own mind, Astell's solution focuses on a woman's interior life or her moral character. Her study plan prompts women to think about "what sorts of persons" they should be, rather than "what sorts of action are right or obligatory." Astell herself concedes that "[t]he Men therefore may still enjoy their Prerogatives for us, we mean not to intrench on any of their Lawful Privileges" (SP II, 179) "our only endeavour shall be to be absolute Monarchs in our own Bosoms" (SP II, 180).

In light of this interior focus, Astell's proposal might be criticized for its failure to rectify women's disadvantages in the external world. Some critics might point out that not only does Astell's moral philosophy fail to address the social and political inequalities between men and women, it positively reinforces them. In the Proposal, Astell promotes certain character traits—such as charity (an attitude of benevolence or loving kindness toward others), generosity (a remedy to anger and resentment), and courage (in the face of physical and psychological threats)—that encourage women to submit to, rather than challenge, the external status quo. The virtue of justice, which might have enabled Astell to promote the notion of women "receiving benefits according to merit,"[20] is curiously absent from her feminist thought. In short, while Astell's ethical theory might be described as feminist in intention, on the surface it would appear to be indistinguishable from any anti-feminist theory that sought to perpetuate women's political subordination by focusing on internal happiness at the expense of external freedom.

Nevertheless, in my view, Astell's theory of virtue might still hold some interest for modern-day feminist ethics, and her emphasis on excellence of character might be considered a strength rather than a weakness of her feminist philosophy. In a recent article, Alison Jaggar identifies two assumptions shared by feminist ethicists: "The first of these is that the subordination of women is morally wrong; the second is that the moral experience of women should be treated as respectfully as the moral experience of men" (1990, 97–98). Though a modern feminist might not accept every aspect of Astell's approach, her moral philosophy meets these broad criteria for a feminist ethic. Astell accepts that the subordination of women is morally wrong *in some sense*, and she consistently treats the sexes as morally on a par. More importantly, in her theory of virtue, she envisions "morally desirable alternatives that will promote women's emancipation" (Jaggar 1990, 98).

Above all, Astell implicitly challenges those moral theorists who regard women as inferior in terms of their moral status and their capacity for practical judgment. Aristotle famously held the view that husbands are justified in ruling over their wives because women lack the capacity for phronesis or prudence, the prime virtue of rulers.[21] Women are unable to acquire prudence because they cannot control their passions and act upon their rational deliberations in situations that call for moral action. For this same reason, according to Aristotle, it is not possible for husbands and wives to have equal character friendships with one another. So long as women are in the position of the ruled and men are the rulers, men and women will remain unequal partners in friendship. Women might still be virtuous, but they will have a different kind of virtue than men, and are incapable of acquiring the highest virtue. By contrast, Astell allows that women can cultivate prudence, and that they have the capacity to be as virtuous as the best of men. Admittedly, in some passages, Astell extols the traditional "feminine" virtues of her time, such as modesty and chastity; but in others, she deliberately rejects those virtues typically recommended to women alone—especially the virtue of obedience. She warns women that "[a] blind Obedience is what a Rational Creature shou'd never pay . . . a blind Obedience is an Obeying *without reason*, for ought we know, *against it*" (RM, 75).

In addition, Astell reconceives the classical virtues of courage, friendship, and generosity as essential tools in the service of female emancipation. In her study of *Plato and the Virtue of Courage* (2006), Linda R. Rabieh comments on some recent feminist critiques of courage as a macho-military quality, typically associated with war and violence. Rabieh points outs that "[b]ecause they [the feminist critics] treat it from the outset as a sickness, they do not investigate its many facets. As a result, feminist critics miss the possibility that a dialectical investigation of courage and what kind of virtue it is cannot only uncover a healthy conception of a courage but can also shed greater light on a genuine human excellence" (2006, 17). Three

32   Feminist Interpretations of Mary Astell

hundred years earlier, Astell had already reconceived of courage in terms that were amenable to feminist thought. For her, it was not the capacity to face death and injury without fear, but rather the strength to face criticism and ridicule for embracing a singular lifestyle as a woman. In Astell's philosophy, the character trait of courage becomes a feminist virtue when it is put to service in the fight against custom, especially those customary practices that thwart a woman's moral and intellectual advancement.

Along the same lines, Astell maintains that female friendships can act as props or support networks for women who hold unconventional views about women and their place in the world.[22] Such friendships can provide women with a moral vantage point from which to identify, and then challenge, customary practices that are detrimental to their happiness and well-being. More recently, Marilyn Friedman (1993) has argued that friends can help us to reprogram our moral thinking and reflect critically on our moral starting points, such as our families, churches, schools, and neighborhoods. For her, friendship can be a socially and politically disruptive force: it can lead us to challenge the subjection of women in our communities of origin, and thus initiate sociopolitical reform. Astell likewise promotes the power of female friendships to counter the customs and preconceptions of early modern society, especially those that obstruct a woman's moral and intellectual advancement. For Astell, the value of female friendship lies in promoting and nurturing values that will enable women to overcome the prejudices of their upbringing and find true and lasting happiness.

Finally, we have seen that Astell also valorizes the Cartesian virtue of generosity as a species of legitimate self-esteem for women. Of this virtue, Lisa Shapiro notes that "the first step in acquiring generosity is to recognise that we are freely willing . . . and that this recognition comes principally with a critical reflection on what we find ourselves taking for granted. For it is precisely with this reflection, which essentially involves turning our thoughts away from those to which we are predisposed, that we exercise our freedom" (1999a, 257–58). While such a revolution in thinking might not be a sufficient condition in itself for feminist emancipation, it is undoubtedly a necessary one. Any attempt at feminist consciousness-raising must begin with instilling this attitude of "critical reflection on what we find ourselves taking for granted." This is what Astell's *Proposal* does: it encourages women to see that they have the means to their liberation—and their moral development and self-esteem—within themselves. Every woman, with the help of a "generous Resolution," might decide to throw off the "Yoke of Impertinent Customs" and attain firmness of mind

(*SP II*, 74, 73). Herein lies a point of enduring relevance in Astell's feminist theory of virtue.

Abbreviations

AT XI René Descartes, *Les passions de l'ame*, in *Oeuvres de Descartes*, vol. XI (1967)

CR Mary Astell, *The Christian Religion, as Profess'd by a Daughter of the Church of England* (1705) (cited by page number)

CSM I René Descartes, *Passions of the Soul*, in *The Philosophical Writings of Descartes*, vol. I (1985)

L Mary Astell, *Letters Concerning the Love of God* (2005)

RM Mary Astell, *Reflections upon Marriage* (1996)

SP I Mary Astell, *A Serious Proposal to the Ladies, Part I* (1997)

SP II Mary Astell, *A Serious Proposal to the Ladies, Part II* (1997)

TCP John Norris, *A Treatise Concerning Christian Prudence* (1710)

Notes

1. Opinions about women's innate inconstancy and lasciviousness were prevalent in popular jest books and marital advice manuals of the period. See, for example, [Gould and Brown] (1682); Anonymous (1685); and Sprint (1699).

2. See Porter (2001).

3. Astell was the author of several pamphlets in defense of High-Church Anglicanism. See Astell (1704a, 1704b, 1704c). The last two works are republished in Astell (1996).

4. My modernized version of the 1717 second edition, Astell (2013), has recently been published in The Other Voice in Early Modern Europe: Toronto series.

5. On the essential requirements of virtue ethics, see Oakley (1996, 138); Trianosky (1990, 335).

6. See Hursthouse (1999, 3).

7. For a modern edition of Astell's correspondence with Norris, see Astell and Norris (2005). The Astell-Norris correspondence (1693–94) was originally published in 1695.

8. On this topic, see Kremer (2000).

9. On this topic, see Broad (2007).

10. Here Astell echoes Descartes's views about the passion of admiration or wonder (AT XI, 373; CSM I, 350).

11. In her second *Proposal*, Astell acknowledges her indebtedness to both More's *Account of Virtue* and Descartes's *Passions of the Soul* (see *SP II*, 165). There are various unnamed references to Descartes's *Passions* in her other works (CR, 286–87; Astell 1709, 140).

12. On Cartesian generosity, see Brown (2006, 188–209); Shapiro (1999); and Tilmouth (2007). On Astell's concept of generosity, see Sowaal (2007, 228, 232).

13. Mary Astell to Ann Coventry, July 26, 1714; in appendix C to Perry (1986, 370). In this letter, Astell appears to be paraphrasing *A Discourse Concerning Generosity* (1693), an anonymous work (sometimes attributed to John Somers) that is heavily indebted to Descartes's concept of generosity in the *Passions*. Unlike Descartes, Astell never explicitly affirms that this virtue is "the key to all the other virtues" (AT XI, 454; CSM I, 388).

14. Mary Astell to Ann Coventry, July 26, 1714; in appendix C to Perry (1986, 371).

15. See Cocking and Kennett (2000).

16. On this topic, see Broad (2009). On Astell and friendship more generally, see Kolbrener (2007).

17. On this topic, see Cooper (1977, 635).

18. On this same topic in the work of Christine de Pizan, see Green (2005, 2007).

34   Feminist Interpretations of Mary Astell

19. Though Norris did not publish the *Treatise* until 1710, this work enlarges upon the themes of an earlier essay, "A Discourse Concerning Worldly and Divine Wisdom," in the second volume of his *Practical Discourses* (1693). It is likely that Astell was familiar with this essay. There are similarities between Astell's idea of prudence and Norris's Christianized conception of the virtue.

20. On the topic of justice as a virtue, see Slote (2010).

21. See Bradshaw (1991).

22. See Broad (2009).

3

Mary Astell's Account of Feminine Self-Esteem

Kathleen A. Ahearn

In *Letters Concerning the Love of God* (1693), Mary Astell's first publication, she breaks from the subject of her philosophical discourse with her mentor, John Norris, to declare, "Fain I wou'd rescue my Sex, or at least as many of them as come within my little Sphere, from the Meanness of Spirit into which the Generality of them are sunk, perswade them to pretend to some higher Excellency than a well-chosen Pettycoat, or a fashionable Commode" (*L*, 43). This reference to women's meanness in *Letters* demonstrates that Astell's growing preoccupation with feminine self-esteem is present from this first of her publications through her fourth, *Reflections upon Marriage* (1706). By the end of her second and third publications, *A Serious Proposal to the Ladies, Parts I and II* (1694, 1697), Astell has articulated a definition of self-esteem that features universality, "since GOD has given

36   Feminist Interpretations of Mary Astell

Women as well as Men intelligent souls" (SP I, 80); self-preservation, "as every Creature has an aptness to take such courses as tend to its preservation" (SP II, 127); and independence, since self-esteem frees women from falling into the error of "priz[ing] her self on some Imaginary Excellency or for anything that is not truly Valuable" (SP II, 233).

For Astell, self-esteem is not the same as self-love, which she associates with vanity, pride and self-centeredness, vices in women she wishes to root out. She explains, "Self-love, an excellent Principle when true, but the worst and most mischievous when mistaken, disposes us to be retentive of our Prejudices and Errors, especially when it is joyn'd as most commonly it is with Pride and Conceitedness" (SP II, 135–36).[1] When self-love is "true," it is accompanied by benevolence—that is, a humble attitude of goodwill toward the self and others. But Astell contends that benevolence is not sufficient for women to overcome the formidable barriers they face in achieving a kind of self-esteem that features self-preservation, generosity, toward the self and others, and a concept of self that is independent of societal pressures. Further, it does not touch the vice of pride, "this Tumor of Mind" that is a symptom of false self-esteem (SP II, 233).

Astell wishes to assist women in overcoming their "groveling Spirit," a task requiring the proper management of the passions to achieve virtue and happiness for which René Descartes's theory of passions is uniquely made (SP II, 232). But since Astell's project is to raise women up out of meanness that results from societal prejudices and inferior education, her theory necessarily differs from Descartes's on several key points. She argues that women, who live in a society "where the custom is to mock and degrade them," must achieve independence from prejudices concerning their nature, and they must balance generosity with self-preservation, a given in Descartes's system, but not for women who are expected to act in self-sacrificing ways (Sowaal 2007, 232). For these reasons, Astell ties self-esteem in women to God, whom she redefines as good, kind, and just; instead of tying it to the kind of self who has achieved self-mastery, as Descartes does. This move provides an inner refuge for women who need to develop a self-concept that encompasses their innate potential to develop intellectually, emotionally, and morally along the same lines as men develop. Further, elevating the passion of love to the same level as the passion of wonder, which is Descartes's leading passion, emphasizes that loving correctly (i.e., not in self-destructive ways) is the key for women to cultivate feminine self-esteem.

Like Descartes, Astell wants women to be happy in the Stoic sense of achieving inner mastery and tranquility in the face of outer circumstances, whatever they may be. This wish is complicated, however, by the emancipatory nature of her theory. When Astell calls for the development of self-esteem in wives, the tension between her goal of promoting Stoic happiness, on the one hand, and freedom from injustice, on the other, is most acute. For example, in *Reflections*, her most polemical text, she encourages women to use the tools she provides to avoid bad marriages that are characterized by slave-like conditions, for which she views martyrdom as a last resort. Whereas Stoic happiness involves competence and self-care, so that, according to Michael Frede, "one must be good at taking care of oneself, at dealing with the kinds of situations and problems one encounters in life" (Frede 1999, 71), Astell's method puts women's self-care in conflict with societal expectations concerning feminine capacities and wifely duties that may pose barriers to women's pursuit of intellectual, spiritual, and emotional attainments. Her curriculum involves self-care and attention to what she calls women's "Temporal and Eternal Concerns" (*SP II*, 233). In this sense she is most interested in and influenced by what Jacqueline Broad calls Descartes's "guise as a philosopher in search of happiness and the good life"—that is, his moral philosophy. But Astell is also keenly interested in his "skeptical challenge, his rationalist epistemology, and his dualist theory of mind and body," all of which she draws upon in chapter 3 of *Serious Proposal, Part II* to theorize the connection between women's intellectual development and her moral development (Broad 2007, 166).

Ultimately Astell's goal is for women to exert their God-given capacity to "advance and Perfect [their] Being," which will lead to happiness if that inner drive is aligned with God's will (*SP I*, 62). In this sense her theory of self-esteem combines Cambridge Platonist theosophy with Cartesian moral philosophy to emancipate women from inner and outer forms of oppression. This is a paradoxical approach given that her call for dependence on God to foster self-esteem is designed to liberate women from societal prejudices. Even so, throughout her first four publications, Astell's theory unfolds consistently, if complexly, to reveal a method of achieving feminine self-esteem that has practical and theoretical relevance today, especially with respect to balancing relationship commitments and self-care. The following will trace the development of Astell's theory as it unfolds throughout her first three publications and as she applies it in her fourth publication to the fraught case of wives.

Occasionalism and Love

That women are God's instruments rather than men's instruments is a foundational idea to Astell's theory of feminine self-esteem, and this idea emerges in her correspondence with her mentor, John Norris, in her first

38   Feminist Interpretations of Mary Astell

publication, *Letters Concerning the Love of God*. Norris, a second-generation Cambridge Platonist philosopher, was influenced by the French philosopher Nicholas Malebranche, as well as by members of the Cambridge Platonist School, including Henry More and Ralph Cudworth, who combined dualist philosophy with theology to more precisely align rationalism with religion (Mintz 1962, 82).[2] According to Samuel Mintz, the Cambridge thinkers overlaid "clear philosophical thinking and the dialectical search for truth" with what Richard Acworth explains is "a basic approach to God, apprehended as present to the soul in the form of truth" (Mintz 1962, 82; Acworth 1977, 675). Norris's dualism was of a particularly extreme sort in that he believed in a hard and fast distinction between the two substances of mind and body, with no possibility for interaction between these substances. In fact, he adopted Malebranche's causal theory called "occasionalism," whereby it is believed that matter (bodies) is incidental to God's creation.[3] In other words, God alone causes sensations and thoughts to happen in the mind so that the body itself is not really needed; the body is extra, even a nuisance, in Norris's framework.

Because of this stance, Norris was derided as a mystic by some of his contemporaries, who felt that in his attempt to "extend the Cartesian method to theological questions," he went too far (Acworth 1977, 674, 676).[4] Since Norris believes that "God is the only true causal agent" and "is directly, immediately and solely responsible for bringing about all phenomena," then bodies are theoretically incidental to God's creation (Acworth 1977, 626). This is a particular sticking point for Astell, who debates Norris on this point throughout *Letters*. For example, she is suspicious of his claim that "GOD, for instance, can raise the Sensation of Burning in the Soul without any Impression of Fire upon her Body" (L, 83). Withdrawal from society to commune solely with God is the consequence of such a theory, and Astell cannot accept this approach because it contradicts the biblical commandment to love one's neighbors. She replies, "Creatures may be sought for our Good, but not loved as our Good . . . methinks 'tis too nice for common Practice" (L, 86). Indeed, learning to love others for *their* good, a kind of love she refers to as benevolence, is the result of living within a human community.

Astell's response to Norris on this point is indicative of how her mind works in both theological and philosophical registers. Turning to a passage in the Gospel of Luke—"You shall love the Lord your God with all your heart, and with all your soul, and with all your strength, and with all your mind; and your neighbor as yourself" (Luke 10:27)—Astell follows the biblical precedent wherein the love of God, self, and neighbors is intertwined. This model of loving the self in relationship to others and as a reflection of God's will is a cornerstone of Astell's emerging theory because it teaches women to separate two distinct kinds of love that are easy to confuse, desire and benevolence. Desire and benevolence are technical terms for Astell, with desire being a passionate, all-encompassing kind of love that is to be reserved for God and benevolence being a disinterested kind of love characterized by charity and goodwill to others. Desire should be directed toward God, not humans, in order to avoid idolatry and inaccurate conceptions of one's identity and worth.

The following exchange in *Letters* highlights Astell's concern with how loving friends and neighbors with desire rather than benevolence can cause harm. From her own experience, she explains that "having by Nature a strong Propensity to friendly Love, which I have all along encouraged as a good Disposition to Vertue. . . . I have contracted such a Weakness, I will not say by Nature . . . but by voluntary Habit, that it is a very difficult thing for me to love at all, without something of Desire" (*L*, 33). Loving a friend with desire, as opposed to benevolence or "friendly love," causes grief if and when that friendship ends. In the letter to which Astell refers, she characterizes this phenomenon as a weakness, yet she also suggests that this weakness is a result of custom or "Voluntary habit," leaving the reader wondering exactly what she means.

In an addendum to the letter, she clarifies this confusion by stating, "the Writer of this Letter . . . desires to retract what is said in this: For she owns 'tis her Opinion, that next to Sorrow for our own Sins, our Neighbors refusing to receive the Spiritual Good we wish them, is the justest, greatest, and most lasting Cause of Grief" (*L*, 34). When women love God with desire, they are supplied with spiritual goods like self-worth, peace, happiness, tranquility, truth, etc., goods that they cannot obtain in lasting ways from fellow humans. But in this passage, Astell both implies that human beings *can* supply one another with spiritual goods and that rejection naturally and justifiably causes grief. Grief is therefore not a sign of weakness but an indicator of the risk involved in loving others. Further, she contends that desirous love of God purifies benevolent love to humans so that one is assured to love others properly—that is, for their good, not for one's own good. Fortunately, Astell has a philosophical explanation for how this distinction can be made so that these two kinds of love may be properly directed.

Unlike Norris, Astell is concerned to develop a theory according to which the commonsense observation that minds affect bodies holds some truth; she observes, "as the Soul forsakes the Body when this vital Congruity fails,

40   Feminist Interpretations of Mary Astell

so when this sensible Congruity is wanting as in the Case of Blindness, Deafness, or the Palsie, &c. The Soul has no Sensation of Colours, Sounds, Heat and the like" (L, 132). She alludes to Norris's own mentor, the Cambridge Platonist Henry More, who offers a metaphysical explanation for how minds and bodies affect one another. Astell's use of the expressions "vital congruity" and "sensible congruity" in the above passage is an adaptation of More's expression "vital congruity," which is part of his theory of the "spirit of nature" that he describes in The Immortality of the Soul (1659). For More, the spirit of nature is "a substance incorporeal, but without Sense and Animadversion, [that] pervades the whole matter of the Universe and exercises an Plastical power therein" (More 1969b, 169). According to More, the existence of this spiritual substance within matter explains how bodies maintain motion. Vital congruity, by contrast, refers to the predisposition within substances to unite and interact. Thus, the substance, spirit of nature, and the feature of this and all substances, vital congruity, guarantee that mind, matter, and, by proxy, "creatures" not only interact, but also have "causal efficacy," which Norris attributes solely to God.[5]

This explanation not only clarifies for Astell how minds and bodies interact but also accounts for the use of nature within God's creation, a central interest for Astell, who writes in Serious Proposal, Part II, "GOD made nothing in Vain" (SP II, 168). Following More's account of spirit of nature and vital congruity, she explains that matter can "draw forth . . . sensations in the Soul" so that God can act by way of "his servant nature mediately" rather than immediately (L, 132, 131). This is the philosophical point upon which Astell rests her claim in Letters that people can be used by God as his servants to carry out his will with respect to friends and neighbors. But this also lays the foundation for her to argue that women, who tend to be, according to Jacqueline Broad, "intimately associated and intermingled with their bodies," have efficacy and worth as God's servants, not men's servants (Broad 2007, 174). When one directs passionate love toward God, "she has no Pleasure, no Coveting and no Ambition but to partake in the Divine Nature," and benevolent love is purified so that it is not accompanied by jealousy, covetousness, envy, selfishness, etc. In this sense partaking in the divine nature is a cleansing act since "the Soul that centres all her Love on GOD has no Temptation to those Sins that obstruct her benevolence to her Neighbor" (L, 101).

Norris is displeased with Astell's line of reasoning, calling sensible congruity "an absurd and unphilosophical Prejudice" (L, 137). Though she is not dissuaded from the Cambridge Platonist explanation of the interaction between mind and body, Norris's response casts doubt on a part of More's

Astell's Account of Feminine Self-Esteem   41

theory in which he posits that the soul has two parts, one that is superior and cannot be moved by matter and the other that is inferior and interacts with matter. Norris disagrees with this idea, responding, "thus the Stoicks of old and thus you now. . . . I do not see what Advantage accrues of this Distinction" (L, 84). Astell admits she is not convinced by the two-part soul theory either and replies: "As for the Distinction of the Soul into inferior and superior Part[s], I am as little satisfied with it as you can be, and do confess to you ingenuously that I have no clear idea of that which is properly my self, nor do I well know how to distinguish its Powers and Operations" (L, 88). This is a significant moment in Letters because Astell's query into what constitutes a soul leads her to Descartes's mechanistic explanation of the interaction between mind and body, in which he emphasizes "the manifest simplicity and knowability of the self" (Nelson 2005, 400).

In response to Astell's admission of doubt concerning the soul's makeup, Norris quotes Malebranche: "[God] has made thee for himself. Wherefore I shall not discover to thee the Idea of thy Being, till that happy Time when the View of the very Essence of thy GOD shall deface and eclipse all thy Beauties, and make thee despise all that thou art, that thou mayst think only of contemplating him" (L, 95). Though Astell agrees that humans should contemplate God, and she will soon argue that women's self-esteem arises from God, she cannot accept a theory or theology that highlights the self's wretchedness vis-à-vis God. Women already feel wretched when stripped of the trappings of beauty, status, attention, and material goods like fine clothing, social status, etc. Astell wants women to realize that God has made them with the capacity for moral and intellectual greatness, and this goal accords with Descartes's view that freeing the human will from passionate influences "renders us in a certain way like God" (AT XI, 445; CSM I, 384).

Habituation and Resolution

In Passions of the Soul ([1649] 1989), Descartes offers a mechanical explanation for how the soul is moved by matter, and most importantly for Astell, how the soul can retain its sovereignty over outside stimuli. In developing his theory of the interaction between mind and body, Descartes partakes in a systematizing tradition going back to St. Thomas Aquinas, who revised Stoic conceptions of passions by compiling a list of eleven binary pairings with their opposites. In "Traces of the Body: Cartesian Passions," Brown and Normore explain that for Aquinas, "the figure of Christ stands as a

42   Feminist Interpretations of Mary Astell

model for human beings and Christ has no passions except 'propassiones' or intellectual passions, which are not tied to the body in the way the passions are in humans" (Brown and Normore 2003, 88). In *Passions of the Soul*, Descartes is interested in accounting for the role the body plays with respect to passions, which explains Astell's reliance on his theory, especially in *Serious Proposal, Part II*, with its philosophical defense of her curriculum.[6]

On this point Descartes breaks from the Stoic tradition whereby passions are to be rooted out because they lead to "ascensions and recessions to folly" (James 2002, 142–43). Rather, he sees passions as good if managed properly. He writes, "Now that we are acquainted with all the passions, we have much less reason for anxiety about them than we had before. For we see that they are all by nature good, and we have nothing to avoid but their misuse or their excess, against which the remedies I have explained might be sufficient if each person took enough care to apply them" (AT XI, 485–86; CSM I, 403). Astell follows Descartes's holistic approach to theorizing and managing passions, and she adopts the methods he proposes, which employ the tools of habituation and resolution that he claims everyone can learn to implement.[7]

When Descartes fully embraces dualism, he rejects the view of a two-part soul since "it is to the body alone that we should attribute everything that can be observed in us to oppose our reason" (AT XI, 365; CSM I, 346). In other words, the soul cannot struggle against itself as it would if one part of it were passively moved by matter. So when Descartes insists, "there is within us but one soul, and this soul has within it no diversity of parts," he needs another way to account for how bodies affect minds and vice versa (AT XI, 364; CSM I, 346). In *The Passions of the Soul*, he offers this explanation in terms of the pineal gland, which he describes as "a certain very small gland, situated in the middle of the brain's substance and suspended above the passage through which the spirits in the brain's anterior cavities communicate with those in its posterior cavities" (AT XI, 352; CSM I, 340). The pineal gland is passive in that "the slightest movements on the part of this gland may alter very greatly the course of these spirits, and conversely any change, however slight, taking place in the course of the spirits may do much to change the movements of the gland" (AT XI, 352; CSM I, 340).

Since the will in Descartes's system "is by its nature so free that it can never be constrained," it would seem that willing alone could alter the direction of the pineal gland and thereby redirect one's attention from detrimental to beneficial stimuli (AT XI, 359; CSM I, 343). But this is not always the case "because, of all the kinds of thought which the soul may have, there are none that agitate and disturb it so strongly as the passions" (AT XI, 350; CSM I, 339). Descartes signals a close affinity between passion and thought so that in the case of emotions, one must cultivate tranquility to first calm the animal spirits and thereby disentangle the mind from the body. This is important because "until this disturbance ceases they remain present to our mind in the same way as the objects of the senses are present to it while they are acting on our sense organs" (AT XI, 363; CSM I, 345). In the case of very strong passions, the will alone cannot succeed in conquering them; rather, "we must apply ourselves to consider the reasons, objects or precedents which persuade us" to act independently of them (AT XI, 363; CSM I, 345).

In chapter 4 of *Serious Proposal, Part II*, Astell follows Descartes's theory and his method for managing the passions. With respect to the will, she focuses less on its freedom than on the imperative to align the human will with God's will, a move that supports her later claim that self-esteem terminates in God, not in mastery of the self. She explains, "Whenever we oppose our Wills to [God's], we change in a manner the very Constitution of our Nature and fly from that Happiness which we wou'd pursue" (*SP II*, 206). Further, if one's will is not aligned with God's will, it becomes customary to make "unreasonable Choices" which result in "a new and wrong bias to our Inclinations" so that the will pursues happiness in mistaken ways (*SP II*, 207). For Astell, passions are good and "design'd in the Order of Nature for the good of the Body," but when the will, which is "intended for the Good of the Soul," is corrupted, "Spiritual Good" is abandoned for that which "may be Seen and Felt" (*SP II*, 207). A vicious feedback loop into vice then takes hold.

Though the will in Astell's framework is potentially free, it is more limited in its capacity to disconnect from emotions. With the help of Cartesian habituation, however, which involves "a single action and does not require long practice," freedom from emotional bondage is possible (AT XI, 369; CSM I, 348). On this point, Astell shares Descartes's optimism when she writes, "If therefore we assist [a passion] with a little Meditation, it will readily come over; and tho we may find it difficult absolutely to quash a Passion that is once begun, yet it is no hard matter to transfer it" (*SP II*, 223). As mentioned earlier, her approach to handling a strong passion that cannot be "quashed" is holistic. She writes, "all she can do is to Continue the Passion as it was begun, or to Divert it to another Object, or Heighten or to let it Sink by degrees, or some way or other Modifie and Direct it" (*SP II*, 214). The active verbs in this sentence—that is, "divert," "heighten,"

44   Feminist Interpretations of Mary Astell

"modify," and "direct"—attest to the inner agency required to perform habituation, "the due performance of which is what we call *Vertue*" (*SP II*, 214).

Astell demonstrates the importance of self-preservation to her theory when she emphasizes the injury that strong or violent passions can inflict on an individual. By contrast, Descartes welcomes the challenge that these kinds of emotions have with respect to strengthening the soul. Astell, however, is concerned that women avoid self-harm, and she advocates constant vigilance with respect to managing strong passions that may be injurious. From her vantage point, Descartes's method will require "Patience and constant Perseverance thro the whole course of our Lives" (*SP II*, 140). She does not welcome the test of violent passions because she doubts women can successfully handle them due to their inferior education and lack of practice. She warns, "we cannot well discern what Objects most sensibly touch us; which is our weakest side; by what means it is Expos'd or Strengthened; how we may Restrain or rightly Employ a Passion we cou'd not Prevent, and consequently grow strong by our very Infirmities" (*SP II*, 216). The danger is that without vigilance and instruction "the Passions injure us, they violently attack our Reason" (*SP II*, 215). This is a precarious mental and emotional position for women to be in.

Since passions have such a potentially debilitating effect on the will and since they arise within the body and from its senses, calming the body is an essential precursor to practicing habituation, which is a path to virtue. But Descartes thinks of the bodily and mental state of tranquility differently than Astell does; tranquility in his system is more so an outcome, even a reward, of habituation. He writes, "The satisfaction of those who steadfastly pursue virtue is a habit of their soul which is called 'tranquility' and 'peace of mind'" (AT XI, 471; CSM I, 396). "Fresh satisfaction" arises, he writes, "when we have just performed an action we think good" (AT XI, 471; CSM I, 396). For Astell, though, calming the body is a necessary precursor to habituation because women are particularly "sunk into Sense and buried alive in a crowd of Material Beings," a condition that blocks access to the requisite powers within the soul (*SP II*, 212). To cultivate poise, Astell suggests meditation, prayer, scriptural and philosophical studies, and daily conversations with like-minded women in her academy.

In order to perform virtuous actions, the goal of Descartes's theory of self-esteem, one must do more than habituate the mind; one must act with resolution or decisiveness. But this can only occur when one has cultivated knowledge of the difference between good and evil. The passions themselves do not teach individuals to be good; rather, they dispose the will to act in accordance with one's feelings that arise in response to outer stimuli. These stimuli may be good, or they may be harmful since what is appealing to the body via the senses may be harmful to the soul. Resolution, according to Descartes, is one of the soul's "proper weapons," and it consists of "firm and determinate judgements bearing upon the knowledge of good and evil, which the soul has resolved to follow in guiding its conduct" (AT XI, 367; CSM I, 347). To make good decisions, one must engage in what Lisa Shapiro calls Descartes's method of judging. She argues that his "method for judging what is best is analogous to the meditator's method for avoiding error as he articulates it in his resolution at the conclusion of the Fourth Meditation" (Shapiro 1999, 263)." But Descartes's method for judging is different because in daily decision-making, as opposed to theoretical reasoning, "we must come to terms with our limited ability to achieve certainty" (Shapiro 1999, 269). This means that, according to Descartes, "we always do our duty when we do what we judge to be best, even though our judgment may perhaps be a very bad one" (AT XI, 460; CSM I, 391). Descartes's is a forgiving approach to errors, one that Astell cannot afford to share given the import and gravity of decisions that women must make, such as whom to marry.

How then can women gain access to the knowledge of good and evil, a requirement for making wise judgments? Astell suggests that we acquire knowledge of good and evil by disengaging from our senses and understanding "that the Possession of these Worldly Advantages which Mankind so much contend for, is Good if it can procure us Eternal Felicity; and that the Want of 'em is an Evil, if it exclude us from the Kingdom of Heav'n" (SP II, 217). More specifically, she wants women to temporarily "withdraw our Minds from the World" and engage in "Attention and deep Meditation" so that the mind can ascertain "Truth" (SP II, 161). As with managing the passions, "without Attention and strict examination, we are liable to false judgments on every occasion" (SP II, 161). When women calm the body, engage in habituation, meditate, and converse with those "intelligent enough to . . . correct our mistakes," their minds become "Attent and Awakened" to truth, including the knowledge of good and evil that is required to act with virtue (SP II, 162).

Wonder and Generosity

Descartes and Astell have different ideas about what constitutes the highest virtue. For Descartes, the highest virtue is generosity, and generous people

46   Feminist Interpretations of Mary Astell

"esteem nothing more highly than doing good to others and disregarding their own self-interest" (AT XI, 448; CSM I, 385). The habit of generosity arises in those who "have complete command over their passions" (AT XI, 447–48; CSM I, 385). It is, according to Descartes, "the key to all the other virtues and a general remedy for every disorder of the passions" (AT XI, 454; CSM I, 388). As we have seen in her correspondence with Norris, Astell places a premium on generosity, but she also highlights self-preservation in keeping with her observation that women tend to love in self-injurious ways. Therefore, Astell elevates love alongside wonder as a coleading passion in her taxonomy, a move that addresses women's tendency to love in ways that cause self-harm.

In Descartes's taxonomy of passions, there are six "simple and primitive" passions that he lists: "Wonder, Love, Hatred, Desire, Joy and Sadness." He explains that "all the other passions are either composed from some of these six or they are a species of them" (AT XI, 380; CSM I, 353). Wonder is the leading passion for Descartes; he defines it as "a sudden surprise of the soul which brings it to consider with attention the objects that seem to it unusual and extraordinary . . . and worthy of special consideration" (AT XI, 380; CSM I, 353). In "Cartesian Generosity," Shapiro explains that wonder for Descartes is connected to learning and education in that it "leads us to learn more about what we initially wonder at" (Shapiro 1999a, 260). Astell is concerned that women become attentive to and learn about their nature, their minds, and God's will. For this reason, she agrees with Descartes that wonder or admiration as she calls it, "gives Rise to all the Passions; for unless we were Affected with the Newness of an Object, or some other remarkable Circumstance, so as to be attentively engag'd in the Contemplation of it, we shou'd not be any wise mov'd, but it wou'd pass by unregarded" (SP I, 218).

A problem with wonder as a primary passion, however, is that it is neutral. Descartes explains that it "has as its object not good or evil, but only knowledge of the thing that we wonder at" (AT XI, 381; CSM I, 353). This can be problematic because we may "consider with attention" things that are bad for us (AT XI, 380; CSM I, 353). Thus, Descartes concludes that with wonder, we may both strengthen "thoughts in the soul which it is good for the soul to preserve," or we may strengthen and preserve "others on which it is not good to dwell" (AT XI, 383; CSM I, 354). Astell is similarly concerned. For her, the problem with wonder is that it causes one to be caught up in "*little* things, or to busie our Minds about 'em'" (SP II, 218). More specifically, it can cause women to overvalue men. Her remedy is to combine wonder with love as coleading passions, thereby emphasizing the

Astell's Account of Feminine Self-Esteem   47

importance of loving correctly—that is, without confusing benevolence with desire or vice versa. It also highlights the love of God as primary, a move that accords with her Cambridge Platonist intellectual roots. This is why she claims love is "at the bottom of all the Passions" and that when "our Love be Right, the rest of our Passions will of course be so" (*SP II*, 219).

Wonder is connected to self-esteem in Descartes's system because when we practice mastery over the emotions, we wonder or are awed by the will's sovereignty. Descartes explains this connection when he writes that "wonder is joined to either esteem or contempt, depending on whether we wonder at the value of an object or at its insignificance. Thus we may have esteem or contempt for ourselves" (AT XI, 373–74; CSM I, 350). We become great or magnanimous, in Descartes's view, by acting sometimes in a contrary or a better way than we desire to act. This is because, as Shapiro explains, with wonder we "see that things may in fact be quite otherwise than the way they appear when we are in the grips of the passions" (Shapiro 1999a, 253). When we see things as they really are, we may act wisely, or for Astell's purposes, with self-preservation. Cartesian mastery is a kind of inner freedom based on the realization "that one need not think, or act, as one feels impelled to" (Shapiro 1999a, 258). Cartesian generosity arises when we realize that we are free from the influences of our passions, a realization that inclines us to believe that others may achieve the same freedom. Descartes explains, "those who possess this knowledge and this feeling about themselves readily come to believe that any other person can have the same knowledge and feeling about himself, because this involves nothing which depends on someone else" (AT XI, 446; CSM I, 384).

An important feature of Cartesian generosity that sets it apart from other and earlier notions of generosity is its independence from social rank or any other kind of unearned privilege. Stephen Voss, editor of an edition of Descartes's *Passions of the Soul*, calls Cartesian generosity an "artificial aristocracy" whereby self-worth is linked with benevolence and is divorced of social trappings that might compel individuals to follow or outdo the example of their noble ancestors (Voss 1989, 109).[8] Descartes's is a novel way of looking at generosity, and his democratic perspective on it appeals to Astell because in her society a woman's soul is thought to be weaker in that it "allows itself to be carried away by present passions" (AT XI, 367; CSM I, 347).[9] Though Astell vehemently disagrees with this prejudice, as when she writes sarcastically in *Reflections*, "I know not whether or no Women are allow'd to have Souls, if they have perhaps, it is not prudent to provoke them too much, lest silly as they are, they at last recriminate," she uses the prejudice as leverage to prove that women can, in fact, achieve

48   Feminist Interpretations of Mary Astell

self-mastery (*RM*, 59). This argument is bolstered by Descartes's claim that "even those who have the weakest souls could acquire absolute mastery over all their passions if we employed sufficient ingenuity in training and guiding them" (AT XI, 370; CSM I, 348).

A final point needs to be made about Cartesian generosity and pride. For Descartes, self-esteem is false when it is based on pride. He explains, "all those who conceive a good opinion of themselves for any other reason [than merit], whatever it may be, do not possess true generosity, but only a vanity which is always a vice" (AT XI, 448; CSM I, 385). The worst kind of pride, Descartes explains, occurs in people who "are vain for no reason at all—that is, not because they think they have any merit for which they ought to be valued, but simply because they do not regard merit as important: imagining pride to be nothing but self-glorification" (AT XI, 448; CSM I, 385). False merit impels vain people "to humble everyone else: being slaves to their desires, they have souls which are constantly agitated by hatred, envy, jealousy, or anger" (AT XI, 449; CSM I, 386). Gaining mastery over the passions is therefore crucial for acquiring generous behavior toward others, and this idea accords with Astell's goal of promoting both self-preservation and ethical behavior in women.

The distinction that Descartes makes between pride and virtuous humility aligns with the distinction Astell makes between self-love and self-esteem. Astell's conception of pride is almost identical to Descartes's view, but the outcome of indulging in this vice can be different for women. She argues that self-esteem is natural to all humans and that women err when they esteem themselves on false or imaginary grounds. Following Descartes, such grounds have little to do with mastery (in which few women have been trained) than in taking credit for God-given gifts, talents, and favorable circumstances like outward beauty, a high birth, or both. Astell writes that "the Proud on the contrary is mistaken both in her Estimate of Good, and in thinking it is her Own; She values herself on things that have no real Excellency, or which at least add none to her" (*SP II*, 223). Such "things" in Astell's case exist outside of women's field of control, like male attention and flattery, and are thus "sandy Foundations to build esteem upon" (*SP I*, 111).

Because the vestiges of self-esteem that come from such an unstable source must be fiercely guarded, women fall into vices such as envy, vanity, and jealousy in order to guard themselves, and they further distort their natures by taking on traditional feminine virtues to preserve a thin sense of self-esteem. According to Nancy Snow, feminine virtues like, "Humility and Self-Denial, Patience and Resignation" can "set identity conditions . . .

that deny women's full humanity" (*RM*, 62; Snow 2002, 46). Women rarely realize this is happening because, as Alice Sowaal points out, "they believe their natures are defective and that God is an entity that has created them in this defective manner" (Sowaal 2007, 86). In a vicious cycle, women seek self-esteem in ways that reflect society's biases concerning women's supposed inferior nature and capacities. Under the influence of what Sowaal calls the "Woman's Defective Nature Prejudice" (or the WDN prejudice), beauty, docility, and passivity seem laudable but can really be symptoms of an inner weakness or poverty (*RM*, 62). Independence of thought that could free women from the WDN prejudice is especially difficult since under its influence women "have no desire to improve their minds and they lack an ability to understand their perfections" (Sowaal 2007, 231). Astell thinks that by basing feminine self-esteem on God, "the most substantial ground," women free themselves from this debilitating prejudice and escape from "the great Honor and Felicity of their Tame, Submissive, and Depending Temper!" (*RM*, 30)

Feminine Self-Esteem and Neighbors

On the surface, Astell's claim that women should base their self-esteem on God seems anti-feminist, especially to contemporary readers given the biblical commonplace that women were created by God to serve and obey men, their superiors, not just in strength but also in reasoning and virtue. Astell is not, however, thinking along these lines when she argues that feminine self-esteem, unlike Cartesian self-esteem, begins and ends with God. To understand the emancipatory nature of her claim, it is useful to refer to the concept of self-possession, a cornerstone of the Lockean social contract that Astell alludes to throughout *Reflections*.[10] In chapter 2 of *The Second Treatise of Government*, Locke writes of inherent human freedom and natural equality in the following passage: "For men being all the workmanship of one omnipotent and infinitely wise maker, all the servants of one sovereign master, sent into the world by his order and about his business, they are his property whose workmanship they are, made at last during his, not one another's, pleasure" (Locke 2003, 264). Astell similarly calls women "God's Workmanship," and she does so to assert that men cannot own women or define their purpose and value (*SP II*, 223). Just as men are not, as Locke states, "made for one another's uses, as the inferior ranks of creatures are for ours," women in Astell's view are not made for men's uses and are not essentially inferior (Locke 2003, 264).

50   Feminist Interpretations of Mary Astell

Being "God's Workmanship" means that women are "endow'd by him with many excellent Qualities, and made capable of Knowing and Enjoying the Sovereign and Only Good" (*SP II*, 223). This claim directly counters the WDN prejudice whereby women are taught to believe God has made them without such capacities. For her claim that "Self-Esteem does not terminate in her Self but in GOD" to be emancipatory, however, Astell must emphasize aspects of God's nature that are favorable to women's flourishing (*SP II*, 223). She does so in *Serious Proposal II* when she writes of God's goodness and justness in the following passage: "Thus from the Agreement which we plainly perceive between the Ideas of GOD and of Goodness singly considered, we discern that they may be joyn'd together so as to form this Proposition, *That God is Good*: And from the evident disparity that is between GOD and Injustice, we learn to affirm this other, *that He is not Unjust*" (*SP II*, 172). Women's alignment with God's goodness ensures women's goodness, and God's justice ensures that oppressive conditions in women's marriages are customary, not natural. Under the right (i.e., nonprejudicial and just conditions) women can realize that their "soul was created for the contemplation of Truth as well as for the fruition of Good" and can thus, like men, attain virtue (*SP I*, 90).

Sharon Achinstein argues that Astell's call for "our intire dependence on GOD, for what we Know as well as for what we Are" is reactionary (*SP II*, 117). Achinstein classifies this theoretical move on Astell's part as one of "radical dependence" in an "anti-social and otherworldly" sense (Achinstein 2007, 24). She further claims that it "undercuts the possibility of the expression of human agency" (Achinstein 2007, 24). As we have seen, however, Astell's call for dependence on God for a woman's identity and self-worth is emancipatory since it frees women from false and prejudicial notions about her nature and capacities. Further, when combined with the Cartesian method of attaining self-esteem, it promotes agency with respect to self-mastery, as we have also seen. The master-slave dynamic that Achinstein thinks Astell advocates is evident only in the social realm from which women cannot escape. This is clear when Astell claims "that whatever other Great and Wise Reasons Men may have for despising Women, and keeping them in Ignorance and Slavery, it can't be from their having learnt to do so in Holy Scripture" (*RM*, 28). Astell is arguing against, not for, a "Tyrannous Domination which Nature never meant" (*RM*, 31).

In regard to obedience, Astell turns to the second feature of God's nature which she views as favorable to women's flourishing—namely, justice. Women, she argues, should not passively obey male authority figures "unless they can prove themselves infallible, and consequently Impeccable too" because this could contradict God's will (RM, 75). This is the case because "blind Obedience is an Obeying *without Reason*, for ought we know *against it*. GOD himself does not require our Obedience at this rate" (RM, 75). The nature of reason itself argues against this kind of obedience because reason "requires us to continue our Enquiries with all the Industry we can, till they've put us in Possession of Truth" (SP II, 179). In Astell's society, women cannot openly debate with authority figures without social repercussions, so a tension arises between women's nature, which is characterized by reason and freedom, and the social and political reality of women's lives. Astell exposes this tension when she sarcastically asks in *Reflections*, "can it be thought that an ignorant weak Woman shou'd have patience to bear a continual Out-rage and Insolence all the days of her Life?" (RM, 117) Ironically, her method of achieving feminine self-esteem calls for the stoic bearing of injustice in the oppressed circumstances in which women live. She writes, "there is no surer Sign of a noble Mind, a Mind very far advanced towards perfection, than the being able to bear Contempt and an unjust Treatment from ones Superiors evenly and patiently" (RM, 58).[11]

Astell's emphasis on God's kindness, however, mitigates what might seem like a harsh, sacrificial approach to women's self-development. She writes that "GOD is too Kind and Bountiful to deny us any Pleasure befitting our Nature," meaning that pure self-sacrifice and asceticism do not lead to self-esteem; rather, self-care does (SP II, 221). In her academy, Astell exhorts women to take "care about that which is really your *self*, and do not neglect that particle of Divinity within you, which must survive" (SP I, 53). Self-care in this sense reflects an understanding of one's worth, as she explains in the negative when she writes, "we always Neglect what we Despise, [and] we take no care of its Preservation and Improvement" (SP II, 223). Like reason and freedom, both characteristics of human nature, Astell understands self-preservation, which is strengthened by self-care, as an innate quality in that "every Creature has an aptness to take such courses as tend to its preservation" (SP II, 127). In other words, self-care disposes one to engage in self-preserving acts. In this way her theory anticipates Nancy Snow's definition of self-esteem in *Virtue and the Oppression of Women* as "liking oneself and being willing to take care of oneself" (Snow 2002, 57). And like Snow, Astell promotes friendships among women because these "can be important sources of courage, strength, and self-esteem" (Snow 2002, 59).

52   Feminist Interpretations of Mary Astell

Astell sees so many obstacles in front of women that her optimism concerning their potential to "live up to the Dignity of our Natures, scorning to do a degenerate and unbecoming thing" is mitigated by caution, sometimes in the extreme (*SP I*, 111). Even in her "happy Society" which is characterized by a "general Amity," she advises guardedness among friends (*SP I*, 87). She writes, "But tho' it be very desirable to obtain such a Treasure, such a Medicine of Life [as a friend] . . . yet the danger is great, least being deceiv'd in our choice, we suck in Poyson where we expected Health" (*SP I*, 99–100). If friendships inside Astell's academy can be poisonous, then relationships outside of it are a special cause for alarm. With respect to neighbors, she warns, "And as to the Influence that another Person's Passion may have on us, enough has bin said to warn us, not to dally with the Flame when our Neighbours house is on Fire, lest we be consum'd in it. . . . But when we discern that the Plague is begun, let's remove with all possible speed out of the infected Air" (*SP II*, 231). In other words, if helping neighbors will "infect" oneself, it is best to refrain from helping, even to flee.

Avoiding danger before one cannot escape it is Astell's way of promoting feminine agency. This is especially evident when she writes of the perils of courtship. If a woman should exercise caution with female friends and be ready to flee from impassioned neighbors, she "had need be very sure that she does not make a Fool her Head, nor a Vicious Man her Guide and Pattern" (*RM*, 49). Her warnings concerning courtship read like an SOS signal. She writes, "Preserve your distance then, keep out of reach of Danger, fly if you wou'd be safe, be sure to be always on the Reserve, not such as is Morose or Affected, but Modest and Discreet, your Caution cannot be too great, nor your Foresight reach too far ; . . . all is hazarded by the other" (*RM*, 74). The "other" in this case is scheming, tyrannical husbands, who have the "power to reduce you to your first obscurity, or to somewhat worse, to Contempt; you are therefore only on your good behavior" (*RM*, 45). Since husbands have "Sovereign Power," against which "neither Law nor Custom afford her that redress which a Man obtains," Astell's call for extreme vigilance with respect to courtship is warranted (*RM*, 46). She wants women, at the very least, to "demean themselves better" in marriage, with a pun on the seventeenth-century meaning of "to demean" as both to conduct and to maltreat (*RM*, 74).

Conclusion

Astell, like Descartes, envisions the cultivation of self-esteem as a communal endeavor. She observes "we stand not singly on our own Bottom, but are united in some measure to all who bear a Human Form, especially to the Community amongst whom we live" (*SP II*, 210). She is in agreement with Descartes on this point in that he conceives of learning itself as a communal endeavor, as he indicates in a letter to Princess Elisabeth of Bohemia in 1645 when he writes, "Though each of us is a person distinct from others, whose interests are accordingly in some way different from those of the rest of the world, we ought still to think that none of us could subsist alone and that each one of us is really one of the many parts of the universe" (AT IV, 293; CSMK, 266). Cartesian self-esteem is democratic because anyone can do it, and it is social. These dual emphases influence the development of Astell's theory, which must account for the WDN prejudice and the deficiencies in women's education that reinforce it. Simply put, developing healthy self-esteem in women is complicated.

Astell unravels the complexity. Her view is that for women to develop self-esteem they first need to distinguish the different kinds of love (benevolence and desire) and employ them properly with respect to the objects of their love. If this is done, the love of God becomes primary, the love of self secondary, and the benevolent love of others, including husbands, tertiary. Since women have been habituated to base their self-worth on the changeable feelings, attentions, flatteries, and motives of others or on external, unearned qualities such as beauty or social ranking, the process can be arduous, and some women will not succeed. But helping other women who are gripped by passions is the right thing to do, in Astell's view, because it is ethical to "shew 'em the unsuitableness of those Objects which Irregular Affections pursue, and persuade them to a willing use of such methods as we take to Cure our own" (*SP II*, 229). This can, however, be a fruitless task because "if the Train has took, if she is entangled in the Snare, if Love, or rather a Blind unreasonable Fondness . . . has gain'd on her, Reason and Perswasion may as properly be urg'd to the Folks in *Bethlem* [Bedlam] as to her" (*RM*, 68). Such women are not only self-destructive, but they offer little to society. Astell's academy is designed to remedy this problem so that women "may safely venture out" with the spirit of "*doing much Good in* [the world]" (*SP II*, 232).

It can be argued that Astell's academy is a model of Cartesian generosity, described by Timothy Reiss as "knowledge and sharing of sameness among subjects" (Reiss 2000, 31). But sameness, for Astell, does not necessarily connote equality of knowledge, experience, or rank; it does, however, connote equality of self-worth and capacity. In her academy, women will meditate to calm the mind and body, pray to know and unite with God's will, practice engaging in benevolent friendships, and discuss serious topics and authors such as "*Des Cartes, Malebranch*, and others . . . *French Philosophy*

54   Feminist Interpretations of Mary Astell

. . . the Famous *Madam D'Acier* Etc. and our own incomparable *Orinda*" (*SP I*, 83). This style of learning approximates Descartes's Jesuit education which, according to Reiss, was steeped in inquiry and debate, "an intellectual style embedded in commentary, controversy, and public intercourse, making all their work intensely communal" (Reiss 2000, 31). Astell is thinking along similar lines when she writes in *Serious Proposal*, "Why do we Trust our Friends but because their Truth and Honesty appears to us Equivalent to the Confidence we repose in 'em?" (*SP II*, 174). In this kind of learning environment, women gradually come to know that "we are surrounded with [truth], and GOD has given us Faculties to receive it" (*SP II*, 174).

Her optimistic tone in *Serious Proposal, Part I*, followed by her philosophical style in *Serious Proposal, Part II*, culminates in the sarcastic polemic of *Reflections*. The evolution of her tone in these texts may reflect Astell's awareness that her academy would not be funded.[12] At the time of writing *Reflections*, her optimism has receded, and she advises women to employ sound reasoning and wise judgments to reflect upon "the Good and Evil of a Married State, and . . . either never consent to be a Wife, or make a good one when she does" (*RM*, 75). This is not a time, Astell observes, "when Sex shall be no bar to the best Employments, the highest Honour; a time when that distinction, now as much us'd to her Prejudice, shall be no more" (*RM*, 75). She therefore advises women to take what liberties they can in their compromised social positions. Though she writes, "I don't say that Tyranny *ought*, but we find in *Fact*, that it provokes the Oppress'd to throw off even a Lawful Yoke that sits too heavy," she stops short of advocating rebellion (*RM*, 78). This kind of activism will come later, by other polemicists, though her emancipatory theory of feminine self-esteem, with its foundation in "the Union between our Soul and Body," anticipates it (*SP II*, 148).

Abbreviations

AT   René Descartes, *Oeuvres de Descartes*, vols. I–XII (1996) (cited by volume and page number)
CSM   René Descartes, *The Philosophical Writings of Descartes*, vols. I–II (1985) (cited by volume and page number)
CSMK René Descartes, *The Philosophical Writings of Descartes*, vol. III (1991) (cited by page number)
L   Mary Astell, *Letters Concerning the Love of God* (2005)
RM   Mary Astell, *Reflections upon Marriage* (1996)
SP I   Mary Astell, *A Serious Proposal to the Ladies, Part I* (2002)
SP II   Mary Astell, *A Serious Proposal to the Ladies, Part II* (2002)

Notes

1. In the seventeenth century, self-love is associated pejoratively with self-centeredness and vanity. However, a second meaning emerges in the late seventeenth century, not coincidentally, within John Norris's *Theory and Regulation of Love* (1699, v. 51). In this text, Norris equates benevolence with charity or goodwill to both the self and others.

2. In *An Antidote Against Atheism* (1653), More sets out to prove that God exists in the face of skeptical and empirical onslaughts on his worldview. He writes, "The grand Truth which we are now to be imployed about and to prove is, *That there is a GOD*: And I made choice of this Subject as very seasonable for the Times we are in, and are coming on, wherein Divine Providence [is] more universally loosening the minds of men . . . and permitting a freer perusal of matters of Religion than in former Ages" (More 1969a, 3).

3. In the *Cambridge Dictionary of Philosophy*, "occasionalism" is defined as "the doctrine that all finite created entities are devoid of causal efficacy" (Audi 1999, 626). In espousing an occasionalist framework, Norris believes that material objects serve only as "occasions" for God to cause sensations in the human soul.

4. Damaris Masham, a patron of Locke and critic of Norris, considered Norris to be a religious enthusiast. She writes sarcastically, "And when he is ascended to the highest Degree, he is then got above Reason itself; being first melted and brought to nothing, and then lost and swallowed up in God" (Masham 2004, 4–5).

5. I am indebted to Alice Sowaal for clarifying the distinction between spirit of nature and vital congruity within the Cambridge Platonist framework.

6. Descartes wrote *Passions of the Soul* in response to correspondence he had with Princess Elisabeth of Bohemia. Princess Elisabeth asked Descartes to clarify his account of interaction between the mind and body and relate it to her commonsense observation that her bodily condition affected her mental and emotional condition. For further details on their correspondence and Elisabeth's contribution to the softening of Descartes's dualist philosophy, see Lisa Shapiro's essay "Princess Elisabeth and Descartes: The Union of Soul and Body and the Practice of Philosophy" (Shapiro 1999, 503–20).

7. By "holistic" I mean that Descartes and Astell accept that passions, even extreme and violent ones, exist and that they both advocate working with passions as opposed to eliminating them or removing oneself from society to manage them.

8. In Castiglione's *Book of the Courtier*, the customary conception of generosity against which Descartes bases his theory is evoked in the following passage: "For if a gentleman strays from the path of his forebears, he dishonours his family name and not only fails to achieve anything but loses what has been achieved" (Castiglione 1980, 54). Generosity in this framework arises from social pressure as opposed to inner mastery.

9. Patricia Springborg points out that Nicholas Malebranche believed that the fibers in women's brains were deficient. Because of this deficiency, he believed women were not capable of understanding philosophy. She explains, "Malebranche thus persuaded women to forget philosophy and concentrate on 'deciding on fashion, choosing their words and discerning good tone and nice manner'" (*SP I*, 81n3). Unsurprisingly, Astell encourages women to study philosophy and forget about fashion.

10. In "Mary Astell and John Locke," Mark Goldie argues convincingly that the real target of Astell's "vehemence" in *Reflections* was not the Lockean social contract theory per se but rather "the Whigs and Dissenters as a body" (Goldie 2007, 67). Astell was, according to Goldie, a keen reader of Locke's *Essay Concerning Human Understanding*, and "she is recommending the intellectual independence that Locke advocates" (Goldie 2007, 78). But Goldie is incorrect when he argues that "Astell's position involves a complete repudiation of the political language of self-preservation," as this essay explains (Goldie 2007, 80).

11. Jacqueline Broad writes that "Astell has a different conception of liberty: not a radical political one, but a strictly philosophical conception of liberty as freedom of the will"; she concludes that

56   Feminist Interpretations of Mary Astell

this concept leads Astell to err on the side of "a calm acceptance of the status quo" (Broad 2007, 178–79). My findings reveal the same. Yet I also find that Astell's equivocal approach to rebellion in *Reflections* suggests that she wishes to balance the stoic emphasis on inaction with the emancipatory strains within contemporary political theory.

12. Springborg writes that Astell believed her academy would be funded by Princess Ann of Denmark, who "toyed with the idea, until dissuaded by Bishop Gilbert Burnet" (Springborg 1997, 182n1). Burnet, according to Springborg, was concerned that her academy would resemble a monastery.

4

Mary Astell and the Development of Vice

Pride, Courtship, and the Woman's Human Nature Question

Alice Sowaal

Questions regarding human nature and the differences between the nature of man and woman loomed large in the seventeenth and early eighteenth centuries. In this essay, I describe different positions taken by philosophers on the matter of whether human nature is at core good or evil, and I show how Mary Astell counters the paradigm of her day, according to which the nature of woman is evil because it is vice-ridden.

Earlier versions of this essay were presented at Bay Area Feminist Philosophers (2013) and the American Philosophical Association, Pacific Division (2014). I thank Kathleen Ahearn, Jacqueline Broad, Deborah Boyle, Karen Detlefsen, Marcus Ewert, Bruce Folsom, Daniel Gulch, Marcy Lascano, Ruth Sheldon, Susan Starr, Penny A. Weiss, Shelley Wilcox, Norma Young, the two anonymous reviewers of this volume, and students at San Francisco State University for reading and commenting on earlier drafts.

58   Feminist Interpretations of Mary Astell

In doing so, I argue that Mary Astell maintains that people are basically good. According to this reading, Astell thinks not only that we are basically good but also that once we have gone bad, we can become good again. In and of itself, this view may not sound surprising to our twenty-first-century ears, for today there is a general attitude in Western culture that we are each well-intentioned, kind, and loving, even if we do not always live up to our potential. Further, it is often held that, with the right kind of effort and guidance from rehabilitation programs, therapy, and self-help books, we can all reach these moral heights.

When examined in the context of seventeenth-century England, however, Astell's view becomes more surprising. At this time, Thomas Hobbes argued that human nature in the State of Nature is at root selfish and aggressive, and that it leads to lives that are "nasty, brutish, and short" (Hobbes 1994, 76). Though most intellectuals of his period rejected Hobbes's pessimistic views, the Calvinists also maintained a picture of human nature that, at least on some interpretations, is quite gloomy. Because the Calvinists held many major positions in religious, political, and university institutions, this view spread throughout the population. On this reading of the Calvinist view, human nature is evil as a result of the biblical Fall. When God created the first humans, they had a good nature, but, given the original sin that stems from the transgression in the garden, corruption riddles the soul of each human being that is ever to be born. This corruption reaches all faculties—including, importantly, the rational faculties that inform thought and action. A further consequence of the Fall is that people are perpetually separated from God, and there is nothing that they can do to improve themselves. Sin is a necessary part of the human condition. Given the depth of degradation, not one person deserves a better life or help from God; indeed, not one person deserves salvation. At the beginning of creation, God makes an arbitrary decision about which people will be given grace. During this lifetime, all that one can and should do in this regard is to gain a full sense of the reach of one's corruption. In other words, you should cultivate within yourself the feeling of the extreme degree to which you are a sinner. It is possible, if you do this properly, that God's grace will redeem you (Gill 2006, 1–11).

It is against this backdrop that Astell joins other philosophers to put forward views regarding the goodness of human nature [1] In doing so, they offer answers to what Michael Gill calls the "Human Nature Question." This question—or, rather, this collection of questions—concerns the natural connection between humans and good and evil: "Are human beings naturally good or evil? Are we naturally drawn to virtue or to vice? Is it natural for us to do the right thing?" (Gill 2006, 1). Those who offer what Gill calls a "Negative Answer" hold that human nature is basically evil, as do the Calvinists; whereas those who assert a "Positive Answer" hold that human nature is basically good. Gill shows how the Cambridge Platonists—Benjamin Whichcote, Henry More, Ralph Cudworth, and John Smith—fall into the latter category.

I argue that Astell, too, falls into the latter category and, further, that she does so in an original manner. That is, I show how, in addition to addressing the Human Nature Question that Gill outlines, Astell recognizes that another version of the question is in circulation, namely, one that specifically addresses woman's nature. Astell's additional question is not about human nature in general, but about woman's nature in particular. This *Woman's* Human Nature Question concerns the following: Do women have a nature that is basically and invariably set, full of either virtue or vice? Are women invariably drawn toward virtue or vice? Are women connected with God or doomed to be perpetually separated from God? Are women deserving or undeserving of salvation? Astell argues for the Positive Answer in response to each of these questions.[2] By examining Astell closely on these issues, I argue that in *Serious Proposal to the Ladies* (1694, 1697) she develops a psychological theory explaining how women come to demonstrate the vices that others—namely, those who maintain the Negative Answer to the Woman's Human Nature Question—claim are natural to them. I also reconstruct her account of how God helps all people so that they can direct their psychological and intellectual development such that they can further perfect their natures.

In reconstructing Astell's view of how women come to demonstrate the vices that others claim are natural to them, I do three things. First, I present Astell's understanding of the Negative Answer to the Woman's Human Nature Question. Second, I present Astell's own Positive Answer to the General Human Nature Question, showing how her answer employs an account of the faculties of understanding and will in the pre- and postlapsarian states (that is, the pre- and post-Fall states) and an account of "generosity," a provision God gives.[3] We come to see that for Astell: human nature is basically good (versus being bad or neutral); humans can return to the prelapsarian state; and humans are in partnership with God. Third, I return to Astell's account of the Woman's Human Nature Question, reconstructing her example of how easy it is for a young woman to develop vice when meeting a suitor.

60   Feminist Interpretations of Mary Astell

The Negative Answer to the Woman's Human Nature Question

In reading *Serious Proposal*, one gains two impressions about Astell's state of mind regarding women. On the one hand, she is quite passionately interested in offering them a new way of thinking and living that will allow them the best possible life on earth and the promise of eternal blessedness in heaven. On the other hand, she is deeply frustrated by their current behavior. They pass as "little useless and impertinent Animals," who are not making any general contributions to the good of themselves or society (*SP I*, 76). That is, given their poor behavior, women seem to offer evidence to those who hold a Negative Answer to the Woman's Human Nature Question.

It is important to reconstruct just how Astell understands the Negative Answer to the Woman's Human Nature Question. In one passage, she focuses on the claim that there are some vices that are attached to women's natures, ones that are referred to as the "Feminine Vices" of pride and vanity (*SP I*, 62). In another passage, she more specifically gives an account of what I am calling the Negative Answer, and she states her goal in debunking it: "Altho' it has been said by Men of more Wit than Wisdom, and perhaps of more malice than either, that Women are naturally incapable of acting Prudently, or that they are necessarily determined to folly, I must not grant it. . . . The Incapacity, if there be any, is acquired not natural" (*SP I*, 58–59). Here we see that the Negative Answer centers on a claim about natural imprudence in women. This is a claim about what Aristotle called phronesis, practical wisdom, which involves one's ability to think in a way that yields correct action in moral situations. The Negative Answer, then, is the view that women are inherently defective: they cannot make wise decisions in moral contexts (they are imprudent) (*SP I*, 58–59), they take undue credit (they are vain), and they are excessively focused on themselves (they are proud).

According to Astell, this view circulates in society as a prejudice and affects women in particular ways. This prejudice can be called the Woman's Defective Nature Prejudice (Sowaal 2007, 229–33). By "prejudice," I mean to refer to a thought that is held as a prejudgment—an assumption that has not been tested by critical thought. Astell holds that the Woman's Defective Nature Prejudice is held by both men and women. However, she also maintains that it affects women in a very specific manner—it becomes a habit of thought that "fetters" the understanding and a "custom" that "manacles" the will such that women remain in ignorance (*SP II*, 139). Ultimately, the prejudice becomes something that rational argument alone cannot address (*SP II*, 120).[4]

Astell and the Development of Vice   61

A further point implicit in Astell's view is that when women are trapped in the Woman's Defective Nature Prejudice, they are not able to usefully engage in the rationalist method of education outlined by Descartes's method of doubt. The problem, Astell explains, is that women who hold this prejudice face a daily skeptical predicament, thinking that their natures are inherently defective. That is, they do not have the kind of esteem for themselves that Descartes thought one must have in order to engage the method of doubt. Indeed, in *Discourse on the Method*, he notes that the method of doubt is not effective for all people, but only for those who have strong self-esteem and have previously practiced calling custom into question (either because of their schooling or their experience in travel) (AT VI, 9–16; CSM II, 115–19). In article sixty-one of *Passions of the Soul* ([1649] 1989), he discusses esteem further, noting that those with strong self-esteem may have it due to "good birth." One can read "good birth" here in different ways—that is, as involving either biological or social influences. Among the social influences can be one's upbringing (from one's family in particular and from society in general), which encourages one to have esteem for oneself based on one's true human value. This positive, nurturing childhood is opposed to an upbringing that encourages one to have a sense of one's value and nature as degraded (AT XI, 453–54; CSM I, 387–88).

Many of the women whom Astell addresses lack the experiences that lead one to develop the self-esteem to which Descartes refers in these passages. They do not have the experience of travel and schooling that can lead one to call custom into question; further, they have been encouraged to understand their own natures as defective. Despite the class status that some of them may enjoy, they will still suffer from Woman's Defective Nature Prejudice if they are already steeped in self-doubt. The employment of the kind of philosophical skepticism Descartes articulates will not lead them to knowledge. Indeed, it may further entrench them in a doubt from which they will not be able to escape.

The Negative Answer, then, is not just a harmless view held by a few people, people whom others can easily ignore. Rather, it is a pervasive social force that has a detrimental effect on the intellectual and ethical well-being of women. It is imperative that the Negative Answer be replaced with a Positive Answer. Astell does just that.

Astell's Positive Answer to the General Human Nature Question

Astell's Positive Answer involves her account of the ontology of mind, that is, her views on the understanding and the will.[5] In Astell's view, the

62   Feminist Interpretations of Mary Astell

understanding and the will work together to enable a person to make judgments about truths (in metaphysical contexts) and about correct courses of
action (in moral, practical contexts). The understanding is the capacity to
receive and compare ideas; the will is the power of preferring and directing
thoughts and motions (*SP II*, 205). There is a teleological aspect to Astell's
view in that each of these two faculties has a proper object. The proper
object of the understanding is truth, which has "being from Eternity in the
Divine Ideas" (*SP II*, 137); the proper object of the will is the good, which
is God's will (*SP II*, 206). When the understanding is healthy, it has knowledge (*SP II*, 130). When the will is healthy, it is "regular"—that is, it is in
conformity with God's will and is guided by the understanding (*SP II*, 130,
205, 209).[6] Given that the understanding and will have proper objects,
they are neither bad nor neutral faculties. Rather, they are good faculties:
the understanding is a truth-disclosing faculty, and the will is a good-
pursuing faculty. In this regard, Astell's ontology of mind composes a central aspect of her Positive Answer.

So far, what I have said about Astell's ontology of mind describes the
understanding and will when they function properly. But what about
when they do not function properly? Astell discusses the mind in the
pre-and postlapsarian states, connecting it with the biblical Fall:[7] "Morality is so consonant to the Nature of Man, so adapted to his Happiness,
that had not his Understanding been darkn'd by the Fall, and his whole
Frame disorder'd and weakned, he wou'd Naturally have practis'd it" (*SP
II*, 143). In the postlapsarian state there is a "darkn'd" understanding and
a "frame" that is "disorder'd and weakned." I interpret this as meaning
that the understanding on its own does not always "maintain its ground
against Passion and Appetite," and that it is "weak" and does not "oppose
incursions of sense" (*SP II*, 143–44). In such a context, the unruly will
takes direction not from the understanding, but from one or more of the
following: the senses (e.g., perceptions such as images, sounds, and feels);
the appetites (e.g., desires such as thirst and hunger); and the passions
(e.g., emotions such as pride and vanity). With such wild governors, the
will neither seeks the good nor restrains itself, and thus the understanding has no opportunity to connect with its proper object of truth or to
gain the requisite clarity that could be used to guide the will. This situation does not bode well for further judgments. It is in stark contrast to
the mind in the prelapsarian state, which has an enlightened understanding and a "frame" that is ordered and strong, such that the person
naturally practices morality and is thoroughly happy and naturally
balanced.[8]

Astell and the Development of Vice   63

Of course, even a person with a disordered understanding and will still has an understanding and a will that are good. That is, the elements of each person's mind are good even if these elements are currently being inappropriately employed. This again speaks to Astell's Positive Answer.

Another aspect of Astell's Positive Answer concerns our relationship with God, namely that God is close to us and that we work for our salvation by being in partnership with him. One important element of this view is that with God's help we can return to the prelapsarian state and again have pure happiness and easily be moral. This comes about in part when we retrain our understanding such that it perfectly governs the will and retrain our will such that it is perfectly regulated by the understanding. When we do this, distractions from sense, appetite, and passion will be properly managed. However, according to Astell, it is important to emphasize we do not make the return to the prelapsarian state *on our own*. God must help us do so. Astell writes that God, the author of our nature, knows of our fallen condition and gives us provisions to help us. One of these provisions is a principle called generosity (*SP II*, 129, 141).[9] Astell writes, "But the Author of our Nature to whom all the Inconveniences we are liable to in this Earthly Pilgrimage are fully known, has endow'd us with Principles sufficient to carry us safely thro them all, if we will but observe them and make use of 'em. One of these is *Generosity*, which (so long as we keep it from degenerating into Pride) is of admirable advantage to us in this matter" (*SP II*, 141). Notice here what is implied about our partnership with God: God helps us return to the prelapsarian state when he gives us provisions to remedy any disorders that develop.[10] God does not act alone in returning us to our previous state, but rather gives us a principle so that we can put ourselves into a position to return.[11] Of course, to make this return, we must use these provisions properly.[12] Consider another passage in which Astell again highlights this partnership: "Nature as bad as it is and as much as it is complain'd of, is so far improveable by the grace of GOD, upon our honest and hearty endeavours, that if we are not wanting to our selves, we may all in *some*, tho' not in an *equal* measure, be instruments of his Glory, Blessings to this World, and capable of eternal Blessedness in that to come" (*SP I*, 61). Again in this passage, we see that there are two elements that must come into play in order for our improvements to come about—our work and God's work. Indeed, Astell holds that these two elements must be joined together: (1) we make our "honest and hearty endeavours" to improve ourselves, and (2) God grants us grace. Further, through this partnership with God, we become instruments of God, aiding God's glory by improving this world. Ultimately, we become worthy to enjoy the blessedness of salvation.[13]

64   Feminist Interpretations of Mary Astell

In Astell's view, we do not return to the prelapsarian state solely because of *our will* to do so. Given this, Astell's position on salvation is not subject to the Pelagian heresy, one aspect of which involves the claim that one's salvation is entirely in virtue of one's own efforts. But neither do we return to the state solely because of God's grace, the Calvinist position. For Astell, God, in grace, has given us a provision we can use to retrain our understanding and will such that the will is properly regulated by the understanding; once our minds are retrained, God can, in grace, save us.[14]

We can now turn to the practical way in which God helps us by giving us generosity. We can, Astell argues, either use this passion to return to our prelapsarian state or we can allow it to degenerate into pride. In order to understand generosity and how it degenerates into pride and vanity, it is useful to examine one of Astell's metaphors, which has resonances with Jesus's parable of the sower:[15]

> The Soil is rich and would, if well cultivated, produce a noble Harvest, if then the Unskilful Managers not only permit, but incourage noxious Weeds, tho' we shall suffer by their Neglect, yet they ought not in justice to blame any but themselves, if they reap the Fruit of their own Folly. (*SP I*, 60)

> For that Ignorance is the cause of most Feminine Vices, may be instanc'd in that Pride and Vanity which is usually imputed to us, and which, I suppose, if thoroughly sifted, will appear to be some way or other, the rise and Original of all the rest. These, tho very bad Weeds, are the product of good Soil; they are nothing else but Generosity degenerated and corrupted. A desire to advance and perfect its Being, is planted by GOD in all Rational Natures, to excite them hereby to every worthy and becoming Action; for certainly next to the Grace of GOD, nothing does so powerfully restrain people from Evil and stir them up to Good, as a generous Temper. (*SP I*, 62)

Because metaphors can be interpreted in multiple ways, they are notoriously difficult to pin down. This one is no exception. What is important for our purposes is that Astell aligns our rational nature with good soil, and implies that it may or may not be well educated (cultivated); she also states that God plants generosity—another good thing—in our rational nature; further, she implies that generosity, when grown in uncultivated soil, will degenerate into vice. Note that there are no original bad parts of our nature: no inherently bad soil (rational nature), no original bad seeds (ori-

Astell and the Development of Vice   65

gins of our passions, tempers), no essentially bad plants (passions, tempers). Everything is originally good; though our nature can become bad, if it does develop in that manner, it can also again become good.[16]

We saw earlier in this essay that Astell maintains that generosity is a principle, namely, a principle that God gives us as a provision so that we can return to the prelapsarian state. This implies that generosity is a principle of the understanding. In the metaphor above, Astell implies something additional about generosity: a "generous Temper" is the same as the "desire to advance and perfect [one's] Being." Given this, generosity is also both a kind of temper and a desire. As a desire, generosity may be a passion or a state of the will.[17] Further, generosity is described as a "desire to advance and perfect [one's] Being" that will "excite [people] to every worthy and becoming action" and "powerfully restrain people from Evil and stir them up to Good" (SP I, 62). In sum, Astell makes four different claims about the ontological status of generosity—namely, that it is a principle of the understanding, a state of the will, a passion (a desire), and a kind of temper. It is beyond the scope of this essay to iron out all of the details of Astell's view of the ontological status of generosity. However, it is evident that generosity plays a large role in Astell's moral theory.

One question that may arise at this point is about how odd it is to use the term "generosity" for the desire to perfect. For example, it is unclear how this account captures the other-regarding perspective that is usually implied by the term "generosity." That is, we think about generosity as involving something that prompts us to share resources with others and not expect anything in return. But it seems at least plausible that one could have a "desire to advance and perfect its Being" (SP I, 62) and still be self-centered and self-serving. At least at first glance, it seems problematic that Astell describes generosity as a striving to perfect oneself at all.

Let us see how Astell's texts can be read as supporting the view that generosity involves more than self-serving passions and behaviors. In what follows, I will argue that, for Astell, being generous involves the desire to be a perfected member of a perfected social whole. Though Astell does not put her view in precisely this manner, once we consider other related points that she does make, we can see that the notion of generosity includes this wider perspective.

First of all, let us look more deeply at Astell's claim that generosity is a striving to perfect and advance one's being. For Astell, perfecting and advancing one's being involves, at the very least, perfecting one's understanding and will. The meaning, however, is not restricted to intellectual contexts; it extends to moral ones as well. That is, generosity involves a

66   Feminist Interpretations of Mary Astell

striving to be moral, to be prudent. Second, for Astell, one advances one's being as part of a metaphysical whole that includes other people, for doing so involves doing God's will and promoting God's glory (versus when one advances one's being out of selfish motives). *Serious Proposal* abounds in statements about God's glory—specifically, that it is our proper end and that it is connected with doing God's will (*SP I*, 61, 74; *SP II*, 136, 142, 195, 226, 233–34). In addition, Astell writes that being in conformity with God's will "is at once both the Duty and Perfection of all Rational Beings" (*SP II*, 227). Astell maintains also that friends grow perfect together (*SP I*, 74)—that is, that God has given us different locations in life so that we can be mutually useful to each other's advantage (*SP II*, 153–54), that we should look at our acquisitions (moral and otherwise) as a general treasure in which the social whole has a right, and that we find our own improvement in the improvement of every part of that social whole (*SP II*, 153–54). In brief, the components of generosity are two desires: the desire to be a perfected, virtuous being and the desire to be a member of a perfected social whole.[18] Generosity does not involve the individualistic, selfish behavior of using other people as a means to an end. Note also that this way of understanding generosity is consistent with how Astell describes generosity as a desire that excites us "to every worthy and becoming Action" (*SP I*, 62).[19]

Given this account of generosity, we can now turn to how generosity can degenerate into pride and vanity. One relevant point here is Astell's claim that ignorance is the source of all sin (*SP I*, 61). Given that pride is a sin, then pride must come from ignorance. Further, given that Astell also says that pride arises as a degenerated form of generosity, pride must come from generosity when one loses knowledge and becomes ignorant. Astell does not specify what kind of ignorance must one have in order to acquire pride. But given the reconstruction I offer above, the ignorance must involve lack of knowledge of oneself and God. That is, one must become confused about what it is to be a perfected member of a perfected social whole.

Passages in support of this reading come from related texts in which Astell discusses pride in contrast with the virtue of humility. The humble person has knowledge about her perfections (that is, knowledge of her true self) and the origins of her perfections (that is, knowledge of God). Astell writes that such a woman "does not prize her self on some Imaginary Excellency, or for any thing that is not truly Valuable; does not ascribe to her self what is her Makers due" (*SP II*, 233).[20] The proud person, on the other hand, "is mistaken both in her Estimate of Good, and in thinking it is her

Own; She values her self on things that have no real Excellency, or which at least add none to her, and forgets from whose Liberality she receives them: She does not employ them in the Donors Service, all her care is to Raise her self" (*SP II*, 233). The proud person commits two errors: she does not grasp what her perfections are, so she misapplies her striving for self-perfection to the wrong kind of perfections; she does not recognize the source of her perfection in God, but rather thinks that she herself is the source of her perfection, and also that her perfections are for her alone to enjoy. That is, she does not put her true talents to God's service (God being her "Donor"). This has the further effect that she does not appreciate God's creation, that is, God's glory.[21]

Another way Astell describes the humble person is in terms of where such a person places her esteem. This view is related to her views on honoring God and God's creation in the proper way. The humble person has properly developed an esteem that terminates in God, not in herself: "[N]or [does she] Esteem her self on any other account but because she is GOD's Workmanship, endow'd by him with many excellent Qualities, and made capable of Knowing and Enjoying the Sovereign and Only Good; so that her Self-Esteem does not terminate in her *Self* but in GOD, and she values her self only for GOD's sake" (*SP II*, 233). We can describe the proud person, in contrast, as locating esteem in the wrong place. Esteem that should end in God instead ends in her own self. This means that the proud person and the humble person will respond to praise in different ways. Upon being complimented for one's talents, the humble person redirects the praise to God; her feeling of esteem is a celebration of God and God's overall creation. In contrast, the proud person absorbs the praise herself—and so garners this improper esteem—and she celebrates her separateness from creation.

Astell's Positive Answer to the General Human Nature Question involves claims about the goodness of human nature, how humans can return to the prelapsarian state, and how humans are in partnership with God. Human nature is good insofar as it is composed of an understanding and a will, the former of which is a truth-disclosing faculty and the latter of which is a good-pursuing faculty. Humans are in partnership with God in that God sees humans in their fallen state and gives provisions to help them do work such that he will then return them to the prelapsarian state. That is, God does not act alone in returning us, nor do we act alone in trying to be returned; rather we must work as partners with God to succeed at this goal. One such provision is generosity, which Astell variously describes as a principle of the understanding, a state of the will, a passion of the soul, and a

68   Feminist Interpretations of Mary Astell

kind of temperament. To use this provision properly, we need knowledge; when we lack this knowledge, our generosity can develop into pride and vanity. Thus, vices are not natural to us, and even the person who is steeped in vice can follow a path that can lead back to the prelapsarian state.[22]

Courtship and the Woman's Human Nature Question

According to Astell, vice may be present in humans of all sexes and social classes. Indeed, Astell writes that if men were treated as women are, they, too, would develop the same passions (*SP I*, 57). In this regard, her view constitutes a Positive Answer to the *General* Human Nature Question, which concerns the nature of man and the nature of woman. However, given the prevalence of the *Woman's* Human Nature Question, Astell specifically addresses the development of vice in women. She does so with the example of how women's vices are involved in courtship. Here we see a fuller illustration of Astell's claim that women work under specific disadvantages in their moral maldevelopment.

In examining the context of courtship, we are asked to consider the young woman who has underdeveloped intellectual perfections and over-developed physical and economic ones. Given her current state, this young woman mistakenly focuses all of her striving for perfection on her physical perfections, and she also takes sole responsibility for them. Thus, her generosity degenerates into pride.

Pride develops as an intricate problem in courtship, a time in which a woman receives praises for her perfections from family, friends, and suitor. Such praises reinforce her sense of personal responsibility for her physical perfections, allowing for the possibility that her esteem, which she properly owes to God, terminates in her own self. This combination leads to an additional form of vulnerability when she is with her suitor. First, she comes to feel a specific obligation to the man who praises her for the "Perfections" she has been developing. Astell writes, "[S]he who has nothing else to value her self upon, will be proud of her Beauty, or Money, and what that can purchase; and think her self mightily oblig'd to him, who tells her she has those Perfections which she naturally longs for. Her inbred self-esteem and desire of good, which are degenerated into Pride and mistaken Self-love, will easily open her Ears to whatever goes about to nourish and delight them" (*SP I*, 62–63). This feeling of indebtedness may lead to an additional problem. If the suitor has ill intentions, he will quickly get the upper hand in the growing relation-

Astell and the Development of Vice   69

ship, for the young woman's feeling of indebtedness will leave her vulnerable in a new manner:

> [A]nd when a cunning designing Enemy from without, has drawn over to his Party these Traytors within, he has the Poor unhappy person at his Mercy, who now very glibly swallows down his Poyson, because 'tis presented in a Golden Cup; and [she] credulously hearkens to the most disadvantagious Proposals, because they come attended with a seeming esteem. She whose Vanity makes her swallow praises by the whole sale, without examining whether she deserves them, or from what hand they come, will reckon it but gratitude to think well of him who values her so much; and think she must needs be merciful to the poor despairing Lover whom her Charms have reduc'd to die at her feet. (*SP I*, 63)

The "Traytors within" are imprudence, pride, and vanity in the young woman. These vices are now employed by the malevolent suitor—the "Enemy"—to his ends.[23] The suitor claims to have been slain by her physical perfections—that is, he is "despairing" and "reduc'd to die at her feet." The woman's pride and vanity lead her to think that she must be merciful, for she appears to be responsible for his purportedly vulnerable condition.

What she does not realize is that the tables are turned; she is being manipulated by the suitor, not vice versa. She is not able to evaluate the situation rightly because her ignorance manifests in this social interaction as imprudence. That is, she is so far from having a clear understanding of what she truly is, what her suitor truly is, and what God truly is that she cannot rate things at their proper value, proportion means to ends, or make measured decisions about the proper courses of action. Courtship offers an institutional context for the development of imprudence, pride, and vanity, now vices that both distance her from God and grip her such that she cannot act otherwise.

Conclusion

Astell's account of the young woman in courtship is bleak indeed. With "help" from her "friends" and family, the young woman's vices fashion her shackles and create her own prison. That is, vice leads her to accept a contract that will bind her into a hierarchical relationship that she does not understand and that, according to Astell, she lacks the right to break.

70   Feminist Interpretations of Mary Astell

However, with a developmental account of vice, Astell provides a much rosier picture of human nature in general—and of woman's nature in particular—than many other views in circulation at this time. Indeed, her account of how generosity couples with ignorance to degenerate into vice constitutes the core of her Positive Answer to both the Woman's and General Human Nature Questions. This means that: (1) any badness in humans is the result of a maldevelopment of generosity, and so the badness itself is not a necessary part of the human condition; (2) by gaining proper knowledge and by then retraining generosity, humans can return to the prelapsarian condition in which they can naturally practice morality; and (3) humans are close to God—indeed, they are aided by God in that their generosity is a gift from God and it is to be used in partnership with God. In posing the Positive Answer to the *General* Human Nature Question, Astell's view is now a far cry from her Calvinist contemporaries. In posing the Positive Answer to the *Woman's* Human Nature Question, Astell anticipates a discussion of essentialism that—though it will morph from a theological to a secular framework—will occupy the attention of many generations of Astell's future feminist colleagues.

Abbreviations

AT   René Descartes, *Oeuvres de Descartes,* vols. I–XII (1996) (cited by volume and page number)
CSM   René Descartes, *The Philosophical Writings of Descartes,* vols. I–II (1985) (cited by volume and page number)
CSMK   René Descartes, *The Philosophical Writings of Descartes,* vol. III (1991) (cited by page number)
SP I   Mary Astell, *A Serious Proposal to the Ladies, Part I* (2002)
SP II   Mary Astell, *A Serious Proposal to the Ladies, Part II* (2002)

Notes

1. It is worth noting that Astell was an Anglican and that in *Christian Religion* she worked to articulate a philosophical basis for the teachings of the Anglican Church.

2. In this chapter, I address Astell's views on vice, leaving aside her account of sin.

3. One may wonder about Astell's use of the term "generosity" (which Descartes used as well) and its relation to "magnanimity" (which was used by other philosophers, notably Aristotle, Cicero, Augustine, Aquinas, and Descartes). For a discussion of Descartes's use of both terms, see Brown (2006, chap. 8).

4. For discussions of Astell on custom, see Broad (2007) and Sowaal (2007).

5. Astell's view about the understanding and will is roughly Cartesian. In order to assess how Cartesian Astell is in this regard, one would need to do the following: choose an interpretation of Descartes on these issues (there are many, and they differ greatly); and assess how Astell understands

Astell and the Development of Vice   71

the distinction between the understanding and will, as well as what she means when she makes claims about related issues, for example what kinds of things can be clearly and distinctly perceived. For an account of Descartes on the intellect and will, see Nelson (2007). For an account of Descartes on clear and distinct perceptions, see Sowaal (2011).

6. For more on this reconstruction of Astell's account of the mind, see Sowaal (2007).

7. Note that Astell does not say that ignorance is in itself a vice, though she implies that it is better to have knowledge than lack it. In this essay, I am using the terms "virtue" and "vice" to refer to moral actions, not to epistemic states.

8. One may wonder how this view explains the possibility of the first transgression.

9. This implies that in our prelapsarian state, we did not have generosity (at least we did not have it in the form that God gives us once our natures are disordered). Therefore the transgression in the garden must come from something other than a vice that develops when generosity degenerates.

10. In addition to the points I make about this passage, there are two additional interesting points to consider. First, Astell writes that these provisions God gives us are *sufficient* to carry us through our inconveniences. If she means the term "sufficient" in the technical sense that philosophers most often do, then these provisions are enough to save us from our difficulties—if we employ them, we need not seek any additional provisions. Second, Astell does not make the claim that these provisions are *necessary*. That is, she leaves open the possibility that there are other routes we can take to navigate our difficulties and failings—for example, God may choose to save us even though we have not used the provisions.

11. On Astell's view, both the desire for praise and the related desire to do things that will lead to praise are additional provisions that God has given to us to help us escape our postlapsarian state. Astell writes: "It was not fit that Creatures capable of and made for Society, shou'd be wholly Independent, or Indifferent to each others Esteem and Commendation; nor was it convenient considering how seldom these are justly distributed, that they shou'd too much regard and depend on them. It was requisite therefore that a desire of our Neighbors Good Opinion shou'd be implanted in our Natures to the end we might be excited to do such things as deserve it, and yet withall a Generous neglect of it, if they unjustly withheld it where it was due" (SP II, 141).

12. A full account of how this return from vice to virtue comes about lies outside the scope of this essay, as it involves a detailed explanation of Astell's method. Proper use of this method can expunge the ignorance (of our true nature and of God's nature) that entered humanity by way of the Fall and give us a way to return to virtue. Part of such an account may consider whether this is a return to a state of innocence, or whether it is growth to a new (third) state. This third state would be one in which a person reaps the benefit of having first existed in a fallen state and then transformed herself, with the result that she again easily practices morality, but now does so with a personal grasp of what happens when one is fallen and then transformed.

13. This account raises an important philosophical question about how (and whether) temporality is involved in the working of this partnership between each person and God. Put crudely, the issue is this: Is it that a person must first do her work and then, once God has reviewed the attempt and found it satisfactory, God finishes the improvement by granting grace? Or is it that first God grants grace, which then strengthens a person to do her work? Both of these views involve temporality. A way of reading the issue in an atemporal manner is to say that the work of a person and the work of God are two ways of describing the same event: a person's work *just is* God's grace at work in her (and vice versa). In *Serious Proposal*, Astell does not seem to explicitly choose one of these views to defend. But she is clear about another issue at stake—both our work and God's work must be at play for us to improve. In this regard, she is far from the Calvinist picture, according to which a person's work to improve herself and prepare for salvation is independent of God's grace. In that view, there is no partnership to be considered.

14. There are two deep ironies here, neither of which seems to be addressed by Astell. One is that a provision God gives us—namely, generosity—develops properly only with the very thing that we lack in our fallen condition: knowledge. Indeed, it seems as though something that God has given

72   Feminist Interpretations of Mary Astell

us to remedy our fallen condition only works when we are not in that condition. The other irony is that if we misuse our provision, we stray even further from our original Fall. In other words, we not only fall, but we tumble aimlessly. Ultimately, I suspect Astell's view can be understood to encompass machinery (within her writings on method) that sheds light on both of these issues such that these "ironies" do not present true puzzles that reveal deep problems with her system. However these are resolved, Astell's view is still positive in that it maintains that no person is irretrievably full of vice; there are always paths out of the bad habits of thought and action we have developed; these paths involve a partnership with God. Further, precisely because these paths involve a partnership with God, and because people have some role to play in that partnership with God in order to bring about their own salvation, Astell is again quite far from her Calvinist contemporaries.

15. One place in which this parable is presented in the New Testament is in Matthew 13:1–23.

16. An interesting question arises here regarding whether or not pride and vanity become intrinsic aspects of one's nature.

17. Note that for Descartes, generosity is a passion and a virtue (*Passions of the Soul*, section 161: AT XI, 454–55; CSM I, 388), and desire is both a passion (*Passions of the Soul*, section 57: AT XI, 374; CSM I, 350) and a mode of the will (*Principles of Philosophy*, I, section 32: AT VIIIA, 17; CSM I, 204). For Malebranche, desire just *is* the will (Malebranche 1980, 5).

18. What does this perfected whole look like? Further, are the hierarchies embedded in our society part of this perfected whole? In explaining Astell's view on the first issues, it may be useful to think of her as an "enthusiast." During this period, the term "enthusiast" is used (often as a pejorative) to refer to those philosophers, theologians, and religious people who think that individuals can commune with others—God or other people—in special and direct manners; see Myers (2012). These two questions together are important, especially in light of the fact that Astell does not critique many aspects of (what we today see as) imbalance in society with respect to gender and social station. One way of answering these questions is to interpret the perfected whole as quite different from anything we experience in our temporal lives, namely as an otherworldly, spiritual entity that arises after the biblical final judgment. On this reading, the perfected whole is one in which there are only minds (not mind-body unions), and thus neither markings of our temporal lives (e.g., sexed bodies) nor hierarchical social locations (e.g., marriage). I thank Shelley Wilcox and Daniel Gulch for conversation on this issue.

19. More could be said about how Astell's account of generosity connects with the two commandments often associated with the New Testament: to love God and to love your neighbor as yourself. These are stated in several places in the New Testament (e.g., Matthew 22:37–40); they are also present in the Hebrew Bible (e.g., Deuteronomy 6:4–5 and Leviticus 19:18).

20. Claire Pickard connects this quote with Astell's poem "Ambition," noting that, for Astell, "true greatness can be achieved only through humility" (2007, 124).

21. There are other relevant quotes in *Serious Proposal*. One is "to be ambitious of perfections is no fault, tho to assume the Glory of our Excellencies to our selves, or to Glory in such as we really have not, are" (*SP I*, 62). Another is "She who rightly understands wherein the perfection of her Nature consists, will lay out her Thoughts and Industry in the acquisition of such Perfections. But she who is kept ignorant of the matter, will take up with such Objects as first offer themselves, and bear any plausible resemblance to what she desires; a shew of advantage being sufficient to render them agreeable baits to her who wants Judgment and Skill to discern between reality and pretence" (*SP I*, 62). And a third is "Whence is it but from ignorance, from a want of understanding to compare and judge of things, to chuse a right End, to proportion the Means to the End, and to rate ev'ry thing according to its proper value; that we quit the Substance for the Shadow, Reality for Appearance, and embrace those very things which, if we understood we shou'd hate and fly; but now are reconcil'd to, merely because they usurp the Name, tho' they have nothing of the Nature of those venerable Objects we desire and seek?" (*SP I*, 64–65).

22. Astell implies that generosity is innate, for it is given to us before we are born. However, if generosity is innate and it requires knowledge that is to be acquired during our lives, then generosity seems to require something that we do not have at birth. I thank Deborah Boyle for this point. A

Astell and the Development of Vice   73

similar problem may arise with other passions that Astell maintains are innate, namely self-esteem and our desire for our neighbor's good opinion. About self-esteem, she writes that when a woman lacks knowledge of her true goods, "Her inbred self-esteem and desire of good, which are degenerated into Pride and mistaken Self-love, will easily open her Ears to whatever goes about to nourish and delight them" (*SP I*, 62–63). About our desire for our neighbor's good opinion, see note 11 above.

23. On Astell's disapproval and distrust of male suitors, see Wilson (2004, 288–91). Wilson examines the social history of this distrust to evaluate whether it was warranted. See also Perry (1986, 145ff.) and Hilda Smith (2007, 203).

5

Custom, Freedom, and Equality

Mary Astell on Marriage and Women's Education

Karen Detlefsen

Few suppose that feminism in the seventeenth century was as sophisticated and advanced as are the feminisms of today, or that our seventeenth-century forebears could have imagined as fully as we do women's emancipation in all the forms we imagine it. But is it the case that to speak of feminism three to four hundred years ago is to commit a "vile anachronism" (Janes 1976, 121; cf. Duran 2006, 86)? Or is speaking of feminism an appropriate recognition of the fact that some thinkers of the 1600s were indeed concerned with women, men, and their social roles precisely so as to push back against at least some of the constraints women experienced simply because of their sex? It is certainly worthwhile to carefully consider the nature and meaning of feminism, and how feminism might have evolved over the centuries.[1] Nonetheless, in this essay on Mary Astell's related views on marriage and education, I assume—and indeed will provide evidence throughout for the assumption—that we can acknowledge a sort of protofeminism in early thinkers who did indeed challenge some constraints that seventeenth-century women encountered. Astell is, according to this approach, one of the earliest feminists—perhaps the first English feminist (Hill 1986)—even if a conservative one (Kinnaird 1979; c.f. Hartmann 1998), a conservativism that has led to much ink being spilt over serious tensions found within her philosophy on women (e.g., Duran 2000, 148; 2006, 77; Hill 1986; Kinnaird 1979, 55; and Smith 1982a, 117).

In this chapter, I focus on one specific tension. Astell believes that women enjoy natural equality with men based on the fact that both have unsexed rational souls, which share an essential humanity; women, no less than men, are made by God to be rational creatures. On the other hand, Astell also believes that women are socially unequal to men, with perhaps the most troublesome example being her belief that wives are subordinate to their husbands within marriage. Because of her socially and politically conservative views, including her beliefs about marriage, there has recently been a suggestion that we reject Cartesian epistemology as the source of whatever feminism we might find in Astell (Broad 2007). For while Cartesianism might give rise to Astell's thoughts on male-female equality, she does not go so far as to subscribe to Descartes's radical skepticism regarding custom, as is evidenced by her acceptance of social and political practices that are deleterious to women. I argue that there is no tension between Astell's views on male-female natural equality and social inequality, and that no less than Descartes, her epistemology leads her to urge humans to radically question custom. It's just that much less falls into the sphere of custom for her than for Descartes; specifically, Astell does not believe that some very conservative social-political relations that rightly give feminist pause are customary. I also argue that the most promising way of lessening (albeit not eliminating) the antifeminism of Astell's thoughts on marriage is to focus on her Cartesian epistemology, for it can lead to a recognizably feminist theory of freedom in Astell, a theory that eases some of the burden on women of their social inequality. Before turning to these two related goals, I give a brief overview of Astell's Cartesianism, how others have noted that she uses it for feminist ends, and the precise nature of the tension I will thereafter examine.

Astell's Cartesianism: Ontology, Epistemology, Education

Perhaps the majority of commentators identify Astell's Cartesian roots as the source of her feminism (e.g., Kinnaird 1979, 61–62; O'Neill 1999, 242;

76   Feminist Interpretations of Mary Astell

Perry 1984, 22–23; 1985, 473–91; and Smith 1982a, 119). According to this approach, Astell has a roughly Cartesian metaphysics and epistemology, and these, together with a commitment to the logic and method of Port Royal, lead to her own feminist philosophy of education. In this section, then, I give a brief overview of these elements of her philosophy to show the points of overlap and divergence with Descartes's thought, and to draw out the feminist character of her Cartesianism.

Astell's feminism starts from a commitment to a Cartesian ontology of the human, specifically Descartes's dualism of soul and body (e.g., CR, 251), according to which the thinking soul (L, 1–2) is the mark of the divine within each of us and is our human essence.[2] While the soul may be embodied during our time on earth, it will eventually be free from the body after death (SP I, 52–53). Since sex attaches to bodies and not to souls, women's human essence is identical with—and thus equal to—that of men. This is the bedrock of Astell's feminism, and it informs her prescription for how women ought to treat themselves. For example, she says to women, "I suppose then that you're fill'd with a laudable Ambition to brighten and enlarge your Souls, that the Beauty of your Bodies is but a secondary care" (SP II, 122; cf. SP I, 54). Astell departs, however, from Descartes on the issue of individual differences. While Descartes believes that the powers of reason are "naturally equal in all men" (AT VI, 2; CSM I, 111) and quite possibly women as well,[3] Astell believes that humans have different degrees of rational capacity (e.g., SP II, 153, 186), even though all humans have the same essential kind of nature. Nonetheless, she is adamant that individual differences in rationality are not sex-based. It is a "ridiculous Pretension" to believe that men and women have different intellectual differences solely due to their sex: "that a Man is Wiser than a Woman merely because he is a Man! . . . [H]e who has no more Understanding than to argue at this rate, must not take it amiss if he is Esteemed accordingly" (CR, 171).[4]

Astell's Cartesian ontology encourages her to adopt a broadly Cartesian epistemology.[5] God created souls with finite rational capacity (SP II, 152), but they nonetheless contain some truths communicated by God, truths which are "clear and distinct" (SP II, 146). All humans have different "Modes of Understanding" (including faith, science, and opinion [SP II, 149]), but "knowledge in a proper and restricted sense" (SP II, 149) belongs to the scientific mode of understanding because it starts from premises clearly and distinctly known and reaches conclusions through deduction (SP II, 149–53).[6] Astell contrasts science with opinion and faith variously: "Now tho there's a great difference between Opinion and Science, true

Science being immutable but Opinion variable and uncertain, yet there is not such a difference between Faith and Science as is usually supposed. The difference consists not in the Certainty but in the way of Proof" (*SP II*, 150). Truths understood through faith are no less certain than those understood through science. The scientific mode of understanding is starkly contrasted with the senses, through which we may be conscious but not obtain certain knowledge (*SP II*, 150). Part of our task as knowers is to understand our various cognitive capacities, recognize our limits, and constrain ourselves therein (*SP II*, 152), another obviously Cartesian point.

From this taxonomy of cognitive abilities and their relation to knowledge follows an essentially Cartesian method for gaining knowledge, with the Cartesian-inspired Port Royal logic of Arnauld and Nicole (*SP II*, 166) also playing a key role. Astell sums up her account with six rules, the sixth being crucial for my purposes: "To judge no further than we Perceive, and not to take anything for Truth, which we do not evidently Know to be so" (*SP II*, 178). This rule commands us to accept as truth that which we believe through science or faith, but to reject as potentially not true that which we believe through opinion. Astell also alerts us to various sources of error that normally derail us from the path to true knowledge; crucial sources of error are the senses and related aspects of our embodied nature, such as the passions (*SP II*, 154–55). She thus encourages us to "withdraw ourselves as much as may be from Corporeal things, that pure Reason may be heard the better" (*SP II*, 164). Two feminist advantages emerge from Astell's epistemology and method. First, echoing a point central to Descartes, the certainty of scientific method—that is, of starting from clear and distinct perceptions and reasoning stepwise through deduction to conclusions—is contrasted with the uncertainty of mere opinions, and the scientific mode of understanding is highly individualistic. Astell thus allows the individual to challenge traditional beliefs held by members of a society at large. In other words, a woman can challenge customary beliefs that undermine women, such as the belief that their beauty matters more than their intellect. Second, Astell strongly links rationality with human essence while also disengaging the passions from our human essence, and this applies equally to men and women alike. She thus rejects the traditional pairing of women with irrational passions and men with rationality, a rejection that has obvious benefit for women.

The purpose of Astell's general Cartesian ontology, epistemology, and method is much more clearly articulated by Astell in her formal works than it is by Descartes, whose purposes, including laying metaphysical foundations for a new physics, are more clearly laid out in private correspondence

78   Feminist Interpretations of Mary Astell

(AT III, 298; CSMK, 173). Astell's purpose is resolutely theological (much more so, I would venture, than is Descartes's): to prepare the soul for the afterlife (*SP II*, 187–89, 200), and to serve God in this life at least in part by helping others perfect their souls. This latter point alerts us to one aspect of the tension within Astell's feminism. Astell believes that in this life, women ought to serve God in a specific, gendered way; by having knowledge, a woman finds "very great use of it, not only in the Conduct of her own Soul but in the management of her Family. . . . Education of Children is a most necessary Employment [and] . . . shou'd be laid by the Mother, for Fathers find other Business" (*SP II*, 202; cf. *CR*, 296). Astell clearly believes that while human nature is unsexed and therefore equal, humans have gendered roles to play, at least insofar as we find ourselves in specific social settings. I return to this tension in the next section.[7] At this juncture, I underscore the religious element of Astell's thought thus far explicated: God, and serving God, is our end (e.g., *SP II*, 142–44).

Developing our God-given rationality is the means by which we attain our end of serving God, and the way in which we develop our God-given rationality is to pursue a good education.[8] Let us suppose that education belongs properly to the sphere of custom; Astell herself often connects education and custom (e.g., *SP I*, 67, 77, 94–95). I follow Jacqueline Broad in her view that, for Astell, "custom inclines us to judge an action as right or wrong for no other reason than that such an action has been deemed right or wrong by long use and by the sanction of our forebears" (Broad 2007, 168). Given Astell's constant refrain *against* custom and *in favor of* our true nature, most notably in A *Serious Proposal to the Ladies* (e.g., *SP I*, 55, 67–68, 77, 94, 101; *SP II*, 126, 130, 133, 139–40, 170), it would seem that she is opposed tout court to the customary ways of humans. And this is, by and large, a fair interpretation of her reaction to the empirical facts of her time. But while Astell does find much fault in the majority of contemporary customs, it is not necessarily custom per se that is at fault. For customs, and thus education, can be good or bad depending upon how well they are aligned with, or serve, our true, God-given nature. Bad customs are those that pervert our natural selves, and bad education is one that does not develop our God-given rationality, thus robbing us of the means by which we attain our end of honoring and serving God. "This Ignorance and a narrow Education lay the Foundation of Vice, and Imitation and Custom rear it up" (*SP I*, 67). Conversely, good customs cultivate our natural, God-given selves, and good education develops and perfects our God-given rationality, thus enabling us to attain our end of honoring and serving God, including by helping others perfect their rationality.[9] Indeed, this last

Astell on Marriage and Women's Education   79

point is *the* point of Astell's *Serious Proposal*, in which she lays out the
details and foundations of a good education precisely, I suggest, to bring
about better customs for generations after Astell's own.

For women—Astell's singular focus—good education should occur in a
religious retreat, a women-only educational institution. This is because *bad*
customs are so widespread in a world dominated by men "who under pretence of loving and admiring [women], really serve their *own* base ends"
(*SP I*, 74), that women's true nature simply cannot be developed in that
wider world. A number of points about this religious retreat should be
emphasized. First, it is a *religious* retreat, in keeping with Astell's overall
theological purposes. The religious retirement will draw women's attention
away from the worldly, bodily concerns that currently dominate their
attention, and it will turn women's attention toward the cultivation of her
soul "so that here's a vast treasure gain'd, which for ought I know, may
purchase an happy Eternity" (*SP I*, 89). Second, it is especially important
for *women* to be afforded such a retreat because of the disproportionate
burden women bear living in the world of bad customs (*SP I*, 56–73
passim). Third, women-only retreats cultivate the value of true female
friendship—"a Vertue which comprehends all the rest" (*SP I*, 98). Female
friendship is valuable not only for its own sake but because it helps women
to develop the ability to withstand bad customs that tempt them away
from their God-given ends of self-perfection and perfection of others' souls,
customs to which they will once again be exposed should they be forced to
leave the retreat (*SP I*, 100). And women *will* have to leave the retreat: "It
is not my intention that you shou'd seclude your selves from the World, I
know it is necessary that a great number of you shou'd live in it; but it is
Unreasonable and Barbarous to drive you into't, e're you are capable of
doing Good in it, or at least of keeping Evil from your selves" (*SP II*, 231).

Astell, like Descartes, thus connects two crucial elements in her philosophy. First, the ontology of the human, and the related epistemology
and method which follow from this ontology, allow a woman to rely upon
her own God-given nature—especially her rational capacities—in order to
reach whatever truths about the world she is able to reach. Second, developing one's rational capacities allows a woman to reject customs which her
own rational nature tells her are wrong. And yet, in Astell, this connection of two crucial elements is not, seemingly, fully realized. Some social
relations that we might justifiably think are positively detrimental to
women are relations that she at worst lauds, and at best, does not challenge. I hinted at this above when noting her acceptance of special gendered duties that women seem to bear. For the remainder of this essay, I

80   Feminist Interpretations of Mary Astell

address this issue by focusing on Astell's views on marriage as articulated in her *Some Reflections upon Marriage*.

In keeping with the exposition of her views thus far, Astell argues in that work that women are not *naturally* inferior to men (e.g., RM, 14–15). Nonetheless, and due to humanity's fallen state in which we are not guided by reason, women must be *socially* subordinated to men in private families so as to maintain stability (RM, 15). In perhaps the most (in)famous passage in her oeuvre, Astell writes:

> She who Elects a Monarch for Life [in marriage], who gives him an Authority she cannot recall however he misapply it, who puts her Fortune and Person entirely in his Powers . . . had best stay till she meet with one who has the Government of his own Passions, and has duly regulated his own desires, since he is to have such an absolute Power over hers. . . . And Covenants [contracts] betwixt Husband and Wife, like Laws in an Arbitrary Government, are of little Force; the Will of the Sovereign is all in all. (RM, 48–49, 52)

So, Cartesian epistemology should lead to a radical intellectual independence, which in turn should lead to the radical challenging of customs. Yet, contrary to this logical trajectory, Astell espouses traditional social and political values. For this reason, Broad has suggested that we downplay Astell's Cartesian epistemology as the grounds for Astell's feminism, such as it is (Broad 2007, 167). I take it there are two related issues with Cartesian epistemology. First, Astell cannot be a fully committed Cartesian with respect to epistemology; if she were, she would espouse much more radical attitudes toward traditional social and political relations than she actually does. Second, because of the limits to her Cartesian epistemology, we have to turn to some other aspect of Astell's philosophy to locate a source for a viable feminism. Broad suggests we turn instead to Astell's Cartesian ethics (Broad 2007) as the more likely and promising source of that feminism. In focusing on Astell's ethics, I think Broad accurately captures Astell's most explicit response to the social inequalities between women and men. But from a feminist perspective, I think there is more hope in Astell's Cartesian epistemology than that which is to be found in her ethics. In the remainder of this chapter, I first make sense of Astell's seemingly contradictory approach to custom—both constantly deriding it and yet seeming to embrace some customs that are most detrimental to women. I do so by underscoring the fact that these social relations are not (human) customs for Astell but rather are divinely instituted. I then argue that the best way

Astell on Marriage and Women's Education   81

of easing the blow to feminism of Astell's embrace of women-unfriendly social relations in fact stems from her Cartesian epistemology and method, for these are the source of a decidedly feminist strain of freedom implicit in her philosophy. Further, this freedom will be most effective in rooting out women-unfriendly social relations, which Astell so astutely recognizes are rampant in her time.

Custom and Nature: Astell's Ambivalent Feminism

In examining Astell's views on marriage, I start with a caveat: *Reflections* is dripping with irony (Lister 2004, 63–64), and as a result, it is sometimes difficult to ascertain Astell's true beliefs therein.[10] That said, I think the following is a defensible interpretation of Astell's thinking. Human relations, such as male superiority over women in marriage, have come about due to the Fall, and these relations ensure stability, where otherwise there would be chaos (e.g., RM, 15). This situation leaves the sanction of the hierarchical marriage relation unclear in Astell's thought. Sometimes, Astell seems to suggest that husbands' power over their wives is simply a factual description of what men, through a power grab, have usurped for themselves, without the further prescriptive judgment that this unequal relation is right. "And Covenants [contracts] betwixt Husband and Wife, like Laws in an Arbitrary Government, are of little Force; the Will of the Sovereign is all in all. Thus it is in Matter of Fact, I will not answer for the Right of it" (RM, 52; cf. RM, 26, 30, 33). On other occasions, Astell seems to assert that the inequality between men and women in marriage is right, not because of divine sanction, but rather because of the civil stability such a hierarchy can afford (e.g., RM, 15).[11] According to either of these first interpretations, the hierarchical relation between men and women in marriage would indeed be a case of human custom. Yet, at still other times, Astell seems to indicate that the unequal marriage relation is sanctioned by God, such that husband-wife inequality is both descriptively actual and prescriptively good, with the highest degree of ratification for that goodness. This view is strongly implied by her claim that marriage is a "Christian Institution" in which women have gendered roles such as the education of children (RM, 37) and implying that men also have gendered roles therein. Astell also explicitly acknowledges what she takes to be the truth of the biblical claim that wives ought to "submit themselves to their own Husbands" (RM, 20).[12] Indeed, both the bulk of her claims and the nature of her religious commitments favor this last interpretation, and so

I accept it as capturing Astell's beliefs: the marriage relation, characterized as it is by the husband's power over the subordinate wife, is authorized
by God.

Given this interpretation, Astell's acceptance of the structure of marriage, a structure that has traditionally been deleterious to women as wives,
is nonetheless entirely coherent despite her repeated sharp criticisms of
customs that are harmful to women. In other words, *marriage, with its
attendant hierarchy, is not a custom.* God made human beings, all of whom
are equal insofar as all have rational capacities which are intrinsic and
essential to them. Any custom, such as bad education, that undermines
the natures that God has given humans should be actively worked against.
God also made the marriage relation, within which husbands (as husbands)
are superior to wives (as wives), all the while preserving the natural equality of men (as men) with women (as women). God ordained the husband-
wife relationship, but this relationship is not intrinsic to men's or women's
nature; what is intrinsic to human nature is their shared rationality. Outside the marriage bond, women can freely choose whether to enter into
marriage. Once within a marriage, a wife has consented to subordinate
herself to her husband socially, but not to thereby consider herself to be
inferior in her nature. Within marriage, how a husband chooses to behave
is up to him. He can choose whether or not to follow the God-given purposes that, as a man, are intrinsic to him. Likewise, he can choose whether
or not to contribute positively to his wife's attempts (should she be so
inclined) to follow her God-given purposes that, as a woman, are intrinsic
to her. When a husband cultivates his own rational nature as a man, when
he acknowledges and contributes to the cultivation of his wife's rational
nature as a woman, and when a wife cultivates her own rational nature as
a woman, then individuals within marriage do not need to take on conflicting roles, such as an individual taking on the conflicting roles of a
rational woman and of a wife treated as less than fully rational by her
husband. Moreover, a marriage without such conflicts will be a happy one.

However, when a husband does not cultivate his own rational nature as
a man, when he does not acknowledge and contribute to the cultivation of
his wife's rational nature as a woman, or when a wife does not cultivate her
own rational nature as a woman, then individuals within marriage will
take on conflicting roles. But an individual taking on the role, for example,
of mistreated wife (mistreated because treated as less than fully rational),
does not take away from her intrinsic nature as a fully rational human. She
can be, at one and the same time, both subordinated, mistreated wife and
equal, rational woman; the former role is extrinsic to her and follows from

her relation with her husband, while the latter role is intrinsic to her and follows from her own treatment of herself. The marriage bond, in which there is a rift between the role of wife and the role of woman, is a bad one. Nonetheless, having consented to enter into this divinely instituted relation, a woman cannot leave it. At the same time, Astell notes two factors that she believes mitigate the challenges of such marriages. First, and in keeping with her Cartesian ontology, epistemology, and method, no matter how badly treated a wife might be, if she has cultivated her God-given rationality through excellent education before entering into that bond, she can continue to develop and find comfort in her rational, contemplative nature even within that bond. Her God-given nature as a rational being ensures that this is within her own power. Second, as wife, enduring a bad marriage is an excellent testing ground for Christian virtues, helping to cultivate and develop those virtues through the endurance of the bad marriage (e.g., Duran 2006, 91).

Five points from the above deserve emphasis. First, to the degree that one can find a strain of feminism in Astell's account of women, it is squarely grounded in Cartesian ontology and epistemology. A woman's essential nature is her unsexed rational soul, and she can develop and use this rationality equally with men (nongendered, individual differences aside). Furthermore, this view leads to the conclusion that customs, such as unequal education, which violate God-given human rationality are customs which ought to be opposed.

Second, to the degree that one can find strains of antifeminism in Astell's account of wives, it does seem to be due to a departure from Cartesian epistemology. That is, certainty that marriage is divinely instituted comes neither from what Astell would call science (which proceeds from clear and distinct perceptions and deduction) nor from opinion (which could not secure the certainty of the claim), and so must come from faith (cf. Duran 2006, 82). Moreover, beliefs from faith depend not upon the self but upon testimony of a person we believe (SP II, 151). Indeed, Astell's turning to biblical evidence to shore up this belief indicates that faith is the source of that belief. And so, faith delivers fairly substantial beliefs for Astell, including the certain belief that wives are socially subordinate to their husbands in marriage, whereas for Descartes, the role that faith plays in delivering beliefs is radically more constrained.[13]

Third, this antifeminism is, however, not as strong as it might initially seem. For while the institution of marriage, together with the unequal relationship between the husband and wife therein, are divinely instituted, I take it that the way men and women choose to conduct themselves within

84   Feminist Interpretations of Mary Astell

that institution is merely customary and can be changed if their behavior is bad. This flexibility can mitigate the negative impact upon women who find themselves within a marriage. In the final section, I argue that the way men and women improve their behavior within marriage is firmly grounded in Cartesian epistemology, which gives rise to a feminist-friendly account of freedom.

Fourth, for the feminism identified in the first point above and for the cultivation of good behavior identified in the third point above to be realized, women must be educated prior to marriage. If they are not, then their intrinsic and equal rational nature will not be developed and they will fail to realize their God-given nature *as women* within marriage, should the marriage be bad. Marriage is not a custom but a divinely instituted relation; human rationality is no less divinely made. To pay due heed to God, *both* human rationality *and* marriage must be fully respected. Entering into marriage without first having developed the resources to withstand its tumults and protect one's God-given nature will necessarily result in an injury to God; either a woman will break the God-instituted marriage bond in order to put herself into a more tolerable situation such as one in which she can cultivate her God-given rationality, or a woman will respect the God-instituted marriage bond and in doing so, will fail to cultivate her God-given rationality. Excellent education prior to marriage is *essential* for equipping women to fully respect God by both staying within marriage and being able to maintain their essential rational nature therein, no matter the quality of that marriage. Astell's call for excellent women's education, then, is not only for a woman's sake but also a call meant to pay due heed to God.[14]

Fifth, Astell's position is nonetheless limited from a feminist point of view. For even if women do enjoy the sort of education that allows them to paid due heed to their nature as rational beings, it is women who are nonetheless subordinated in marriage and who will therefore bear the largest burden should the marriage be bad. Further, Astell assumes a psychologically unrealistic split between women's inner and outer lives. For even if a woman has been well educated before marriage such that she has realized her rationality—the very inner quality that she must continue to cultivate even after marriage—the outer conditions of marriage may be so exacting that she simply cannot realize her duty to God to continue to focus on her rational capacity, and expecting her to do so is both unrealistic and unfair.

Broad's suggested solution to the threat to feminism articulated in this fifth point is to turn to Astell's ethics, specifically, "a pursuit of Cartesian ethical ideals [which] might result in a calm acceptance of the status quo.

Astell on Marriage and Women's Education   85

While we cannot master our external circumstances, including "the cruel tyranny of an abusive husband," Broad interprets Astell as saying, "we can master our own inner aspirations. The culmination of our re-direction of the passions toward a love of God is an inner tranquility and peace of mind, regardless of 'what happens without us'" (Broad 2007, 179). It may well be that Astell herself suggests this approach. But it is an approach that is inherently limited from a feminist point of view, for it disproportionately burdens the woman with the consequences of men's poor treatment of them, and it encourages a quietism on behalf of women in the face of socially debilitating conditions, a quietism that cannot bring about change.[15] So in the next section I suggest an alternate solution to the threats to feminism. It is a solution both strongly implicit in Astell's philosophy and grounded in her Cartesian ontology and epistemology.

Reason and Freedom

Astell has, I will argue, the seeds of a recognizably feminist theory of freedom, a theory that goes a long distance—even if not the *whole* distance— in mitigating some of the less women-friendly elements of her social-political philosophy. Moreover, it is a theory that relies foundationally upon her broadly Cartesian epistemology, which favors the cultivation of the rational capacities that are definitive of our souls. I start with a general account of Astell's theory of freedom, and then draw out its feminist potential.

Astell directly links the development of one's rationality with the ability to freely choose how one will behave, and to choose from one's own undetermined will rather than from the determination by another's will: "If then it be the property of Rational Creatures, and Essential to their very Natures to Chuse their Actions, and to determine their Wills to that Choice *by such Principles and Reasonings as their Understanding are furnish'd with*, they who are desirous to be rank'd in that Order of Beings must conduct their Lives by these Measures, *begin with their Intellects*, inform themselves what are the plain and first Principles of Action, and Act accordingly" (*SP II*, 128, my emphasis; cf. *CR*, 278). A well-developed intellect or rational capacity will allow a woman to formulate clear, rational principles of behavior, and this in turn will allow her will to pursue those principles. This will save her from pursuing a course of action that is in accord with custom and against rational principles. Astell associates the pursuit of customary forms of behavior (presumably those that are bad customs) with the absence of freedom: "Why shou'd we not assert our Liberty, and not

86   Feminist Interpretations of Mary Astell

suffer every Trifler to impose a Yoke of Impertinent Custom on us?" (*SP II*, 120). Finally, Astell connects men's mistreatment of women to women's reduced rational capacity and consequently reduced freedom, and she locates women's ability to push against this reduced freedom in their good sense, or within their own minds: "I dare say you understand your own interest too well to neglect it so grossly and have a greater share of sense, whatever some Men affirm, than to be content to be kept any longer under their Tyranny in Ignorance and Folly, since it is in your Power to regain your Freedom, if you please but t'endeavour it" (*SP II*, 121). Astell's account of human, and therefore women's, freedom is squarely grounded upon Cartesian first principles, namely the fact that all humans are essentially characterized by their souls, which are free, indeed, increasingly more free the more the soul is guided by intellect and not by custom.[16] So in her plan for women's education, Astell it is not just motivated by the fullest possible realization of women's *rational* essence; she is also motivated by the fullest possible realization of women's freedom allowed by that development of reason.

This general account of human (and women's freedom) based in Cartesian principles can be developed into a recognizably feminist account of freedom. To show this, I lay out a brief account of some crucial contemporary ideas on freedom and then turn to Astell's conceptual position in this account.[17] In somewhat recent feminist theory, there has been a great deal of opposition expressed toward the ideal of the free or autonomous agent (Mackenzie and Stoljar 2000, 3). The ideal of autonomy with which these feminists take issue assumes a self-sufficient, independent, and "atomistic" agent, and is thus seen as exalting hyperindividualism. Because this ideal of autonomy distances itself from emotional commitments such as care, it is also seen as hyperrationalistic. This conception of autonomy is further seen to be masculinist because historically the traits of self-sufficiency, independence, nonconnectedness, and rationality have been associated with men, while interdependence, reliance on social communities, trust and care, and thus emotions and passions, have been associated with women. So, according to this feminist line of thought, any theory of freedom which lauds the former list of traits and portrays them as central to a fully and freely lived human life, and which disparages the latter list of traits, is a masculinist theory.

Lately, a number of feminist theorists, including Marilyn Friedman, Nancy Hirschmann, Diana Tietjens Meyers, and Natalie Stoljar, to name a few, have argued forcefully that we should recognize the critical importance of freedom for feminist ends.[18] Without women and men being free or autonomous agents, it is unclear how we can engage in the project of pushing against and overcoming oppression of women. Yet these theorists are still mindful of the important feminist criticisms levied against the ideal of autonomy sketched above. And so, recent theorists suggest we "refigure" rather than reject the concept of the autonomous or free individual. Central to one such refiguring is the acknowledgment that we just are in social relations, and that these relations are crucial to how we understand our freedom because of the range of human actions that our relations can permit or disallow. The kind and quality of our relations are important in understanding freedom or autonomy, according to these thinkers, insofar as agents just are "intrinsically relational because their identities or self-conceptions are constituted by elements of the social context in which they are embedded," and insofar as social relations shape the range of options open to people (Mackenzie and Stoljar 2000, 22). Many have dubbed this feminist account of freedom or autonomy "relational autonomy." According to this theory, we can give a feminist account of freedom if we expect that women and men alike acknowledge the subjectivity and projects that others wish to pursue, and that women and men alike modulate their behavior in their relationships so as to allow others the freedom to pursue their projects, even if this requires the individual to curb one's own freely pursued projects.

I contend that we find such an account of freedom in Astell. To make my case, I turn to one of the crucial features found within her religious retreat: the power of female friendship. According to Astell, human creatures deserve the love of benevolence from one another; this is to be contrasted with the love of desire we owe to God (L, 282–85).[19] Benevolence is the source of our friendship with others, and in the female-only religious retreat, it is benevolence women feel toward one another. Such a friendship

> has a special force to dilate [open] our hearts, to deliver them from that vicious selfishness, and the rest of those *sordid Passions* which express a narrow illiberal temper, and are of such a pernicious consequence to Mankind. . . . But by Friendship I do not mean any of those intimacies that are abroad in the world, which are often combinations in evil and at best but insignificant dearnesses. . . . But I intend by it the greatest usefulness, the most refin'd and disinteress'd Benevolence, a love that thinks nothing within the bounds of Power and Duty, too much to do or suffer for its Beloved; And makes no distinction betwixt its Friend and its self. (SP I, 99)

88   Feminist Interpretations of Mary Astell

A true friendship cannot be developed hastily, for it requires that "we look into the very Soul of the beloved Person, to discover what resemblance it bears to our own" (SP I, 100). Astell underscores the purpose of such a friendship: "The truest effect of love being to endeavour the bettering of the beloved Person" (SP I, 100), which for Astell must mean the cultivation of the friend's rational capacities so she can honor and serve God.

Two elements of Astell's account of female friendship encourage the belief that she holds, at least implicitly, the seeds of the theory of relational autonomy in contemporary feminism. First, her account of female friend-ship rests upon an individual recognizing the subjectivity of others. This is supported by her belief that true friendship requires that we come to know the soul of another and to acknowledge the likeness of that soul to one's own; both are subjects. Indeed, true friendship "makes no distinction" between the other and the self, showing that the true friend acknowledges the other's subjectivity just as we acknowledge our own. Second, acknowl-edging the other's subjectivity requires one to modulate one's own behavior toward the other precisely so as to allow the other to better herself by devel-oping her mind, which in turn, as we saw above, increases her freedom.

Thus far, my account of Astell's implicit endorsement of relational autonomy does not go far enough to tease out a feminist account of free-dom from Astell's works. For Astell's relational autonomy, thus far pre-sented, simply applies to women's freedom outside the unequal marriage bond. Once condemned to marriage, women will continue to suffer the burdens of marriage in a way men will not. Nonetheless, Astell imagines that her prototheory of relational autonomy could hold not only among women in the religious retreat but also between a woman and a man in the marriage bond. This harks back to my discussion of the good marriage outlined in the previous section. My readers will recall that there I sug-gested that, for Astell, a good marriage would be one in which, among other things, a husband acknowledges and contributes to the cultivation of his wife's rational nature as a woman. This view bears both marks of the relational autonomy that, I suggested, we find in Astell's account of friend-ship: it requires that a man recognize a woman's subjectivity (the fact that she is a rational creature), and it requires that a man modulate his own behavior so as to allow the woman to freely cultivate that nature (he can-not, for example, behave in any way he wishes lest his behavior stand in that way of the woman's project to develop her mind).

And indeed, in Reflections, Astell does characterize a good marriage as one in which the woman and man are friends. She explicitly rejects more traditional reasons for marriage. So, for example, one should not marry for the other's estate (*RM*, 38), or "that the Family must be kept up, the ancient Race preserv'd" (*RM*, 43). Rather, a woman should marry a virtuous man "who has the Government of his own Passions, and has duly regulated his own desires, since he is to have such an absolute Power over hers" (*RM*, 49). Moreover, Astell explicitly notes that a man's contributing to a woman's rational development is crucial to a happy marriage: "Men ought really for their own sakes to do what in them lies to make Women Wise and Good, and then it might be hoped they themselves would effectually Study and Practise that Wisdom and Vertue they recommend to others" (*RM*, 45). And finally, a woman and man in marriage should be friends:

> Is it the being ty'd to *One* that offends us? Why this ought rather to recommend Marriage to us, and would really do so, were we guided by Reason, and not by Humour or brutish Passion. He who does not make Friendship the chief inducement of his Choice, and prefer it before any other consideration, does not deserve a good Wife, and therefore should not complain if he goes without one. Now we can never grow weary of our Friends; the longer we have had them, the more they are endear'd to us; and if we have One well assur'd, we need seek no further, but are sufficiently happy in Her. (*RM*, 37)

Taken together, Astell's pronouncements on what a good marriage should look like contain the seeds for an account of husband-wife relations based on the ideal of relational autonomy, an ideal very promising from a feminist point of view. It is also an ideal which is, in Astell's works, based ultimately on the development of the human's God-given rationality—a Cartesian epistemic principle at the core of Astell's fundamental philosophy. In developing one's rationality, both man and woman will recognize the damage that can be done to husbands and wives by following customary reasons for marriage choices and customary treatment by men of women within marriage. That is, this very promising feminist seed in Astell's work requires a Cartesian epistemology that leads to the radical questioning of customary features of human behavior within the marriage bond, a questioning that is truly Cartesian. Interestingly, the individual's development of his rationality along Cartesian lines leads him to acknowledge the importance of good communal relations, relations which are anything but the highly individualistic person we find in Descartes. So ultimately, Astell's feminism is based upon an acknowledgment of our essential, communal interrelatedness.[20]

90   Feminist Interpretations of Mary Astell

Admittedly, Astell seems to hold out little hope for this happy account of marriage—or of happy female-male relations in general—obtaining in her day. She seems understandably skeptical of men's ability to change (e.g., SP I, 56), and women are left with the lion's share of the work in changing the current situation. And yet, without men making changes in their own behavior at least as radical as those that Astell urges women to make in themselves, the seeds of a relational autonomy that are found in Astell simply cannot develop into a full-grown theory. Perhaps for this reason, Andrew Lister interprets Astell *not* as advocating a feminism grounded in women's rights, but rather as espousing a feminism grounded in a rejection of misogyny (Lister 2004, 46 and 72). Certainly, Astell is committed not to human rights at all but to human duties to God to perfect our natures. But she believes women and men have equal duties on this score. Given this, if I am correct in my reading of a nascent relational autonomy in Astell's account of male-female relations, then not only is her feminism based in a rejection of misogyny (as with Lister), but it is also based in an acknowledgment of a woman's equal duty to develop her God-given rational nature and to be aided in that endeavor by men who are willing to subordinate their base passions in order that their wives may develop their minds. It is a much fuller account of feminism than either the form that focuses only on misogyny or the form that encourages women to develop their virtuous characters in order to better endure a burdensome marriage. Instead it is a feminism that requires some social change—namely, that men allow women greater freedom to flourish as rational beings.

Astell's feminist promise should not be overstated. For a seventeenth-century woman, she was remarkably advanced both in her understanding of women, men, and their social roles, on the one hand, and in her prescriptions for women's education and attitude toward marriage, on the other. Still, even were men and women to achieve the friendship-based relationship within marriage that I contend would lead to increased freedom for women due to men's recognizing women's subjectivity and allowing them to flourish as a result of that recognition, the *institution* of marriage itself would remain an unequal one by Astell's lights. The negative effects of women's subordination to men within marriage may be eliminated in the best of friendships, but the possibility that such effects could always arise again remains, and should such effects of subordination be reasserted, then women would have no recourse to change those effects. That is, the nascent relational autonomy to be found in Astell allows for some social change, but social change that is not particularly far-reaching. Her theology, together with its tenet that marriage is an unequal relationship between men and

Astell on Marriage and Women's Education   91

women instituted by none other than God, precludes a more far-reaching feminism. But since that same theology is the seat of her feminist beliefs, namely her belief in female-male natural equality and her belief in men's duty being to perfect their own souls, which will permit them to see the like duty in a wife (the crucial step in her relational autonomy), this is as radical a feminism that we can hope to find in her philosophy.

Abbreviations

AT   René Descartes, *Oeuvres de Descartes*, vols. I–XII (1996) (cited by volume and page number)
CR   Mary Astell, *The Christian Religion, as Profess'd by a Daughter of the Church of England* (1705) (cited by page number)
CSM   René Descartes, *The Philosophical Writings of Descartes*, vols. I–II (1985) (cited by volume and page number)
CSMK   René Descartes, *The Philosophical Writings of Descartes*, vol. III (1991) (cited by page number)
L   Mary Astell, *Letters Concerning the Love of God* (1695)
RM   Mary Astell, *Reflections upon Marriage* (1996)
SP I   Mary Astell, *A Serious Proposal to the Ladies, Part I* (2002)
SP II   Mary Astell, *A Serious Proposal to the Ladies, Part II* (2002)

Notes

1. Melissa Butler, for example, thinks the study of historical figures like Astell "calls twenty-first century scholars to reexamine those categories [of contemporary feminism]" (Butler 2009, 736).

2. Alice Sowaal has a much more well-developed account of Astell's theory of mind and its relation to key points addressed in this essay (Sowaal 2007).

3. This is not to deny that Descartes's approach fails to recognize the special conditions of women's lives, conditions which might well prevent women from maximizing their rational capacity along the lines Descartes himself suggests. See Ruth Perry (1985), for example, on this point.

4. I must acknowledge one potential worry with Astell's approach, namely that unsexed souls are nonetheless embodied in sexed bodies, which have an influence on the soul (e.g., SP II, 159–60). This is a worry worthy of closer treatment, but here let me just pass over it by noting that Astell uses the embodiment of souls to women's advantage, arguing, for example, that women as embodied souls are more suited for the speculative life, which, as we shall see, better perfects human nature (e.g., SP I, 57; CR, 296).

5. I recognize that her epistemology is not fully Cartesian, for, as Broad points out, there is no commitment to radical doubt in Astell (Broad 2007, 171).

6. As this description of the scientific mode of understanding makes clear, Astell's use of "science" is, of course, different from our own. For Astell, as for others writing in the seventeenth century, "science" derives from *scientia* and refers to certain knowledge such as the sort we might derive from indubitable first principles together with deductive reasoning.

7. John McCrystal reads Astell as defending women's roles against disparagement and thus offering another form of feminism (McCrystal 1992, 157).

8. See McCrystal's argument that women have an equal *duty* to educate their minds, not an equal *right* to education. Developing our minds through education is a duty to God as our proper end

92   Feminist Interpretations of Mary Astell

(McCrystal 1992, 165; cf. Achinstein 2007). On this point, he diverges from those who believe Astell thinks good education is a woman's *right* (e.g., Weiss 2004, 65).

9. Astell's educational theory is thus at one and the same time a perfectionist theory, insofar as it requires that we perfect our rational capacities, and a functionalist theory, insofar as perfecting our rational capacities permits us to take on specific functions such as serving God, including by taking on gendered social roles. See Patricia Ward Scaltsas for an argument that Astell is motivated by perfectionist principles (Scaltsas 1990, 139, 141–42), and Joan K. Kinnaird, who acknowledges the functionalist role of education in Astell's philosophy (Kinnaird 1979, 72–73).

10. See Patricia Springborg's writings for an interesting argument that reading Astell's comments on marriage alongside her comments on the monarch-subject relation alerts us to her true goal, which is to challenge the contract political theories of her contemporaries, especially John Locke (Springborg 1995; 1996; 2005, 113–42). Springborg's position is in opposition to that held by, for example, Kathleen M. Squadrito, who believes that Astell rejects arbitrary power in marriage and uses this to suggest that we also ought to also reject arbitrary power in the state (Squadrito 1991, 94).

11. Weiss argues against this interpretation since in marriage, half the population (women) are in a state of insecurity, not security or stability (Weiss 2004, 72–73).

12. On marriage as a divinely instituted bond, see arguments by Kinnaird and Andrew Lister (Kinnaird 1979, 66ff.; Lister 2004, 66). Springborg also argues that God authorizes the institution of marriage, specifically with men empowered to rules over women therein, even while individual men and women can consent or not to enter into this divinely authorized institution (Springborg 1996, xxff., xxviiff.).

13. At the same time, the radical individualism of Descartes's method might not necessarily lead to a more promising conclusion on the social role of women in marriage than we find in Astell, for his radical challenge of custom was aimed more clearly at the customary acceptance of Aristotelian physics and the metaphysics which grounds it.

14. To be sure, Astell believes that the next best approach would be for women to self-educate. But as Sowaal points out, this underestimates "the degree to which custom has manacled women's wills" (Sowaal 2007, 233), and thus this second best strategy may have little hope of success. Astell herself recognizes that some women are not naturally strong and virtuous (*SP I*, 104), and if so, they will likely fail at self-education.

15. Looking at Astell's poetry, Claire Pickard notes that quietism shifts one's focus to the afterlife, and therefore, to human souls, where women enjoy equality with men. She understands this sort of approach to go hand in hand with Astell's feminism (Pickard 2007).

16. In pushing this account of freedom, I do not deny the claim that women are always embodied in this life, and that we must take account of that embodiment in our understanding of women's freedom. That said, while it may not be the case that the freedom of the *disembodied* mind for self-determination (Bryson 1998, 45) motivates Astell, it is still the case that the soul is *the* source of freedom for Astell, and in developing one's intellect in order to be better able to set rational principles for free action, one is developing the reasoning power of one's *soul*.

17. Material from this paragraph is from my "Margaret Cavendish and Thomas Hobbes on Freedom, Education, and Women" (Detlefsen 2013, 162).

18. For example, see papers collected in Mackenzie and Stoljar (2000).

19. On this aspect of Astell's philosophy, see works by Broad, Sowaal, and Wilson (Broad 2002, 11–20; 2003; Sowaal 2005, §3.1; Wilson 2004).

20. For those who acknowledge and develop in various ways this focus on community over individualism in Astell, see Broad (2007, 167); Hartmann (1998, 246); Perry (1990); Sowaal (2005, §1.2); and Sowaal (2007, 237).

6

Further Reflections upon Marriage

Mary Astell and Sarah Chapone

Susan Paterson Glover

Three centuries ago in England, the philosopher Mary Astell argued that, despite whatever constraints society might lay upon a woman's body, her mind was her own and she could enjoy complete freedom of thought: "Tho' the Order of the World requires an *Outward* Respect and Obedience from some to others, yet the Mind is free, nothing but Reason can oblige it, 'tis out of the reach of the most absolute Tyrant" (RM, 56). She had, however, little use for the religious toleration that such a sentiment might foster, seeing in it only a nursery for sedition and rebellion that continued to threaten the Church of England. Astell's convictions that Anglican doctrine is sound and that the Bible reveals that God granted reason to both men and women in order to equip them for an earthly life that would lead to eternal salvation, were for her quite compatible. Astell's calls for greater

94   Feminist Interpretations of Mary Astell

respect for women's abilities and worth, for access to education, for the pursuit of knowledge and reason in place of vanity and folly, were all grounded in a belief that women's disabilities arose from the limitations of custom, rather than capacity.[1]

Astell's Christian faith provided the raison d'être for the exercise of a reason that led her ineluctably to believe in an equality of mind posited by Cartesian rationalism. God provided the power of reason to men and women alike in order that each might learn to know Him. It was the deployment of that reason in search of truth that prompted Astell to write to the philosopher and divine John Norris in 1693 and ask him to clarify his claims in the third volume of *Practical Discourses upon Several Divine Subjects*, published earlier that year. If God was the efficient cause of our pleasure, and therefore the fit object of our love, she asked, is he not also the author of our pains, and must he not then remain the object of our love in pain as well as in pleasure? The ensuing correspondence between the as yet unpublished Astell and the Anglican author, which unfolded while the first part of Astell's *A Serious Proposal to the Ladies* was in press, honed her intellect and bolstered her confidence. Norris's mentorship contributed the Cartesian underpinnings of her spiritual and philosophical positions; through Norris she was able to refine and expand her thinking on the ideas of Descartes and Nicholas Malebranche. As Melvyn New and E. Derek Taylor suggest in their edition of *Letters Concerning the Love of God*, Norris's Christian Platonism and Cartesian rationalism "must have struck a chord in Astell's similarly tuned mind" (Taylor and New 2005, 11).[2]

Astell's next work, *Some Reflections upon Marriage, Occasion'd by the Duke and Dutchess of Mazarine's Case; Which Is Also Consider'd* (1700), had, as the title suggests, been prompted by renewed interest in the case of the Duchess of Mazarin, the niece of Cardinal Mazarin, who had achieved notoriety by fleeing a disastrous marriage in France. She eventually found refuge at the court of Charles II, but died in poor health and poverty in Astell's neighborhood of Chelsea in 1699.[3] Astell's rhetorically compelling representation of the miseries arising for both husbands and wives from a misguided choice of marriage partner has at times been inaccurately read as an indictment of the institution of marriage. For Astell, the case of the French duchess highlighted the injustice that would leave a woman yoked for life to a violent and mentally ill husband and the too-frequent pattern of young women entering the married state unprepared for what lay ahead. Much of *Reflections* is devoted to a discussion of the faulty motivations that propel men and women alike into wedlock, and the pitfalls against which women in particular needed to guard themselves.

Astell insists that while the "Order of the World" required that some govern and others be governed, all had equal access to "the supreme Good"; the mind's only obligation was to "Reason," and was out of reach of "the most absolute Tyrant" (RM, 56). Maintaining the distinction between the free mind and the "*Outward* Respect and Obedience" owed to others was perhaps more challenging for women who, unlike Astell, were bound within the religious and legal constraints of marriage. What about her women readers for whom it was too late; who were already married and no longer in a position to benefit from Astell's advisory cautions? And for those so unfortunate as to be married to an improvident or brutal partner, was the cultivation of virtue through patient endurance their only option, and how comforting did they find this hard advice? Astell had reiterated repeatedly in *Serious Proposal* that for both men and women the primary task of this life was to prepare for the next. Her primary concern was for women who for the most part had no opportunity to develop the capacities to think and reason required for the spiritual duties God required of them. The stunted and misdirected preparation of most young women for adulthood left them poorly equipped for either an adequate understanding of the obligations of marriage or, more importantly, the obligations of a Christian to prepare for eternity. In the preface to the 1706 edition of *Reflections*, Astell responds to criticism by assuring her readers that she stands willing to be corrected, but cautions that "the only way to remove all Doubts, to answer all Objections, and to give the Mind entire Satisfaction, is not by *Affirming*, but by *Proving*, so that every one may see with their *own* Eyes, and Judge according to the best of their *own* Understandings" (RM, 10). She insists on "this Natural Right of Judging for her self" (RM, 10). Hearsay and custom can no longer serve as authorities; rather "Rational Conviction" is required (RM, 10). Astell wrote explicitly for female readers, determined to improve their lot. But what of the woman who took in her admonitions, followed her directives, and reached other conclusions? What if adopting "this Natural Right of Judging for her self" led to choices other than those of Astell's (RM, 10)?[4]

Literary scholars have commented on the considerable influence that Astell's life and work had on writers through the eighteenth century, most especially on Samuel Richardson and his midcentury triumph, *Clarissa* (1747–48), but also on debates about "Protestant nunneries" that surface occasionally in fiction (including Richardson's) of the period.[5] But what of her readers, the men and women of England who read her arguments about religion, education, and marriage?[6] How can we know the influence that

96   Feminist Interpretations of Mary Astell

her writing had on the lives and minds of those whose ideas have for the most part not been preserved? One remarkable example is recorded in the work of Sarah Chapone, an obscure clergyman's wife living in rural Gloucestershire in the first half of the eighteenth century. From the various extant sources of information about her life (primarily her correspondence with her better-known friends Mary Delany, Charles and John Wesley, and Samuel Richardson), as well as a remarkable pamphlet she published anonymously in 1735 on the legal inequities facing married women, *The Hardships of the English Laws in Relation to Wives*, we can observe Chapone's reception and revision of Astell's arguments refracted through her own hermeneutical engagement with a range of textual authorities: legal, doctrinal, and fictional.

This chapter will examine the evidence that Chapone had read widely in, and absorbed the arguments of, the works of Mary Astell. It will also demonstrate the ways in which she acted upon Astell's advice in rejecting custom for reason in order to reflect further on marriage and the situation of women enduring intolerable situations due to their status as *femes covert*,[7] only to come to rather different conclusions. Astell had dealt eloquently in *Reflections* with the miseries arising from the curse of subjection; indeed, these are some of the most compelling passages in the work, and have prompted some readers to infer that she is thereby condemning marriage. Nevertheless, for Astell the right use of reason was not to find remedies for the pains of earthly life, but instead to see trials as means to train the mind to focus fully on God's love. In her polemic on marriage and the law, Chapone attempts to follow Astell's admonition to prove, rather than simply affirm, and persuasively spells out evidence for the injustices faced by wives under the common law. But documenting those problems carries her away from the soul to a focus on the body and the lived life, to urge not submission but legal redress. Astell's reframing of a gender equality prior to, and somehow still inhering in, a fallen world attempts to bridge the gap between an ungendered reason and scriptural prescription of woman's subjection.[8] Chapone also writes about women and marriage, and similarly attempts to strengthen her claims with scriptural evidence of a prelapsarian equality, but her obviating efforts are less effective, while the force of reason propels the argument for political, rather than spiritual, change. Astell's proposals for a monastery for women's education may have been thwarted, but Chapone's midcentury correspondence with the novelist Samuel Richardson suggests that Astell's "home schooling" program allowed individual women to fulfill at least some measure of her aspirations for the improvement of their minds.

Prior to the seventeenth century, no legal books addressed exclusively the common law concerns of particular relevance to women; those aspects of marriage, property, and inheritance likely to affect most women at some point in their lives were dealt with in works on property law, the most significant of which was Thomas Littleton's *Tenures* (1481–82?), known following Sir Edward Coke's heavily glossed edition as *Coke upon Littleton* (1628).[9] The first work on women's issues was *The Laws Resolutions of Womens Rights* (1632).[10] The book is written in English, but printed in black letter, and includes extensive use of Latin and law French. Lynne A. Greenberg (2005, xxxiv) has found no evidence of women quoting from or alluding to this work in seventeenth-century writing, and the nature of the text would make it virtually inaccessible even to those women who could read. The next significant work on the law as it affected women appeared at the end of the century, *Baron and Feme: A Treatise of the Common Law Concerning Husbands and Wives* (1700). It draws heavily on Coke's edition of Littleton, and is a highly technical treatise written for the practicing lawyer or attorney. Several decades later, *A Treatise of Feme Coverts; or, The Lady's Law* was published in 1732. Like *Baron and Feme*, it relies heavily on *Coke upon Littleton* for its structure and discussion. Its account of the law purports to be written for the female reader: "The fair Sex are here inform'd, how to preserve their Lands, Goods, and most valuable Effects, from the Incroachments of any one" (1732, vii) but again, an understanding of the law is required if the reader is to benefit from its guidance.[11]

In the same year that *Baron and Feme* was published, Astell's *Reflections* appeared. In her study of Astell's rhetoric, Christine Sutherland traces the development of the rhetoric of sermo, an informal discourse of conversation, to the more traditional and public contentio "typical of the law courts and the legislative assemblies" and the subject of most histories and studies of rhetoric (2005, xviii). She argues that Astell makes the shift from sermo to contentio with her publication of *Reflections* (80). Astell did not believe in women engaging in the practice of public speaking; three years earlier in *Serious Proposal II* she had argued, in her advice on speaking and writing clearly and well, that there was no material difference between writing and speaking, and rejects any need to dwell on "*Pronunciation*" as it is unnecessary "since Women have no business with the Pulpit, the Bar or St. *Stephens Chapel*" (*SP II*, 196), the public spaces of male voices in church, law, and government. She sets out a series of rules to guide her female readers in the development of their powers of reasoning. As part of her guide she includes in chapter 3, "*Concerning the Improvement of the Understanding*," a set of rules based, as Patricia Springborg notes (*SP II*, 176n1), on Antoine Arnauld

98   Feminist Interpretations of Mary Astell

and Pierre Nicole's *Logic, or the Art of Thinking* (an English translation had been published in London in 1693), who, in turn, had borrowed them from Descartes's *Discourse on the Method*.[12] Ruth Perry credits John Norris with providing Astell "the philosophical arsenal" to articulate and defend her views, and his influence for the difference between the first and second parts of *Serious Proposal* (Perry 1986, 82). The final rule, following admonishments to have a thorough and "*Distinct Notion of our Subject . . . and of the Terms we make use of*" (SP II, 176), to begin with the simple and ascend by degrees to the more complex, and to leave no part of the subject "*unexamin'd*" (SP II, 177), is Rule VI, drawn from the first rule of Descartes's *Method*; "*To judge no further than we Perceive, and not to take any thing for Truth, which we do not evidently Know to be so*" (SP II, 178). Astell's observations on marriage addressed not the issues of property, inheritance, and descent that so preoccupied families and suitors, but what she believed was the more serious and pressing concern: the barriers that bad marriages and poor education posed to the spiritual fulfillment of women's lives. Her *Reflections* was not a guide to property law, but rather a warning about the folly of using these concerns to determine the choice of a spouse. It was republished (along with *Letters* and *Christian Religion*) in 1730, and it is tempting to speculate on the possibility that this edition might have prompted Chapone to undertake her own, rather different, reflections.

Sarah Chapone was born in 1699, daughter to the Reverend Lionel and Damaris Kirkham in the Gloucestershire village of Stanton, in the Cotswolds. Although a close friendship developed with John Wesley, a friend of her brother Robert who frequently visited the rectory while they were both students at Oxford, in 1725 Sarah married the Reverend John Chapone and spent the remainder of her life in the area. Chapone's lifelong friendship with Mary Delany also dates from her early years, when Delany (then Mary Granville) moved with her family to the nearby village of Buckland.[13] Recalling these years much later in a memoir, Delany remembers Sarah Kirkham as having "an uncommon genius and intrepid spirit" that initially alarmed her father, who "could not bear anything that had the appearance of being too free and masculine" (Delany 1861, 15). They wrote to one another every day and met often in the field between their houses. "Her extraordinary understanding, lively imagination and humane disposition, which soon became conspicuous, at last reconciled my father to her" (16).

Ten years after her marriage, Sarah Chapone published anonymously her polemic on married women and the law, *The Hardships of the English Laws in Relation to Wives. With an Explanation of the Original Curse of Subjection Passed upon the Woman. In an Humble Address to the Legislature*

Further Reflections upon Marriage   99

(1735).[14] There appears to be no personal unhappiness motivating her work; despite the frustrations of financial difficulties and an unsettled living expressed in her letters, she expresses appreciation for a husband who, despite the *feme covert*'s status as dead in law, "lets me be *alive*, and gives me leave to be *some Body*" (51). Her authorship, while kept secret, appears to have been known among her close friends. In a letter written to her sister July 22, 1734, Mary Delany discusses the pleasure of Sarah's company and then adds, "The ingenious MS. was sent in my mama's box; it is an excellent piece of wit and good sense, and when *she* (the author) has rectified the *law part* of it, it will be fit for the press and the perusal of the *smartest wits of the age*" (1861, 487). Evidently the "law part" was amended; V. H. H. Green, one of John Wesley's biographers, notes that Wesley was correcting Chapone's "essay on laws" in 1734, and the work was published the following spring (1961, 294n1). As its title suggests, it was not a treatise providing a methodical exposition of the law, but rather a polemical attack on the legal disabilities of married women. In a pattern of "Cases and Observations," Chapone argues from the specific to the general, by providing first an exposition of a particular legal case or situation, and then a narrative of the consequences of the law or ruling for that woman's life. Chapone's analysis is presented from the point of view of a married woman, a perspective to this point completely absent in English legal discourse.

The Hardships of the English Laws in Relation to Wives begins with the claim that wives, like the males of the kingdom, enjoy "the Privilege of the Free-Born Subjects of *England* to approach their Sovereign, represent their Grievances, and humbly to implore Redress" (1), and she lays out her grievances under three headings. The first, echoing Astell, is that the estate of wives is worse than slavery itself; the second, that wives may be imprisoned by their husbands with impunity; and the third, that wives have no property in their persons, their children, or their fortunes. Her strategy is to prove her claims by offering factual evidence, in a series of cases, and then her observations on these cases.

To demonstrate her first proposition, "That the Estate of Wives is more disadvantagious than *Slavery* itself" (4), she recounts the case of a (deceased) widow whose will from her first marriage was deemed to be invalid. The lawyer defending the validity of the first will used the analogy in court of a Roman who had been held captive in slavery and was later freed, and his will revived. But the court ruled that the analogy would not hold as marriage was a voluntary act, while captivity was the effect of compulsion. The trope of marriage and slavery had been a recurring image in women's poetry since the late seventeenth century. Lady Mary Chudleigh's poem "To the

100   Feminist Interpretations of Mary Astell

Ladies" warns that once "that fatal Knot" is tied, "all that's kind is laid aside" and the wife must "still be govern'd by a Nod, / And fear her Husband as her God" (Chudleigh 1993). Margaret Ezell notes that this work "seems to have appealed strongly to her eighteenth-century female readers" (Ezell 1993, xvii). While Astell's incendiary riposte to Locke, "If *all* Men *are born free*, how is that all Women are born Slaves?" (RM, 18), was intended to rebut Locke's claim that, contra Filmer, all men were born free, one can imagine her female readers missing the allusion. Chapone may have been among them, as she grounds her claims for injustice in the comment that the legal inequities she has outlined can hardly be reconciled with "the Rights and Privileges of a free People" (47).

As evidence that wives may be imprisoned with impunity by their husbands, she recounts a case concerning a woman who left an abusive marriage to seek refuge with her clergyman brother, but who was forced to return home by the outraged husband, where she subsequently died. Another case recounts the story of an heiress married to a rogue who promptly confined her to a country house and spent her money in London. Still another is of a woman kept locked in a garret without heat or adequate food and clothing, and who eventually committed suicide by jumping from a window. Her husband was acquitted, as testimony showed that there had been some hard moldy bread in the room "supposed sufficient to sustain Life" (9) and that he had not actually pushed her out the window himself. Astell had argued that, because a woman "puts her self intirely in his Power" when she marries, "what a Brute must he be who betrays that Trust, or acts any way unworthy of it" (RM, 55). Chapone echoes, "She [a wife] puts her whole Happiness into his Hands, a Trust for which no Man can give a sufficient Security. She has from hence a Title to his Protection in every Distress: If so, how is a Husband's Guilt aggravated, when he beats, confines, or murders his Wife" (13). Astell adumbrated at length the potential for unhappiness, as her unswerving belief in obedience to divinely appointed authority left only an informed choice as a hedge against misery. Chapone is equally cognizant of the risks, but seems either unable or unwilling to school her mind to the consolation of the soul, and suggests that it is the law, rather than the mind, that must adjust.

For her third proposition, that married women have no property in their bodies, their children, or their fortunes, Chapone cites the example of a man who left a considerable fortune to his daughter with the stipulation that she was never knowingly to converse with or visit her mother, else the inheritance would be forfeited to a relation whose dislike of the mother would ensure that a vigilant watch would be kept. She explores the ineq-

Further Reflections upon Marriage   101

uity of redress for adultery, where the husband may sue for damages, an option not available to wives. She also discusses at some length the anguish resulting from women's exclusion from guardianship, where widows can be denied any role in the upbringing and education of their own children. To the charge that women are not qualified to undertake these responsibilities, she offers the refrain familiar to Astell's readers that "[i]f we are accidentally disqualified by a foolish trifling Education, where does that Imputation revert, but upon those Persons under whose Direction and Authority we are so educated?" (21). Astell of course had included among the benefits of her proposed educational institution the employment of the women to provide "the best Education to the Children of Persons of Quality" (*SP I*, 103). Her response to the situation of women was to devise a means whereby they could develop the powers of reason and a life of the mind apart from worldly duties and obligations. Chapone's response to the consequences of their inadequate preparation was to "use this as an Argument why they should find some Redress for their great Calamities" (45).

The work continues with more cases, more examples, and for each Chapone offers her analysis and commentary, offering the evidence of what she has observed. For two of her cases, she conscientiously explains that she has had to rely on "the public Prints" for the details, and "therefore don't take upon my self to say that this Case is truly stated, 'tis possible some material Circumstance may be omitted" (11). Knowing her audience, Chapone anticipates that many of her readers may remain unswayed by her appeals, and so she proceeds with refutation, enumerating possible objections and addressing these concerns. For example, to the objection that an abused wife may turn to the law for relief, Chapone observes that a husband may confine his wife to prevent such an action. A wife may hesitate to swear the peace against her husband and send him to jail if he provides the maintenance for the family, and the consequence is that "she, and her Family must starve."[15] She also notes pointedly that such an action would, as she puts it, expose her to "the Resentment of her Husband at his Return Home" (32).

Recent historical work into the very difficult questions of just how, and to what degree, women were restricted by the doctrines of coverture has investigated various legal mechanisms such as marriage settlements, jointures, pin money, and separate property that allowed women some relief from the rigors of the common law.[16] Astell had earlier observed that "there have been but too many instances of Husbands that by wheedling or threatning their Wives, by seeming Kindness or cruel Usage, have perswaded or forc'd them out of what has been settled on them. . . . A Man

102   Feminist Interpretations of Mary Astell

enters into Articles very readily before Marriage, and so he may, for he performs no more of them afterwards than he thinks fit" (RM, 51). To those who would argue that women in this period were increasingly well protected, Chapone offers a cautionary observation:

> But if we reflect how extreamly ignorant all young Women are as to points in Law, and how their Education and Way of Life, shuts them out from the Knowledge of their true Interest in almost all things, we shall find that their Trust and Confidence in the Man they love, and Inability to make use of the proper Means to guard against his Falsehood, leave few in a Condition to make use of that Precaution. And it is too notoriously known, that it has seldom been of Service to those who have done it, the Husband having so entirely the Disposal of the Wife's Person, that he easily finds Means to bend her to his Will, insomuch that I have heard, that it is a frequent saying of one of our present eminent Judges, "that he had hardly known an Instance, where the Wife had not been kissed or kicked out of any such previous Settlement." (33)

Chapone continues in this vein, responding to a broad range of imagined objections to her petition for changes to the law with refutation grounded in reason, logic, and examples drawn not from case law, which—one presumes—she did not know, but from the experienced realities of women's lives, which she did.

Her powerfully persuasive prose and compelling argument built on the morality of equity, justice, and reason carry her along to the final objection she must address: her ontological status as a woman, and her presumption in speaking out in apparent violation of the laws of God that the husband is to rule over the wife. Here she adopts Astell's strategy, and attempts to plead that women's increased opportunities to demonstrate self-denial, patience, and submission will result in exemplary lives on earth and rewards in heaven; "that Condition which has the most frequent Opportunities of practicing Self-denial in its ordinary Occurrences, will be ultimately the most advantagious" (62). Yet this argument lacks the passionate conviction driving the force of the work to that point, and she candidly acknowledges how difficult it is to force one's will to submit to the dictates of reason.[17] Astell's Serious Proposal II had addressed "the Regulation of the Will and the Government of the Passions" at considerable length, acknowledging the powerful sway of the "Commotions in the Bloud and Animal Spirits accompanying these Inclinations," and prescribing a rather ascetic

Further Reflections upon Marriage   103

regime of practices whereby the mind and soul may gain mastery (*SP II*, 206).[18] Chapone acknowledges that the sex which first gave evidence of a disobedient will should have an additional restraint laid upon it, and that women thereby remain under an obligation to obey their husbands "*till the Fashion of this World passeth away*" (66). God punishes his servants in mercy, she acknowledges, but then bursts out, "yet he never condemned them to be *put under Axes, and Harrows of Iron, nor to pass through the Brick-kiln!*" (66).[19] Repeatedly we see Chapone struggling to contain her deep sense of outrage and injustice within the framework of revealed truth, and there is little evidence of Astell's clear separation of the "the creature" and the soul.

Reading Chapone's correspondence, and particularly her pamphlet on the law, makes Astell's influence abundantly clear; nevertheless, in one significant area Chapone does not follow her preceptor. Treading where Astell had declined to go, Chapone, by arguing for legislative changes to the legal status of women in marriage, is forced to confront the problem posed by the Fall in a way that Astell was not. Astell, possibly alluding to William Whiston's *A New Theory of the Earth, from Its Original, to the Consummation of All Things* (1696), claims a "greater" equality for men and women before the Fall, again reiterating her conviction that woman's primary obligation is to God, and that "a Rational Mind is too noble a Being to be Made for the Sake and Service of any Creature" (*RM*, 11).[20] She suggests that the various New Testament statements on the submission of women were of a piece with St. Paul's injunction that men were not to wear their hair long; both matters of custom only. Astell finds in Paul's statement that "*the Man is not without the Woman, nor the Woman without the Man, but all things of God*" evidence that the relations between the sexes are "mutual, and the Dependance Reciprocal" and thus "no great Argument of the natural Inferiority of either Sex" (*RM*, 13). Perhaps sensing the weakness of her argument here, Astell goes on to suggest that in any case it is unsporting of men to cite scripture as their authority when "[w]omen without their own Fault, are kept in Ignorance of the Original, wanting Languages and other helps to Criticise on the Sacred Text, of which they know no more, than Men are pleas'd to impart in their Translations" (*RM*, 14). She is willing to concede that someone must be granted authority to keep order, but superior power doesn't equal superior abilities and worth, and this leads into her famous homology of tyranny in the state and the family. She marshals an impressive array of scriptural evidence for women's capacities, but in the end her focus is on the hereafter, a goal unimpeded by any sublunary and temporal state of passive obedience to authority here on earth.

104   Feminist Interpretations of Mary Astell

By petitioning Parliament for changes in the law, Chapone as a *feme covert* faces a more formidable barrier, and the biblical support she is able to adduce is more ambiguous and tenuous. Like Astell, Chapone offers theological arguments to mitigate the disability of the curse and propose an original equality. She cites several authorities, including, somewhat reluctantly, Thomas Hobbes, and especially the Reverend Patrick Delany, whose *Revelation Examined with Candour* (1732) had argued that Eve, in the prelapsarian world, had been created as Adam's "associate and companion:—without the least hint of subjection, or dependency" (P. Delany 1732, 76).[21] Again, echoing Astell, she suggests that both men *and* women had been put under obligations, but in a more Lockean mode wonders why, when men did not bear their part of the curse; "*In the sweat of thy Brows shalt thou eat Bread*"—in other words, did not support their families—"with what Equity can they require us, to bear ours?" (66). Chapone opens her polemic with a claim that the rise of Deism was undermining the "noble Principles of Christianity" (2) that should protect wives, and precipitating a "*State of Nature*, in which there can be no Appeal but to the Laws of our Country" (3). The authority of scripture, which to this point had directed a man to "erect a private *Court* of *Equity* in his own Breast" (3), is in decline, leaving women to the unmitigated harshness of the common law. Although both John Toland and Anthony Collins were dead by 1730, the publication of Matthew Tindal's *Christianity as Old as the Creation* that year renewed public attention to the apparent threats of deism. Tindal died in 1733, but a dispute over his will carried on in the pages of the *Grub Street Journal* kept his name, and notoriety, in the public eye.[22]

Nevertheless, it is not to the principles of Christianity, but to the laws of Great Britain to which Chapone looks for redress. Chapone had clearly absorbed Astell's method of logic and her polemical style. Indeed, reading *The Hardships of the English Laws*, it is impossible to miss the acerbic tone and acid commentary of passages in Astell's *Serious Proposal* and *Reflections*. Yet Astell wrote about marriage as an observer—her remarks are incisive, trenchant, acutely observed, brilliantly analytical, and even, from the vantage point of several hundred years, painfully familiar—but as an observer nonetheless. She was able to enjoy to the full her status as a *feme sole* and, with the financial support of several women friends, a degree of independence, which gave her the freedom to comment on social, religious, and political affairs.[23] Astell had painted with brutal frankness the woes of marriage awaiting women, but nowhere does she intimate that the laws governing marriage should be changed, or advocate what we would now think of as rights for women. Astell accepted the biblical injunction

Further Reflections upon Marriage   105

regarding the submission of wives to "the yoke," and in the preface to *Reflections* she reaffirms the authority of husbands, reiterating that "she did not in any manner prompt them [wives] to Resist," not even where "the Laws of God and the Land make special Provision for it" (RM, 9). Despite the caustic and vivid portrayals of the varieties of meanness, pride, abuse, contempt, and scorn all too commonly practiced by husbands, Astell at no point suggests that the laws or demands of marriage be altered: it is "the Institution of Heaven, the only Honourable way of continuing Mankind" (RM, 36). Her deceptively bold claim in the preface is merely to "retrieve, if possible, the Native Liberty, the Rights and Privileges of the Subject" (RM, 8); the "native" liberty here to be "retrieved" is the freedom of the mind, out of reach of any tyrant.[24] The classification of women as "subjects" was a common locution during the English Civil Wars, when women petitioners emerged in the public sphere, but a noticeable, almost startling, claim early in the eighteenth century.[25] Chapone, who frames her work on the inequities of the status of married women as a petition from "his Majesty's faithful *Female* Subjects" for legislative redress, appears to have a more corporeal liberty in her sights, and has begun the shift to a civil definition of "female subject" (2).

One of the most significant sources of information about the life of Mary Astell is the account prepared by the antiquarian George Ballard for his compilation of lives of learned women. Ballard was a tailor with an amateur love for the study of antiquities. Hearing that he was teaching himself Anglo-Saxon, Chapone (his neighbor) arranged an introduction in 1735 to the Anglo-Saxon scholar Elizabeth Elstob, at that time living obscurely and in poverty as a rural schoolteacher. The death of her brother in 1715 had brought an abrupt end to Elstob's scholarly life in Oxford and London. The efforts of Chapone, Delany, and others resulted in financial support from the queen along with a position of governess to the Duchess of Bulstrode's family, thus rescuing Elstob from penury. One of Elstob's unrealized plans was a book memorializing the learned women of England. Ballard took up the project, and it was finally published in 1752 as *Memoirs of Several Ladies of Great Britain: Who Have Been Celebrated for Their Writings or Skill in the Learned Languages, Arts, and Sciences.* As Norma Clarke (2005, 219) notes, his account of Astell draws on accounts of people such as Elstob who knew her, and remains the most important single source of information about her.[26] We know that the works of Mary Astell were read with enthusiasm and admiration by Chapone and her circle through letters Chapone exchanged with Elstob and Ballard, as he worked through the 1740s on the *Memoirs*.[27] The letters in the Ballard Collection of Manu-

106   Feminist Interpretations of Mary Astell

scripts frequently allude to copies of Astell's works being borrowed and returned among the correspondents. For example, we learn that Chapone owned a copy of Astell's *Serious Proposal*; Anna Hopkins writes to George Ballard on December 14, 1741 (Ballard MSS, vol. 43, #106), that she is unable to send him the book because she had returned it to Chapone. On March 12, 1741/2 (Ballard MSS, vol. 43, #132), in a letter to Ballard, Chapone apologizes that she cannot send "the letters to Mr Norris," "the most sublime part of her Works," as her husband has them and they are packed up for a move. A year later, on April 23, 1743 (Ballard MSS, vol. 43, #134), she writes to Ballard to thank him for the loan of "Mrs Astel's Book" (there is no indication which one). Thomas Rawlins writes to Ballard on June 11, 1742 (Ballard MSS, vol. 41, #215), asking if Mrs. Chapone will lend him her "Miss Astell's Proposal to the Ladies" and also "Essay in Defence of the Female Sex" (at the time believed to have been written by Astell, but since attributed to Judith Drake) and indicating that Chapone can borrow his copy of her "Christian Religion."[28] On December 25, 1743 (Ballard MSS, vol. 41, #227), he writes to Ballard that he will return Chapone's copy of *Serious Proposal*.

Chapone had offered Ballard the assistance of the London printer and (more famously) novelist Samuel Richardson, a connection made through Mary Delany and her sister.[29] He and Chapone began a correspondence in 1750, and by the winter of 1752 they were engaged in an intense debate over the civil status of women, real and fictional, arising from their discussion of *Clarissa*; many of the issues from Astell's *Reflections* are back on the table. Richardson had cultivated a wide network of correspondents whose response to his novels he conducted and directed, but the letters exchanged with Chapone are remarkable for the sustained attention to Clarissa's legal position.[30] Having read the epistolary exchange on filial duty between Richardson and Hester Mulso, a young woman who had become part of Richardson's circle (and who would later become her, Chapone's, daughter-in-law; the letters were published in 1807 in *The Posthumous Works of Mrs. Chapone*), Chapone concurs with Mulso's claim that to enter a marriage against one's will is to commit perjury. Richardson, seemingly puzzled by her continuing refusal to accept his views, reproves her for not reading his replies with sufficient care. He is clearly disturbed by her opposition: his letter of March 2, 1752 (*Papers of Samuel Richardson*, F.48.E.6.144), is sixteen sheets long.

Chapone replies with twenty-four sheets in response. She remains unconvinced by his arguments, continuing to insist that a promise to do something contrary to one's will is a deliberate falsehood, and perjury. She insists,

Further Reflections upon Marriage 107

echoing Astell, that submission to authority is an act "of private Judgment, which chuses the Authority to which it submits, and weighs and determines upon the Evidence produced to enforce such Submission." Her ensuing discussion treats of both men and women, and the necessity of will and volition in order to enter into an agreement or contract. She then turns her attention specifically to women, and Richardson's denial of independence to women; when Chapone claimed that women were free to marry without parental consent at the age of twenty-one, he replied that women should not be independent at any age. She responds with the proposition that a woman may consider marriage as a religious institution, not a civil ordinance, and must judge for herself where her duties lie. "To deprive a Woman of her natural Liberty, under Pretence of keeping her out of Harms way, is just such a favour as it would be, to deprive a Man of all Pleasure, and then, in return, graciously decree he should feel no Pain." She acknowledges Richardson's claim that suffering is the test of virtue, but adds that she hopes she is not intended to infer that he therefore advises a woman to marry a man because she believes he would make her suffer. She assures him that she did indeed read his replies to Miss Mulso, but they failed to satisfy all her objections. She boldly confesses that "I was not convinced you were right" and took the liberty of remonstrating (*Papers of Samuel Richardson*, F.48.E.6.145). Richardson is clearly taken aback, and in his twenty-four-page reply on April 18 he carefully goes through the list of her points, responding to each in turn, again accusing her of not attending to his replies to Miss Mulso (*Papers of Samuel Richardson*, F.48.E.6.147).

Chapone's letters provide a glimpse into a mind that has been able to implement fully and skillfully Astell's call to reason. If Chapone is unable to overcome the theological challenge of the doctrine of the Fall (she is, after all, wife, daughter, granddaughter, and sister to Anglican clergy), she nevertheless, in the face of opposition from one of the leading novelists of the day, is able to surmount what Astell had called the "very great Fault to regard rather who it is that Speaks, than what is Spoken" and "submit to Authority, when we should only yield to Reason" (*RM*, 7).

At the close of *Reflections*, Astell admonishes her "Female Reader" that "if Heaven has appointed the Man to Govern, it has qualify'd him for it." Should a reader then go on to ask, if he has not those qualifications, "where is his Right?" Astell refuses to sanction any contractarian rationale for change, or to open the door to any consideration of justice, or "Right"; on the contrary, "I must leave her there" (*RM*, 79). The bare possibility of doubt introduced by the conditional "if" is not taken up, and the "I must" is firm. Nonetheless, Astell had veered dangerously close to advocating

108   Feminist Interpretations of Mary Astell

resistance (she acknowledges in the previous paragraph, possibly in a glance at William III, that usurpers will be ousted when "Power and Opportunity" permit, and that tyranny will provoke "the Oppress'd to throw off even a Lawful Yoke that sits too heavy" (RM, 78).[31] Her acutely drawn demonstrations of the dramatically inequitable conditions that prevailed for many women may have brought readers to that crossroad, however much Astell might urge them not to proceed. Norma Clarke notes that by the time George Ballard's *Memoirs* appeared in the midcentury, Astell was "all but forgotten" (2005, 219). Ballard writes that *Reflections* were thought by some to carry her arguments "with regard to the *birthrights* and *privileges* of her sex a little too far; and that there is too much warmth of temper discovered in this treatise" (1752, 449), although he generously, and somewhat ironically, adds that the "second" edition with its preface is "perhaps the strongest defence that every yet appeared in print, of the *rights* and *abilities* of the fair sex" (450).[32] Half a century later, that defense, refracted through the thought and writing of one her readers, resurfaced in the epistolary exchange of views between Chapone, the relatively unknown woman who had published her own reflections upon marriage two decades earlier, and the renowned novelist who had appropriated elements of Astell's life to create the most influential female character of eighteenth-century fiction. That aspects of his construction were so vigorously resisted reminds us that even Astell's formidable control could not extend to her readers, who learned from her to judge for themselves.

Abbreviations

RM   Mary Astell, *Reflections upon Marriage* (1996)
SP I   Mary Astell, *A Serious Proposal to the Ladies, Part I* (2002)
SP II   Mary Astell, *A Serious Proposal to the Ladies, Part II* (2002)

Notes

1. For a review of the discussion and an analysis of the apparent contradictions between Astell's uncompromising championing of obedience to authority and her acute concern for the inequitable position of, which continue to vex scholars, see Hilda L. Smith (2007). For extended discussions of arguments by eighteenth-century women using custom and reason, see Judy Cornett (1997).

2. Ruth Perry (1986, 71–72, 482n36) has also noted the likely influence of François Poulain de la Barre's Cartesian skepticism; his work on the equality of the sexes, *De l'égalité des deux sexes* (1673), was translated and published as *The Woman as Good as the Man: or, The Equality of Both Sexes* (1677), although she suggests that the editions of the 1690s may have been more influential.

3. Hortense Mancini was raised in the court of Louis XIV and was married by her uncle Cardinal Mazarin, to the Duke of Meilleraye and Mayenne on condition that he take the cardinal's name.

Further Reflections upon Marriage   109

The duke's cruelty drove his desperate wife to flee, and her subsequent life in England under the patronage of Charles II prompted Astell's pity and condemnation. For additional discussion of this background to Astell's *Reflections upon Marriage*, see Perry (1986, 150–60).

4. For a discussion of the theological dimensions of "Judging for her self," see Jacqueline Broad and Karen Green (2009, 282–84).

5. Leslie Richardson (2005), for example, argues that Clarissa is *not* able to retain Astell's freedom of mind, and that the madness and loss of memory that follows her rape are an alienation resulting in loss of self that can be recovered by the exercise of the only control over the body that remains: its death. E. Derek Taylor (2009) explores in detail the numerous textual links with Norris's work and the aspects of Astell's life and thought inscribed in *Clarissa*. For a thorough exploration of Astell as a model for Samuel Richardson, see Jocelyn Harris (2012).

6. Astell was not the first woman to write about women and marriage, but she was among the first to publish her views. For a discussion of "The Womans Right," an essay by Mary More written for her young daughter addressing many of the concerns raised later by both Astell and Sarah Chapone, and a reproduction of the essay, see Margaret J. M. Ezell (1987, 144–60, appendix II). More's essay is also reproduced in Trill, Chedgzoy, and Melanie Osborne (1997, 246–54).

7. *Feme covert* is a legal term for a married woman, *feme sole* for a single woman.

8. For a discussion of Astell's work as the textual creation of a "biblical subjectivity" for women in response to Milton's powerful inscription of Eve's fall in *Paradise Lost*, see Shannon Miller (2008), especially chap. 7, 205–30.

9. First published in 1628 as part of Coke's *Institutes of the Laws of England*, it remained a standard reference on English property law until the twentieth century.

10. Its anonymous author explains that he has written this work as women have "nothing to do in constituting Lawes, or consenting to them, in interpreting of Lawes, or in hearing them interpreted at lectures, leets, or charges, and yet they stand strictly tyed to men's establishments, little or nothing excused by ignorance" and adds "mee thinkes it were pitty and impiety any longer to hold from them such Customes, Lawes, and Statutes, as are in a maner, proper, or principally belonging unto them." *The Lawes Resolutions* (1632, 2).

11. The work was republished under the title *The Lady's Law: Or, A Treatise of Feme Coverts* (1737).

12. For a modern edition, see Antoine Arnauld and Pierre Nicole (1996).

13. Mary's father, Bernard Granville, was a younger brother to George Granville, who became Lord Lansdowne under Queen Anne; Lansdowne's alliance with Anne, and his Jacobite leanings, led to his imprisonment after 1714. Bernard prudently retired with his family to rural Gloucestershire, where his daughter became friends with Sarah Kirkham.

14. A critical edition of this work is in preparation by this author. The attribution to Chapone was first made by Ruth Perry and Janice Thaddeus, and is supported by a letter written by Anna Hopkins on December 14, 1741 (Ballard MSS) stating that Chapone's authorship was well known to her, but that it was to be kept a secret.

15. William Blackstone explains that anyone who feared a physical threat from another person could go to the justice of the peace and demand "surety of the peace against such person: and every justice of the peace is bound to grant it, if he who demands it will make oath, that he is actually under fear of death or bodily harm. . . . This is called *swearing the peace* against another" (Blackstone 1979, 252).

16. For discussion, see Lloyd Bonfield (1983), Amy Louise Erickson (1993), Eileen Spring (1993), Susan Staves (1990), and Lawrence Stone and Jeanne C. Fawtier Stone (1984). For an argument that married women in the eighteenth century had much more freedom of ownership and legal independence than that suggested in Astell's and Chapone's work, see Joanne Bailey (2002) and Amy Louise Erickson (2007).

17. This is possibly an allusion to *Serious Proposal II*, chap. 4, "Concerning the Regulation of the Will and the Government of the Passions." For a discussion of *Serious Proposal II* and Astell's theory of mind framed as an exploration of the will and understanding, see Alice Sowaal (2007).

110   Feminist Interpretations of Mary Astell

18. In the previous chapter, Astell was careful to clarify that her advice was not designed for the woman who was occupied with family cares, who was not to "neglect her Necessary Affairs to amuse her self with nice Speculations" or lock herself in her study "when her Domesticks had need of her direction." It was only those women who had "a good deal of time to spare" who were to replace frivolity with philosophy (*SP II*, 204).

19. The biblical reference is to 2 Samuel 12:31.

20. Patricia Springborg (*RM*, 11n6) quotes the relevant passages from Whiston.

21. Mary (Granville) Pendarves wrote to her sister Ann from Dublin on January 24, 1732/33, that Sarah was "in great Raptures with Dr. Delany's book on Revelation." She later married the Reverend Patrick Delany, whom she had met through Jonathan Swift in 1743, and they spent the remainder of their life together in Ireland, Delany returning to England following his death in 1768 (Delany 1861, 395). For a discussion of Astell's political philosophy read in congruence with Thomas Hobbes, rather than the more customary focus of John Locke, see Penny A. Weiss (2009), chap. 7.

22. Jeffrey R. Wigelsworth suggests that as war came to dominate public concerns for the latter half of the century, deism faded from public attention. Not only were individual deist texts drowned in a flood of orthodox responses, the threat from deism was eclipsed by a new challenge from Methodism (Wigelsworth 2009, 194–97).

23. The most complete study of Astell's life and work is Ruth Perry (1986); an important earlier source is Florence M. Smith (1966).

24. Jacqueline Broad and Karen Green read this passage as a statement of a wife's freedom to pursue the good of her soul by exercising her right to judge for herself about religious matters (2009, 282).

25. Hilda L. Smith argues that the early political participation of the petitioning women of the sectarian movements of the mid-seventeenth century was devoted to promoting the interests of their leaders, or petitioning on behalf of male family members, rather than asserting the political legitimacy of the female subject. Astell, on the other hand, offers "fundamental critiques of women's standing in seventeenth-century England" (Smith 2007, 204). See also Hilda L. Smith (1998).

26. For a modern edition with a comprehensive introduction, see Ruth Perry's edition of George Ballard (1985).

27. Patricia Springborg (2002, 23) reminds us that Astell had more readers than the circulation of her books might suggest: portions of *Serious Proposal II* were included, unacknowledged, in *The Ladies Library*, which went through numerous impressions in the eighteenth century.

28. For evidence of attribution to Drake, see Florence M. Smith (1966, 173–82).

29. Mary Delany's sister Ann Granville Dewes had provided an introduction to Richardson for Sarah Chapone's son John.

30. There is considerable discussion of the legal elements raised in *Clarissa*; see, in particular, Macpherson (2010), Schwarz (1999), Beth Swan (1997), and John P. Zomchick (1993). An edition of the complete correspondence of Samuel Richardson is currently in preparation under the direction of Thomas Keymer and Peter Sabor for Cambridge University Press.

31. Sarah Apetrei (2008, 508) explores the tension between Astell's allegiance to passive obedience and the "antiauthoritarian" undercurrent in her writing evident in a three-way exchange of letters between Astell, the nonjuror George Hickes, and an anonymous female correspondent. In one of her letters, Astell explicitly alludes to William's reign as a "most unjust & notorious usurpation by one who had no manner of right nor ind[d] any presence allow'd by o[r] Laws" (quoted in Apetrei 2008, 514). See also Malinda Zook (2007), who explores the complexity and inconsistencies of Astell's condemnation of nonconforming women who entered into the public sphere to advocate political change.

32. George Ballard incorrectly cites the "second" edition of "1705" as including the preface; the preface first appeared in the third edition of 1706.

7

Mary Astell

Some Reflections upon Trauma

Elisabeth Hedrick Moser

Mary Astell, in *Some Reflections upon Marriage*, outlines the state of a woman's life within marriage in late seventeenth-century England. She analyzes the effects of the manipulation of power in an authoritarian marriage, creating a picture of a husband who too often becomes tyrannical, enjoying full power over his wife's body, possessions, and freedoms; and a wife whose peace, contentment, and wholeness are drained. Astell's reflections reveal that this unjust power structure results in the fragmentation and dissociation of the woman's psyche and body—symptoms that bear striking resemblance to the prolonged consequences of post-traumatic stress disorder. In this chapter, I examine how Astell's prescient exposure of the psychological effects of abusive domestic power structures in seventeenth-century England approaches a description of psychic trauma.

112   Feminist Interpretations of Mary Astell

My analysis does not endeavor to demonstrate that Astell's reflections work as case studies of victims of post-traumatic stress disorder.[1] Instead, my analysis pays attention to the shadowy reflection of traumatic experience troubling the waters of Astell's *Reflections*. Using trauma theory as a lens through which to read Astell makes visible the more insidious layers of the consequences of abusive power. While Astell writes within a specific historical context, her perceptions of the psychological effects of the abuse of power still resonate today. Astell's understanding of the fragmented psychic state of women living within an oppressive power structure becomes a further indictment of societies whose structures endorse and enable the perpetuation of an experience that approximates the traumatic.

Astell composed *Reflections* as a response to the scandal produced when the Duchess of Mazarin, Hortense Mancini, left her husband and then fled court orders to return and submit to him. The Duke of Mazarin was reportedly a "religious fanatic" who "considered sawing off the teeth of his young daughters to make them unattractive . . . to protect them from future sexuality" (Perry 1986, 155). He sought to keep the duchess from socializing with anyone but himself, barred her from enjoying places or people too much, and forced her to travel even when it imperiled her pregnancy. In addition to his iron hold on her life, the duke also, according to the duchess's account, drained her finances. In spite of these offenses, when she demanded "separation and division of property," the court "decreed she should return to her husband and . . . submit to his authority both in and out of the bedroom" (155). When the duchess died in 1699, the trials of her marriage were brought again to public attention and to the attention of Mary Astell. In *Reflections*, composed in 1700, Astell considers how the unequal power distribution in marriage, which produced the case of the duchess, affects the intellectual, emotional, and spiritual life of married women. To a modern reader, Astell's description of the state of a woman's inner life in marriage bears haunting resemblance to the symptoms of a person who has experienced a life-threatening trauma.

The proximity of Astell's description of a tyrannical marriage to a traumatic experience shows Astell's prescience in pointing to the violence that may underlie relationships even when no physical violence is present. Bringing Astell's descriptions of psychological responses to violent relationships alongside contemporary descriptions of the structure of traumatic experience makes visible, by way of juxtaposition, the severity of what Astell describes. Many view Astell as an early predecessor of modern feminism, though she would not have identified as a feminist and would have been repelled by the radical implications of much feminist thinking. In like man-

Some Reflections upon Trauma   113

ner, Astell's implicit theorization of violence at the core of domestic relationships places her as a predecessor to modern feminists who more
explicitly make the connection between violence and unequal power relationships.[2] The reflections of trauma in *Reflections* emphasize the violent
elements of Astell's analysis of tyrannical marriage.

The Structure of Trauma

The structure of trauma provides a helpful paradigm to filter the writing of
Astell's *Reflections* because it makes visible the severity and the prolonged
consequences of the experiential realities Astell describes. By examining
the claims Astell makes about the experience of women subordinated in a
tyrannical marriage alongside the psychological signs of traumatic stress, I
hope to show that the similarity between the experiences evidences the
gravity of the situation to which Astell calls attention. As this paradigm
places Astell's description alongside a structure of traumatic symptoms, it
also provides a way to read Astell's spiritual responses as steps toward
recovery from traumatic stress. Astell offers spiritual advice for the survival
of women within this structure, placing their suffering into a Christian
worldview and transforming it into an inner power. Astell's faith, rather
than detracting from the power of her theories, or being simply a by-product
of her time period, as some critics have argued, is integral to her prescription for survival and recovery within this traumatic system.[3]

Trauma is characterized not the by the kind of event one experiences,
but by the structure of the way one experiences it. Cathy Caruth, in
Trauma: Explorations in Memory, explains, "The pathology consists, rather,
solely in the *structure of its experience* or reception: the event is not assimi-
lated or experienced fully at the time, but only belatedly, in its repeated
possession of the one who experiences it. To be traumatized is precisely to
be possessed by an image or event" (1995, 4–5; emphasis in original). While
Caruth here defines trauma as the experience of being "possessed by an
event," it is not only singular events that may be experienced as trauma.
Traumatic events may also be prolonged and repeated, as in circumstances
of captivity. As Judith Herman states, "[R]epeated trauma occurs only
when the victim is prisoner, unable to flee, and under the control of the
perpetrator. Such conditions obviously exist in prisons, concentration
camps, and slave labor camps. These conditions may also exist in religious
cults, in brothels and other institutions of organized sexual exploitation,
and in families" (1992, 74). Herman speaks of captive situations in prison

114   Feminist Interpretations of Mary Astell

and war, but she also allows for the dynamics she describes to take place within families. Astell's description of marriage does not exclusively or primarily deal with a physically violent situation; the violence she describes may, in some cases, be solely psychological. Can the prolonged event of a marriage lacking in physical violence, yet built upon a foundation of psychological violence, have traumatic effects similar to other forms of captivity, where physical force is typically thought of as the primary conductor of traumatic experience? Listen to Astell's description of the condition of an ill-married woman in *Some Reflections on Marriage*:

> To be yoak'd for Life to a disagreeable Person and Temper, to have Folly and Ignorance tyrannize over Wit and Sense; to be contradicted in every thing one does or says, and bore down not by Reason but Authority; to be denied one's most innocent desires for no other cause, but the Will and Pleasure of an absolute Lord and Master, whose follies a Woman with all her Prudence cannot hide, and whose Commands she cannot but despise at the same time she obeys them, is a misery none can have a just Idea of, but those who have felt it. (RM, 4)

Astell describes a state of tyranny where all, or even randomly selected, impulses of the wife are cut off at the roots by the husband, where desires are quashed and their destruction gives pleasure to the tyrant. Herman asserts that "the desire for total control over another person is the common denominator of all forms of tyranny," be they totalitarian governments, slaveholders, batterers, or sex offenders (1992, 74). Later on, Astell plainly calls the state of marriage "female slavery" (RM, 29) and the action of courting "violent" (37). While Astell has not explicitly described a situation of physical violence, she uses the language of violence to describe common cultural practices.

This kind of marriage deprives the woman "of the comfort and quiet of her life" (RM, 6). Comparing Astell's discussion of power and security with that of Hobbes's, Penny Weiss finds that "despite Hobbes's belief that his powerful state establishes the longed-for security, Astell finds that women—half the population—are still at risk there. Peering into the household as she checks on the security of the citizenry, Astell finds something astonishing: another Hobbesean state of nature" (2004, 73). At a time and under a government where citizens felt they were free from the fear of living within a state of nature, Astell shows that, for women, this

Some Reflections upon Trauma   115

security only exists in the public realm; once a woman enters the gates of the household, the security is nowhere to be found. As Weiss argues, "despite the Hobbesean social contract, men still have rights to women's bodies and to women's property—still have the rights of the state of nature, as defined by Hobbes: 'In such a condition every man has a right to everything, even to one another's body.' Women, it appears, have about the same degree of security in civil marriage that all individuals have in the natural state: next to none" (2004, 74–75). Ironically, after her description of the state of this kind of marriage, Astell asserts that no one can "have a just Idea, but those who have felt it" (RM, 4). Astell herself never married. She argues that those who have not married cannot truly know the feeling of such a state, yet she describes it in detail. While surely she gets much of her understanding from her married acquaintances, she perhaps also indicates that the marriage relationship is a localized, private example of the power dynamics embedded in public, political society. While Astell never felt the particular effects of being subordinated to a tyrannical husband, she most likely understood what it meant to be denied freedom and intellectual and spiritual desires and to be objectified as a body. If the structure of power described by Astell existed within marriage, she more than likely experienced those power dynamics through public society. What are the effects of living in such a state of abusive power? The effects of both a physically and a psychologically abusive relationship are largely invisible to society and may go unnoticed even by close friends. In the situation described by Astell, the intimate relationship between husband and wife is not helping to hold the person of the woman together, but, instead, systematically deconstructs her as a knowing person. Miranda Fricker, in, *Epistemic Injustice*, illuminates, in a contemporary context, the damages wrought by this kind of psychological violence.

Testimonial Injustice and Epistemic Consequences

Fricker reveals the epistemic damages of the experience of losing your voice, of being discounted as a knowing person, which she calls "testimonial injustice." Not only does not having a voice keep someone from speaking her mind, it stunts the growth of the mind, and can even nullify whatever growth had previously occurred. In testimonial injustice, a speaker's opinion is not listened to, not based on the validity of her words, but based on a "negative identity-prejudicial social type," which Fricker defines as "a widely held disparaging association between a social group

116   Feminist Interpretations of Mary Astell

and one or more attributes" (2007, 35).[4] While Fricker speaks about the external forces of prejudice, Sowaal shows how Astell describes a connected problem, wherein women themselves hold this prejudice, believing themselves to have defective natures and so not pursuing intellectual improvement (2007).[5] This prejudice may be seen as operating in the ill-married woman described by Astell in *Reflections*. Astell describes a woman whose "Wit and Sense" are "tyrannize[d]" by "Folly and Ignorance," who is "contradicted in every thing [she] does or says," and whose "most innocent desires" are denied by a facetious master (*RM*, 4).

What are the epistemic consequences of being discounted repeatedly in this way? One obvious consequence is that "knowledge that would be passed on to a hearer is not received" (Fricker 2007, 43). To those who value knowledge qua knowledge, this consequence may carry enough weight to demonstrate the gravity of the injustice. Yet the wrong goes deeper than that: "To be wronged in one's capacity as a knower is to be wronged in a capacity essential to human value" (44). Fricker continues, "The capacity to give knowledge to others is one side of that many-sided capacity so significant in human beings: namely the capacity for reason. . . . No wonder too that in contexts of oppression the powerful will be sure to undermine the powerless in just that capacity, for it provides a direct route to undermining them in their very humanity" (44). Testimonial injustice, as defined by Fricker, and seen operating in Astell's descriptions of marriage, does not simply hurt one's feelings, it undermines a person in the essence of her humanity. Fricker elaborates on this point: "the epistemic wrong bears a social *meaning* to the effect that the subject is less than fully human" (44, original emphasis). Again, how serious is this injustice? Its form is that of an absence: it is the specter of violence, the gap in experience, what should have been born, but is not. How can we name this violence exerted on being that never came to being? How is it connected to that violence done to physical, existing being? The violence exerted by testimonial injustice may be partially named by its proximity to trauma. The state of mind described by Astell reflects the symptoms of post-traumatic stress.

Reflections of Trauma

Trauma occurs in a situation of powerlessness. Judith Herman, in *Trauma and Recovery*, explains, "Psychological trauma is an affliction of the powerless. At the moment of trauma, the victim is rendered helpless by overwhelming force. . . . Traumatic events overwhelm the ordinary systems of care that give people a sense of control, connection, and meaning" (Herman 1992, 33). Essentially, trauma occurs in situations where a person or a group is rendered helpless in some capacity to the power of another person, group, situation, or force. This kind of event takes over the psychological resources that humans naturally use to deal with extremity in a way that filters it and enables the person to continue to live as an integrated person. In ordinary responses to danger, the mind and body brace for action: "The ordinary human response to danger is a complex, integrated system of reactions, encompassing both body and mind. . . . These changes in arousal, attention, perception, and emotion are normal, adaptive reactions. They mobilize the threatened person for strenuous action, either in battle or in flight. Traumatic reactions occur when action is of no avail. When neither resistance nor escape is possible, the human system of self-defense becomes overwhelmed and disorganized" (34). The symptoms of trauma arise from an event, sometimes prolonged, in which the normal responses to danger are crippled, cut off somehow due to a realization that such a response is futile. The functions of the mind, which normally serve to enable a person to escape from danger or to survive intense suffering, become severed from their original intent. The bizarre and seemingly irrational symptoms of trauma make much sense when seen in this light. They are not random malfunctions of the mind and body; they originate from the mind's survival mechanisms for extreme situations. When these mechanisms are overwhelmed, they can become stuck, repeating the survival responses long after the danger has passed. The symptoms of traumatic stress are the residue of overwhelmed survival instincts.

Does the state of a tyrannical marriage described by Astell share any of the qualities of a state of trauma laid out by Herman? How does the state of nature reflect a traumatic state? Astell writes that a married woman "*has in truth no security* but the Man's Honour and Good-nature, a security that in this present Age no wise Person would venture much upon" (RM, 38, emphasis mine). The whole of a woman's "security" is located in her husband. Her well-being is placed at the whims of his good nature—a nature which, Astell says, no wise person should bet on. In addition to this structure of power, wives are bound to their husbands for life. The ideal wife for a tyrannical husband, she writes, is "in a Word, one whom he can intirely Govern and consequently may form her to his will and liking, who must be his for Life, and therefore *cannot quit his Service let him treat her how he will*" (RM, 37). The wife, in this situation, has no recourse to action, has nowhere to turn if her husband should turn violent.[6] The structure of power creates

118   Feminist Interpretations of Mary Astell

a situation ripe for trauma to occur. Indeed, Astell's description of a tyrannical state of marriage mirrors Herman's descriptions of the symptoms
shown by a person who has been traumatized.

The three main categories of symptoms of trauma described by Herman
are hyperarousal—the "persistent expectation of danger"; constriction—
"the numbing response of surrender to danger," the numbing of the emotions, and numbing of their connection to the body; and intrusion—that
is, the recurring, literal experiences of the trauma in dreams, in "play," and
in imagination (1992, 35).[7] In prolonged trauma, as in a captivity situation,
these symptoms are the same, but they manifest in more acute and persistent forms (86). Shadows and reflections of these symptoms are uncannily
present throughout Astell's portrayal of the dangers of marriage. Each
reflected symptom highlights a different aspect of the self which is cut off
as it is limited, thwarted, and quashed by the bounds of her existence as
proscribed by her husband's exercise of his authority.

In language reflecting the state of hyperarousal, Astell tells us that women
should always be on their guard, and that resting from a state of watchfulness may bring about their ruin: "A Woman cannot be too watchful, too
apprehensive of her danger, nor keep at too great a distance from it, since
Man whose Wisdom and Ingenuity is so much Superior to hers, conde-
scends for his Interest sometimes, and sometimes by way of Diversion to lay
Snares for her . . . 'tis no great Matter to them if Women who were born to
be their Slaves, be now and then ruin'd for their Entertainment" (RM, 65).
Even when it may seem like a man has the purest intentions in mind,
Astell warns that he may be only laying a snare for the woman. In this
picture of society, women are never out of danger, are always expecting
someone to violate their bodies, minds, and souls. Astell is speaking here,
not of the state of marriage, but of the place of women in the general
society of men. She continues to describe how women should carry themselves in such society: "perhaps the Lady might be willing enough to throw
off the Intruder at first, but wanted Courage to get above the fear of his
Calumnies, and the longer she suffers him to buz about her, she will find it
the harder to get rid of his Importunities" (RM, 73). She speaks of an
intruder, infusing her discussion of the relationship between the sexes with
the specter of violence. In the world Astell paints for her readers, women
are not free to walk about and talk and enjoy themselves in society with
men. Rather, they must remain in a constant state of vigilance, aware that
slipping for a minute may cost them their lives: "By all which it appears
that she who really intends to be secure, must keep at the greatest distance
from Danger, she must not grant the *least* indulgence, where such ill uses

Some Reflections upon Trauma   119

will be made of it" (RM, 73). It is unclear what kind of danger Astell refers to here, whether she speaks about the danger of rape or the danger of entering into marriage. She uses violent language to make her points, conflating emotional and physical dangers, blurring the lines between them. She tells us that "it were endless to reckon up the divers Stratagems Men use to catch their Prey" (RM, 75). Men are the hunters and women the hunted; hunters seek their prey in order to kill them and then to devour their meat. Through this metaphor, Astell points to the psychological reality happening beneath the surface of the socially accepted methods of courtship and marriage. In a way that may seem perfectly harmless to the woman who has been raised to believe that she was born to marry, the man "will either entertain or serve her as occasion offers, and some way or other gets himself instructed with her Fortune, her Fame or her Soul" (RM, 75). The stakes are high. The woman, entertained by flattery, finds herself suddenly in a situation where she is being devoured as prey, slowly perhaps, from the inside out. There is reason enough here for hyperarousal.

When a person has no recourse to action in a dangerous situation, when resistance will not provide relief but only bring an increase of danger, the result is constriction, a numbing of the body and mind's natural responses to the danger at hand.[8] This kind of numbing has widespread effects: "In avoiding any situations reminiscent of the past trauma, or any initiative that might involve future planning and risk, traumatized people deprive themselves of those new opportunities for successful coping that might mitigate the effect of the traumatic experience. Thus, constrictive symptoms, though they may represent an attempt to defend against overwhelming emotional states, exact a high price for whatever protection they afford. They narrow and deplete the quality of life and ultimately perpetuate the effects of the traumatic event" (Herman 1992, 47). In staying away from situations that could lead to healing from the trauma, traumatized persons withdraw and numb themselves, shutting down systems that are vital for recovery. Notably, Astell suggests that women in a tyrannical marriage do something similar for their survival. She says the married woman must "divest her self even of Innocent Self-love, as to give up the Cause when she is in the right, and to submit her enlightened Reason, to the imperious Dictates of a blind Will, and wild Imagination, even if she clearly perceives the ill Consequences of it, the Imprudence, nay Folly and Madness of such a Conduct" (RM, 35). To survive the whims and dictates of her husband's will, Astell suggests that women shut down their "innocent self-love." This suggestion is tantamount to encouraging women to numb themselves within. Astell realizes what is necessary for survival. However, the woman

120   Feminist Interpretations of Mary Astell

who cuts off, whether intentionally or not, her connection with her own self-love may survive her situation yet lose that vital connection with herself which is necessary if one is to live a full life.

The symptom of intrusion, with its specific psychological phenomena of recurring traumatic dreams, and literal reenactments of the trauma in play and in the imagination, appears at first much more tenuous in connection with Astell's descriptions of tyrannical marriage. The trauma resurfaces in the person's memory in the form of dreams and play. Traumatic memories and dreams are characteristically different than other kinds of dreams and memories in that they are not elaborated or transformed or formed into a coherent narrative. Rather, they replay in blatantly literal form the trauma that the person has experienced (Herman 1992, 47–48). Astell does not speak of the dreams or imaginations of the women she describes, so it is unclear whether or not the images of their particular traumatic experiences haunt their subconscious. Yet it is unnecessary for us to know about the dream lives of these women—reflections of trauma intrude their waking lives. Unconsciously recurring traumas of the sort that Herman describes refer to an event or series of events which the person has survived and which now haunt them. The situation described by Astell is different: the overwhelming event has no end in sight, but forms the very structure of these women's lives. There is no single event to return to haunt their psyches; there is a chain of repeating events that they wake into and fall asleep within each day and night. As Astell relates, "She must follow all his Paces, and tread in all his unreasonable steps, or there is no Peace, no Quiet for her, she must obey with the greatest exactness, 'tis in vain to expect any manner of Compliance on his side, and the more she complies the more she may; his fanatical humours grow with her desire to gratify them" (RM, 30). She is caught in a recurring dream with no hope of waking.[9]

Effects of Trauma

Living constantly in such conditions may shatter the core of human life. Herman argues that one of the most damaging effects of trauma is the way in which it shatters human faith in the goodness of life, of the divine, and of human relationships: "Traumatized people feel utterly abandoned, utterly alone, cast out of the human and divine systems of care and protection that sustain life. Thereafter, a sense of alienation, of disconnection, pervades every relationship, from the most intimate familial bonds to the most abstract affiliations of community and religion" (52). She continues, "A secure sense of connection with caring people is the foundation of personality development. When this connection is shattered, the traumatized person loses her basic sense of self" (52). The trusting connection with other people that is shattered in traumatic experience is not simply a need for friendship to allay loneliness and boredom on a slow afternoon. Herman asserts that the bond of relationships is foundational to the development of a personality and to the very sense of self. McFarlane and Van der Kolk argue that "emotional attachment is probably the primary protection against feelings of helplessness and meaninglessness; it is essential for biological survival in children, and without it, existential meaning is unthinkable in adults" (2007, 24). Trusting relationships are the glue that holds human selves together. In the situation described by Astell, one of the trusting relationships that should help the person of the wife recover from the existential destruction wrought by trauma is, instead, a relationship to the very perpetrator of the violence.

Recovery/Salvation

As Astell's writing makes visible the invisible realities of the psychic damage done to women in an oppressive marriage state, she also ushers them along a path to healing whose steps are likewise invisible. The steps for recovery and survival in Astell's philosophy are along a spiritual path that both parallels and departs from Judith Herman's theory of recovery. Herman writes that recovery must take place in three (admittedly simplified) stages: establishing safety, remembrance and mourning, and reconnection with ordinary life (1992, 155). While recovery from trauma often has a cyclical nature, where the survivor must pass through stages again and again, still "in the course of a successful recovery, it should be possible to recognize a gradual shift from unpredictable danger to reliable safety, from dissociated trauma to acknowledged memory, and from stigmatized isolation to restored social connection" (155). Healing must take place on three levels: that of personal safety, of memory, and of community.

The first goal of recovery is to regain a sense of safety, to restore "a sense of power and control to the survivor" (159). In the case dealt with by Astell, however, how can the sense of power and control be regained by women who find themselves continuing to live in a situation where their power and control is largely in the hands of another? This first and fundamental level of recovery is at least partially blocked off. If she cannot leave her

122   Feminist Interpretations of Mary Astell

home, if her supposed place of refuge is the site of recurring oppression, if the society she lives in itself condones the abuse of power, where will she establish a refuge? If she cannot establish physical security, the woman must establish a spiritual refuge within the center of the self. Acknowledging this reality, Astell focuses on the spiritual nature of the battle these women find themselves in. When there is nowhere to escape, the woman must transform her affliction into spiritual energy, transforming her suffering into virtue: "Affliction, the sincerest Friend, the frankest Monitor, the best Instructer and indeed the only useful School that Women are ever put to, rouses her understanding, opens her Eyes, fixes her Attention, and diffuses such a Light, such a Joy into her Mind, as not only Informs her better, but entertains her more than ever her Ruel did, tho' crouded by the Men of Wit" (RM, 17). Affliction becomes the school wherein she is taught the graces. It becomes even her entertainment and joy. By turning inward, a woman can turn even the affliction of oppression into a light and joy in her mind. Because she cannot physically escape or find a refuge from her situation, she transcends her earthly problems by focusing her energy on the eternal: "She now distinguishes between Truth and Appearances, between solid and apparent Good; has found out the instability of all Earthly Things, and won't any more be deceiv'd by relying on them" (RM, 17). Her affliction has schooled her in the transience of the material world, and thus helps set her free from her dependence upon it. While this may seem like a weak balm for the afflicted, it may be the inner power that can enable oppressed women to survive.[10]

The second stage of recovery is that of reconstructing the trauma in a narrative within one's memory. Whereas normal memory takes place on a narrative level, however convoluted, traumatic memory is "wordless and static" (Herman 1992, 175). It must be transformed from the static into the dynamic plain of narrative. As Dominick LaCapra argues, "When the past becomes accessible to recall in memory, and when language functions to provide some measure of conscious control, critical distance, and perspective, one has begun the arduous process of working over and through the trauma" (2001, 90). Placing the traumatic experience into a narrative relocates and redefines the event from a horror which possesses the victim to one which a survivor claims as part of her testimony, possessing the trauma within her story.[11] Astell takes the nameless suffering of women in oppressive marriages and names their suffering, places their suffering within a spiritual narrative, in which even the most meaningless acts of cruelty they endure are endowed with eternal meaning for the cultivation of the soul. During this stage, the traumatized person must mourn the death

Some Reflections upon Trauma   123

of the person she was before the trauma. By naming the sufferings and the severance of aspects of their personality, Astell enables women to recognize that parts of them have been crushed. It is crucial for them to mourn the old self before they will be prepared to create the new.

In the third stage of recovery, of recreation, a survivor must restore her relationships to others in her community, to herself, and to her faith in the meaning of her life (Herman 1992, 196). Astell recognizes the obstacles blocking this restoration. She ends her piece with a foreboding warning: "For tho' it is very unreasonable, yet we see 'tis the course of the World, not only to return Injury for Injury, but Crime for Crime; both Parties indeed are Guilty, but the Agressors have a double Guilt, they have not only their own, but their Neighbour's ruin to answer for" (RM, 95). She proclaims that women who marry foolishly are guilty of being taken in by flattery through their vanity.[12] Tyrannical men, on the other hand, are in a great deal more trouble. The "aggressors" who cause the women to be guilty of vanity by succumbing to flattery will have to bear a double guilt in the coming Judgment. Astell works throughout the piece on two levels—the experience of the present and the coming of eternity. Astell enacts the power of narrative here, bringing together the disjointed fragments of pain into a narrative where earthly suffering yields spiritual joys. At the same time, she gathers together women who live separated in their isolated homes into a spiritual community of the oppressed. She answers the invisible traumas of oppression with an invisible spiritual reality. Faith in this spiritual existence has the capacity to allow women to not be overwhelmed with the meaninglessness of their pain but instead to view their suffering as preparation for the soul's communion with the divine. This may seem to dismiss the wrongs done to women at the hands of men, but, for Astell, it is just the opposite. Though it is understood that these evils of oppression can produce good qualities of the spirit, it is equally understood that the person through whom the oppression comes will be judged harshly and eternally. This teaching vindicates the women, gives meaning to their pain, and condemns the men who oppress them to eternal suffering.

Yet Astell's meditations on the marriage system did not stop with spiritual advice to women. She had far-reaching visions of revolutionary changes in the community, plans to extend spiritual realities into social life. Strong community is a vital aspect of recovery from trauma, as Herman argues, "Traumatic events destroy the sustaining bonds between individual and community. Those who have survived learn that their sense of self, of worth, of humanity, depends upon a feeling of connection to others. The solidarity of a group provides the strongest protection against terror and

124   Feminist Interpretations of Mary Astell

despair, and the strongest antidote to traumatic experience" (1992, 214).
Astell likewise affirms the necessity for community. Her critique of marriage partners with her plan in her earlier work, A Serious Proposal I (1694),
which imagines an educational retreat for women, an intellectual community where women might escape the boundaries of a life with the only
option open to them being marriage, where they could gather together and
devote themselves to the larger world. While the spiritual narrative told by
Astell in Reflections may help oppressed women survive their day-to-day
lives, Astell sought something better than daily survival. She was well
aware that women had a higher purpose than simply trying to survive the
cruelties of tyrannical husbands. Thus, she envisioned a world where a
community of women could band together and learn to live in the fullness
of their spirits, their minds, and their bodies, to reclaim those aspects of
the self that had been lost and to live into their full personalities.

Astell's descriptions of insidious psychological violence in tyrannical
marriage continues to make a case for the community she envisions in
Serious Proposal I, where Astell "advocates a 'Religious Retirement' or
female academy where women could retreat, worship, learn, and teach, and
in general lead the intellectual lives to which they had a right and for
which they had the ability" (Weiss 2004, 65). Such a community would
speed the healing of the traumas as a result of the unequal power in society. Herman writes that "[t]he recreation of an ideal self involves the active
exercise of imagination and fantasy, capacities that have now been liber-
ated" in the recovery from trauma (1992, 202). Full recovery involves a sort
of re-envisioning of the self, reclaiming the parts that have been lost and
shedding the parts that have attached themselves to a person in reaction
to the trauma, refusing to be identified as a victim any longer. At the same
time that the person distances herself from the trauma victim's identity,
she can look at that person with understanding and compassion, even
admiration for the capacity of the mind to withstand such psychological
violence. As the new self is forged, it needs to be forged within community.
The academy envisioned by Astell stands as a sort of utopian vision for
female society, wherein women could heal the wrongs of their oppression
through recreating themselves in educational and religious pursuits. Alessa
Johns's description of the religious retreat proposed by Astell makes clear
that this female monastery would provide a space for this fullness of being.[13]
She argues that "Astell's is a deeply conceived utopianism that constitutes
the core of her feminism: women achieve subjectivity and independence in
the context of an ideal society in which they do not assert identity but
model themselves after each other, imitating the copies of heavenly origi-

nals they experience around them. In the process, metaphysical and physical realms are joined; Astell conceives a system that integrates emotional impulses and the needs of the mind" (1996, 60). Astell envisions an ideal community for women that would contribute to the healing of their personalities and the reintegration of the parts of their being that had been silenced and put to death through their lack of education and treatment as lowly slaves. However, when it became clear that this community would not be funded, Astell went on to write *Part II* of the *Proposal* (1697), where she details "inward strategies" for women to engage in new practices to respond to the power structures governing their culture (Sowaal 2007, 234).[14]

Astell perceives that the damage done to women living in oppressive situations is not confined to the harms they suffer daily but extends to the absence of the good they would enact, the beauty they would create in the larger world were they free to live in the fullness of their being and exercise the full extent of their spiritual, physical, and intellectual capacities. In *Reflections*, she asks, "Is it not then ill Manners to Heaven, and an irreligious contempt of its Favours, for a Woman to slight that nobler Employment, to which it has assigned her, and thrust her self down to a meaner Drudgery, to what is in a very literal Sense a caring for the things of the World, a caring not only to Please, but to Maintain a Husband" (RM, 41). Her vision of healing from the trauma of the oppressive marriage system includes healing of the society that contains it.

Astell's analysis of the structure of marriage reveals that the oppressions resulting from authoritarian relationships can fragment and dislocate essential aspects of a person's being. The repetitive testimonial injustice in such a relationship enacts psychological violence to the extent that the effects of that violence approximate the symptoms of post-traumatic stress disorder. Astell's reflections therefore encourage us to look beyond the visible traces of violence in physical abuse, to see also the psychological wounds which may prevent the oppressed from living as whole persons. Learning to name and to make visible these invisible acts of violence brings us one step closer to bringing into being the creative capacities suppressed through long injustice.

Astell's analysis of the position of women in tyrannical marriages recognizes that their recovery from these invisible wounds depends on their cultivation of likewise invisible spiritual practices. Trauma theorists are increasingly beginning to recognize the importance of religious work in recovering from trauma. Alexander C. McFarlane and Bessel van der Kolk argue that "religion fulfills the critical function of providing a sense of purpose in the face of terrifying realities by placing suffering in a larger

126   Feminist Interpretations of Mary Astell

context and by affirming the commonality of suffering across generations, time, and space. Thus, religion can help people transcend their inbedded-ness in their individual suffering" (McFarlane and Van der Kolk 2007, 25). What modern psychologists are beginning to pay attention to, Astell rec-ognized in the seventeenth century. If we attend to her feminist analysis of women's subordination and the damaging effects of tyranny in marriage without attending to her religious vision, then we receive the diagnosis and ignore the prescription for a cure. Astell's religious vision, as the kind of religious practice McFarlane and Van der Kolk describe, is not solely an individual practice, but takes place within community. This unity of indi-vidual spiritual transformation with the support of a community of women devoted to one another's spiritual good is a formula for recovery from trauma both at the individual and the societal level.

Abbreviations

RM   Mary Astell, *Reflections upon Marriage* (1996)

Notes

1. Of course, the category of post-traumatic stress disorder was not current in Astell's day and only gained official diagnostic standing in 1980, when it was accepted by the *Diagnostic and Statisti-cal Manual of Mental Disorders*, 3rd ed. (Weisaeth, and Van der Hart 2007, 61).

2. I think particularly of Virginia Woolf's *Three Guineas*. Indeed, in this work, Woolf draws on Astell's *Serious Proposal I* as evidence of the longevity and persistence of women's desire for educa-tion. The analysis of psychological violence in relationships makes another point of contact between the two thinkers. In this epistolary analysis of the roots of war, Woolf argues that the British will never succeed in expelling fascism from the continent until they recognize and eradicate the fascist elements of violence in domestic relationships and in the structure of a society which bans women from the professions and from formal education. More contemporary feminist theorists who make connections between violence and patriarchal domestic relationships include Catherine MacKin-non, Andrea Dworkin, and bell hooks, to name a few.

3. Some feminist critics of Astell either dismiss her faith or view it as incompatible with her "feminism" and thus do not consider it as key in her thoughtful response to the situation she con-fronts. An example of this treatment can be seen in Duran (2006). Work has been and is being done, however, which treats Astell's religious thought in its own right as connected to her views on gender and tries to read Astell on her own terms, rather than seeking to make her fit into contemporary secu-lar feminism. The scholarship of Kolbrener and Michelson (2007) provides an excellent example.

4. In her first published book, *Serious Proposal I* (1694), Astell more directly addresses societal prejudices against women as knowers.

5. Alice Sowaal explains that "Astell is focused on disengagement from prejudice, and in par-ticular from the prejudice that women 'naturally' have 'feminine vices'—vanity and pride" (2007, 231). Sowaal calls this prejudice the Woman's Defective Nature Prejudice and has shown how Astell understands it to have far-reaching effects. At the societal level, this prejudice "perpetuates a society in which women are devalued" (2007, 231).

Some Reflections upon Trauma 127

6. While the avenues of escape for a woman in this kind of situation may be blocked off, it is important to remember that she may still have recourse to resistance. As Sarah Lucia Hoagland points out, the apparent helplessness of women can often be a façade for acts of "sabotage" (1982, 92). What I am discussing here is the damage that can be wreaked on the psychology of a woman by the blocking of those avenues of escape and what happens when certain capacities of existence are dislocated by the enforcement of an authoritarian husband, acknowledging, however, that even within these disabilities, women may always be exercising secret, resistant abilities.

7. For more information on the symptoms of PTSD and the structure of traumatic experience, see also Van der Kolk, McFarlane, and Weisaeth (2007).

8. This symptom seems strangely in opposition to the foregoing symptom of hyperarousal, where the person is overaware of danger. Indeed, as Herman explains, this tension between opposing symptoms is characteristic of trauma. The traumatized person's psyche swings between extremes of arousal and numbness, between intense pain and dissociation, forming part of what Herman calls "the dialectic of trauma" (1992, 47–48). Bessel van der Kolk and Alexander C. McFarlane cite one possible reason for this seeming paradox: "Roughly speaking, it seems that the chronic hyperarousal of PTSD depletes both the biological and the psychological resources needed to experience a wide variety of emotions. . . . [A]s intrusive memories come to dominate their thinking, people with PTSD become more and more sensitized to environmental stimuli that remind them of the trauma. Thus, over time, they become less and less responsive to various stimuli that are necessary for involvement in the present" (2007, 12).

9. The lack of clear symptoms of intrusion in Astell's work highlights that the experiences Astell describes are not necessarily symptomatic of post-traumatic stress, but are reflections of such symptoms. Intrusion—the literal return of the traumatic event in dreams and in waking flashbacks—the most dramatic symptom of PTSD, is clearly differentiated from other forms of stress. If an experience were akin to the traumatic, but not fully displaying all the symptoms of PTSD, this symptom would be most likely the least represented. At the same time, the literal return of the trauma in intrusive symptoms occurs on the unconscious level and is by definition not available to the person's consciousness. The trauma that repeats itself in the person's mind is not representable in rational language. Hence, signs of this symptom must be found outside of linguistic representations. If this symptom does exist in the experiences Astell describes, we would need other forms of evidence—fragmentary dream evidence, visual, or poetic traces of the trauma.

10. This strategy of living in two simultaneous realities resonates with the altered consciousness Herman identifies in the practice of captives: "Through the practice of dissociation, voluntary thought suppression, minimization, and sometimes outright denial, they learn to alter an unbearable reality" (1992, 87).

11. Cathy Caruth makes a similar argument in Unclaimed Experience: Trauma, Narrative, History. She asserts that trauma is not a wound that can be simply healed, because it "is experienced too soon, too unexpectedly, to be fully known and is therefore not available to consciousness until it imposes itself again, repeatedly, in the nightmares and repetitive actions of the survivor. . . . [S]o trauma is not locateable in the simple violent or original event in an individual's past, but rather in the way that its very unassimilated nature—the way it was precisely not known in the first instance—returns to haunt the survivor later on" (1996, 4). Hence, traumatic experience is that which has not been claimed by the consciousness; one step of the healing process is beginning to consciously claim the trauma's reality through the ambiguous realm of language. Traumatic experience simultaneously "defies and demands our witness." As such, it must be conveyed in "literary" language, in a way that "defies, even as it claims, our understanding" (1996, 5).

12. Yet throughout the piece, she seems to argue that they really are not wholly at fault for this foolishness, because they have no access to education.

13. See also Alice Sowaal (2007). Sowaal contextualizes Astell's proposal within her larger theory of mind and demonstrates its implications for a critique of society; see also Deidre Raftery (1997). Shannon Miller argues that Astell proposes an Edenic space where knowledge becomes redemptive for women (2008).

14. For a detailed description of these "inward strategies," see Sowaal (2007).

8

"From the Throne to Every Private Family"

Mary Astell as Analyst of Power

Penny A. Weiss

I begin this exploration of Mary Astell's political thought with a disheartening but not unusual claim about the history of feminist theory: "From the point of view of feminist political theory, what is interesting about the earliest writings is not so much the details of what individual writers of the time had to say, for these did not yet constitute an analysis of power relations or any kind of political programme, but rather the fact that debates over women's role in society that include a recognizably feminist perspective go back further than had been commonly assumed" (Bryson 1992, 11). It is certainly true that "debates over women's role in society that include a recognizably feminist perspective go back further than had been commonly assumed," since until very recently the "common assumption" was that women did not write *any* political theory throughout most of history, feminist or otherwise. To this day, most anthologies in the history of philosophy and political theory include not a single woman, though a few female figures are starting to appear more than once, including, most commonly, Mary Wollstonecraft, Simone de Beauvoir, and Hannah Arendt (Weiss 2009).

More controversial than Bryson's claim about the invisibility of feminist thinkers, however, is her assertion above that their "earliest writings . . . did not yet constitute an analysis of power relations." At the very least, hers seems a premature conclusion, given that there is not a single feminist thinker on whom we have produced a sufficiently large and sophisticated literature to justify us saying with such authority whether she has an analysis of power relations or what exactly it looks like; there are dozens of feminist theorists about which very little has been written at all. Why jump to Bryson's conclusion? It might be more reasonable to assume the opposite, since anyone who writes from "a recognizably feminist perspective" is likely to have a rich understanding of unequal power and abuses of power; a vision of more equitably shared power and constructive power; and some thoughts on how power works that could inform us how to get from the former to the latter. This alternative assumption fits well with Amy Allen's understanding of feminist theory.

> It seems undeniable that much work in feminist theory is devoted to the tasks of critiquing women's subordination, analyzing the intersections between sexism and other forms of subordination . . . and envisioning the possibilities for both individual and collective resistance to such subordination. Insofar as the concept of power is central to each of these theoretical tasks, *power is clearly a central concept* for feminist theory. . . . [However,] it is one that is not often explicitly discussed in feminist work . . . [and must] be reconstructed from feminist discussions of other topics (Allen 2005, 1, my emphasis).

So few analyses of historical women writers search the range of their work for ideas on particular themes, like power, community, human nature, or justice. The reason is *not* that these thinkers do not have well-developed ideas on particular themes that evolve over the course of their lives and through the body of their work. The explanation, instead, is that we have indeed not studied "the details of what individual writers of the time had to say." We simply cannot acknowledge that we have not read women theorists with the attention to detail that careful exegetical scholarship rightly demands, and simultaneously conclude that the details of their work are

130   Feminist Interpretations of Mary Astell

not "interesting" and do not form part of "an analysis of power relations or any kind of political programme" (Bryson 1992, 11).

In this chapter, I offer some evidence against Bryson's claim by taking up Allen's challenge above to "reconstruct" Astell's "concept of power" from her "discussions of other topics" as well as from her thoughts explicitly on the subject. In the end, I hold, these discussions do indeed amount to and constitute "an analysis of power." Positively, I find Astell to be a fascinating analyst of diverse aspects of power and authority, someone who came at the subject from many angles, and who provides an early modern understanding I have not yet seen anywhere else. A less noble reason for taking on this topic is my "Foucault fatigue." Those who read political theory today, even including feminist political theory, might understandably reach the erroneous conclusion that Foucault's writing on power was without precedent (especially without female precedent). I think, however, that feminists have been urging us for several centuries down many of the paths Foucault has more recently and much more famously traveled regarding power, but, as many women know, it often takes a man expressing your ideas for them to be heard. Astell, in fact, knew this, too: "The World will hardly allow a Woman to say any thing well, unless as she borrows it from Men, or is assisted by them" (RM, 23). She mourns that women are "buried in silence" and urges her readers to "remember . . . the famous Women of former Ages" (SP I, 53–54) and to resist and rectify the marginalization of these figures and their ideas, as she does herself by naming and using many of them. Incidentally, these quotes already begin to reflect Astell's insights into the workings of power, from the politics of voice and resistance to the varied practices that sustain inequality. It might seem inappropriate and anachronistic to associate Astell with concepts like voice, marginalization, resistance, and silencing (and even feminism), which are central to theorizing about oppression today. Yet only those who are strangers to the history of feminist theorizing and activism assume that these ideas (not always expressed in identical terms) were but recently developed. And only those with a narrow definition of feminism would be stopped and stumped by Astell's religiosity and Toryism, when the variety of frameworks used to argue, variously, for sexual equality, respect for women, and inclusion continue to evolve and to interact with a plethora of religious, political, and cultural practices and ideals. Again, it is unimaginable that someone with a generally "feminist perspective" would be identifiable as such without deep and persistent reflections on power. The time is ripe to listen to what "Women of former Ages"—or one in particular, here—have to contribute

Astell as Analyst of Power   131

to the conversation about power, and for that we need not constantly reference Foucault.

In what follows I look at Astell's analysis of power from two angles. First, using the topic of education as a tool, I touch on the range of issues she covers and how she approaches them, to show something of her breadth and methodology. Then I explore three subjects in greater detail, to give a sense of the depth of her analysis of power. Among the many possible themes that give insight into Astell as analyst of power, I choose to treat patriarchy, incredulity, and resistance. These themes cover the general nature of oppressive power, one concrete epistemological practice and consequence of unequal power, and challenges to domination; they build on each other in a way that provides a relatively cumulative sense of her ideas on the subject; and they set the stage for possible links to contemporary feminist theory and activism.

Breadth: "From Empires Down to Private Families"

Methodologically, in order to analyze power, even in a single relationship or regarding a single issue, Astell approaches the problem from multiple angles. This tactic reflects her understanding that rather than being static and one-dimensional, power evolves and adapts, and consists of a series of generally cooperating forces, arrangements, and practices that enable some to do more (diverse, interesting, things of their choosing), know more (especially of what is currently deemed the most important and difficult knowledge), and have more (efficacy, credibility, advantages) than others. Any single power difference, such as unequal access to resources, or assignment to passive vs. active roles, involves a series of social practices that enact, maintain, justify, and adjust with the difference. So, using here Astell's views on education as an example, I make visible how those views depend upon, develop, and reveal a profound understanding of power capable of rivaling contemporary approaches.

Starting with the basics, Astell notes that in education,

> Boys have much Time and Pains, Care and Cost bestow'd on their Education, Girls have little or none. The former are early initiated in the Sciences, and made acquainted with Antient and Modern Discoveries, they study Books and Men, have all imaginable encouragement; not only Fame . . . but also Title, Authority, Power and Riches

132   Feminist Interpretations of Mary Astell

... are the Reward of their Improvement. The latter are restrain'd, frown'd upon, and beat, not *for* but *from* the Muses; Laughter and Ridicule . . . drive them from the Tree of Knowledge. . . . [They are] star'd upon as Monsters, Censur'd, Envy'd, and every way Discourag'd. (RM, 28)

In this quote, Astell notes that to understand the existing intellectual differences between the sexes, one must grasp the degree and diverse forms of social support or hostility their educations receive (from immediate encouragement and long-term rewards to apathy and even disincentive; the economic, social, and political standing of the un/educated of each sex, etc.). Her insights into the workings of power lead her, and encourage us, to see that power involves a multitude of forms of support and dissuasion, many of which rely upon (and ultimately reinforce) other social, political, economic, and cultural institutions and practices. Too, by bringing marginalized groups into discussions, Astell ends up developing broader understandings of politics and epistemology. For example, what does hostility toward the (educational) pursuits of some reveal, about the sexes, the pursuit itself, what is at stake in education, and the force of custom and opinion, politics and policy?

In looking at educational inequality, Astell also explores what is taught to whom, when, with what consequences. She mentions not only the more obvious differences, such as that boys alone "are early initiated in the sciences, and made acquainted with Antient and Modern Discoveries" and "Books and Men" (RM, 28), but the less formal and less visible yet sometimes more costly differences, such as that only a boy is "acquainted with . . . the Follies, the cheats, . . . and warn'd of the Application and Design of those who will make it their Business to corrupt him" (RM, 64), while women are left ignorant of these motives and methods, and thus made considerably more vulnerable, dependent, and manipulable. This focus on the broad social effects of educational inequality, especially "the ill effects of a bad Education" (RM, 64), is common in Astell, for it provides a sense of how much is at risk personally, socially, and politically. Different educations are less troubling if the differences have few or no important implications. But both directly and indirectly, intentionally or not, unequal education of the sexes affects who has access, who has authority, who is vulnerable to whom. Although language like "epistemology of ignorance" (Mills 1999) and "epistemological injustice" (Fricker 2007) are quite contemporary, in fact the Astellian approach to questions about power leads her to ask questions about what counts as un/desirable knowledge and as un/desirable ignorance for women and for men, with what consequences.

Astell also considers who or what the educators are of each sex. Recall that three centuries later, Virginia Woolf wrote about the "unpaid-for education" of women, where the teachers were "poverty, chastity, derision, and . . . freedom from unreal loyalties" (1938, 78). Part of the power of Woolf's analysis is her concept of the "outsider" who is the product of this "other" education, and the possibility that this outsider can be a critic of the status quo of war and inequality, rather than an advocate (Bechtold 2000). Centuries earlier, intriguingly, Astell similarly documents how "Affliction, the sincerest Friend, the frankest Monitor, the best Instructer, and indeed the only useful School that Women are ever put to, rouses her understanding, opens her Eyes, fixes her Attention, and diffuses such a Light, such a Joy into her Mind, as not only Informs her better, but Entertains her more than ever her Ruel did" (RM, 40).[1]

Again, while Astell does not have access to contemporary phrases like "subordinated knowledges" and "local knowledge," she notes how often that (education, labor, expertise, etc.) which is associated with the subordinated is ignored or underestimated. Astell thus also explores what today is called "the powers of the weak" or "the powers of the powerless." She does this most famously when she suggests that women "erect a Monastery, or . . . a Religious Retirement, . . . a Retreat from the World . . . [where you can] enlarge your Minds" (SP I, 73, 75). But it is a recurring theme. Despite then-common assumptions about and attention to women's intellectual inferiority, Astell questions not only its causes but even its existence: "The Incapacity, if there be any, is acquired not natural" (SP I, 59, emphasis added). We must regularly ask questions about education that involve power, as Astell does. What counts as "an education"?[2] Are there alternative, if unacknowledged, sources of knowledge available to the subjugated? Might these mitigate or counter certain effects of inequality? Are there negative aspects or effects to the education of the dominant that are ignored or not taken seriously? Are there positive ones to the education of the subordinated? How does who or what teaches affect what is taught? What do "uneducated" and intellectually second-rate women know?

Another aspect of this theme of "the powers of the weak" emerges when Astell discusses overvaluing the education (and achievements, contributions, etc.) associated with the dominant group. As she talks of the benefits of women's education and the defects of men's training, she sometimes ridicules men's oft-celebrated "accomplishments." She is urging a reassessment of both the overrated contributions of the powerful and the discounted

134   Feminist Interpretations of Mary Astell

wisdom of the subjugated, and even considers what can make these reconsiderations more credible, with different appeals, for example, to women and to men.

It is worth emphasizing how Astell drives home questions that later become central to political theorists and activists from Marxists to radical feminists alike, among others: Whose interests are and are not served by various inequalities of power? How are certain practices rationalized? What is in women's interest? Are only certain women counted in this calculation? She challenges familiar assessments in part by employing the distinction between real and apparent interests. Thus, for example, she notes how "Men never mistake their true Interest more than when they endeavour to keep Women in Ignorance" (RM, 62).

Finally, Astell also studies the propaganda surrounding education—the social use and manipulation of existing inequalities. "Abuses . . . are not the less because power and Prescription seem to Authorize them" (RM, 7). Among the broad range of effects Astell mentions is the fact that women's intellectual weaknesses can be blamed on them (RM, 65) and used as evidence of their inferior nature, so that miseducation both directly maintains and actively and indirectly reproduces inequality generally. Once again, while feminist philosophers today easily access the gendered dimensions of "objective" science, Astell, too, long ago, explored and challenged respected claims about the causes and consequences of sex differences, in education and other spheres, and showed how some differences were used as evidence of other differences, in a vicious and illegitimate cycle. She questioned what evidence justifies (and fails to justify) claims about, for example, "natural" inequality, or assertions that certain inequalities necessarily have specific social ramifications. This is surely at least a giant step toward today's inquiries into what often wrongly passes for explanation, evidence, objectivity, etc., and into alternative standards of knowledge that should supplement or replace these.

Altogether, writing confidently and convincingly, Astell offers a material analysis of education that contrasts mightily with the characterization of women as uneducated or uneducable. She discloses the power of the powerful to name what knowledge and ignorance are and to shame those denied access to what the privileged have. She understands the way multiple social forces (from standards of evidence and definitions of group "natures" to practices of exclusion and the sway granted "custom") work together to bring about certain ends, which can make inequality more difficult to locate and challenge, and make it seem more akin to that which is "natural," "timeless," and "inevitable" (Enloe 2004, 1–2).

Astell as Analyst of Power   135

Remedies to inequalities are similarly complicated, broadly approached down multiple avenues in Astell's framework for understanding and contesting power. One cannot open schools to girls by fiat and expect them to assume equal power in society if public opinion is not addressed, if demands on girls for household labor are unaltered, if their education is held against them by potential mates, if what they study reinforces their subordination, etc. This complexity does not lead Astell to defeatism. She urges us to understand that "single Medicines are too weak to cure such complicated Distempers, they require a full Dispensatory" (SP I, 72). She knows that remedies must emerge in as many varieties and guises as do the disincentives and misrepresentations. Her own work provides a model of this by its use of multiple strategies, including biblical reinterpretation, introduction of neglected historical examples, application of principles to numerous subjects, recommendations for institutional reorganization, and a wealth of reason, sarcasm, argument, and irony in response to diverse opponents. Finally, she reminds the female reader that "[a]n Ingenious Woman is not a Prodigy to be star'd on, for you have it in your power to inform the World, that you can every one of you be so, if you please your selves" (SP I, 120). This single sentence condemns public opinion, treats women as rightful arbiters of their own fates and evaluators of their competence, and uses a phrase that appears repeatedly in her writing: "you have it in your power." I offer up the possibility that looking at power relations in so many aspects on the practical level leads Astell to look at these relations theoretically through multiple lenses as well, and vice versa.

Astell's breadth is also visible in the range of topics she addresses. As Francis Bacon said that to understand light you have to study the sun, shadows, prisms, etc., so Astell considers ecclesiastical, domestic, and governmental authorities; the relation of power to freedom, custom, civility, virtue, religiosity, and reason; better and worse occasions and means for resisting authority; the costs and benefits of having and not having personal authority; and the uses of power, from its reasonable, legitimate exercise for the benefit of others, to its destructive, arbitrary exertion for personal gain. Often the angles she explores include ones not commonly part of many more famous people's acknowledged "analyses of power," from family and patriarchy to courtship and community, because of the value and centrality in much of her work to the voices and experiences of women.

An example of Astell's attention to less common political themes is her attention to the relationship between power and civility. In a move that may be something of a tradition among feminists, Astell sees the negative effects of unequal power on civility as a compelling argument for greater

136   Feminist Interpretations of Mary Astell

equality (Mary Wollstonecraft and Anna Julia Cooper are among later examples [Weiss 2009]). Describing the tyrannical husband, she remarks that "he who would have every one submit to his Humours and will not in his turn comply with them . . . he's not fit for a Husband, scarce fit for Society, but ought to be turn'd out of the Herd to live by himself" (RM, 37). She associates his dominance with a lack of sociability. More broadly, Astell argues that "no Man can endure . . . to treat a reasonable Woman civilly, but that he thinks he stands on higher ground" (RM, 30). Domination prevents or destroys existing community through incivility. On the other hand, inequality may keep the subordinated from these same vices and, were we to use them, could provide us with alternative wisdom. "But it must not be suppos'd that Women's Wit approaches those heights which men arrive at, or that they indulge those Liberties the other takes. Decency lays greater restraints on them, their timorousness does them this one, and perhaps this only piece of Service, it keeps them from breaking thro' those restraints and following their Masters and Guides" (RM, 42). Subordinated women are often more dependent upon and more devoted to sustaining the bonds of civility and community.[3] This can make them sources of knowledge that society needs as it moves toward greater equality and civility, though forms of sociability and community that reproduce subordination will need to be discarded. Astell sees women as capable of virtue, social as well as personal, even in their second-class status. Oppressors should more often be discussed as uncivil, destructive of necessary social connections and practices.

Astell looks at the negative effects of unequal power on those with more and less of it, though representing the lives of those with less is clearly her priority. She writes at length about the consequences of living with someone who has power over oneself, power that is unearned, undeserved, and, too often, put to ill use. In fact, her perspective is quite distinct and persuasive in portraying the oft-neglected lives of those with less power, even bringing them to center stage. "To be yok'd for Life to a disagreeable Person and temper; to have Folly and Ignorance tyrannize over Wit and Sense; to be contradicted in every thing one does or says, and bore down not by Reason but Authority; to be denied ones most innocent desires, for no other cause but the Will and Pleasure of an absolute Lord and Master, whose Follies a Woman with all her Prudence cannot hide, and whose Commands she cannot but despise at the same time she obeys them; is a misery none can have a just Idea of, but those who have felt it" (RM, 34–35). Astell was especially focused on making visible and understanding the nature and structural causes of unhappiness in the lives of the less powerful partners in personal relationships. Centuries before Betty Friedan tackled the unhappiness of the housewife (1963), before Judy Syfers, as sarcastically as Astell, revealed "Why I Want a Wife" (1971), and Pat Mainardi unveiled "the politics of housework" (1970), Mary Astell analyzed power and its consequences in personal relationships, in essence arguing that the personal is political.

Not only the range of topics, but fine distinctions among them, are distinguishing features of Astell's complex writing on power. She demonstrates a broad understanding of what having more or less power affects, intellectually, psychologically, interpersonally, politically, and epistemologically. She analyzes separately the dynamics of a husband's or a wife's fate when one marries "above" or "below" their station (RM, 50–53). She distinguishes what power looks like in the hands of "usurpers" vs. "a Lawful Prince" (RM, 55). There are conditions that can make subordination better or worse: "Are there regular, reasonable opportunities for redress of wrongs?"; "Do those made 'miserable' receive pity or are they told it is their fate, their duty, not so terrible?" (RM, 18); "Is subordination used to improve or degrade those on the bottom?"; "Is the 'bitter Cup' of obedience 'sweetened as much as may be,' or is there "that nauseous Ostentation of Power which serves to no end or purpose but to blow up the Pride and Vanity of those who have it, and to exasperate the Spirits of such as must truckle under it" (RM, 54)? Astell explores the consequences of equal power between spouses, as well as the costs of "entering into an unequal Yoke" (RM, 36), for the husband and wife alike. She distinguishes the institution of marriage ("Marriage, considered in its self") from "the ill Choice, or foolish Conduct of those who are in it" (RM, 36).

Overall, then, we can get an important sense of the breadth of Astell's treatment of power through an appreciation of how dynamically she understands power relations, the range of topics she links to power and the subtlety with which she examines each, her refusal to oversimplify the causes, character, or consequences of unequal power, her interest in examining power in a range of locales, from religious rites to interpersonal rituals, and the contribution she makes to studying inequality by looking at the lives of the subordinated. How unanticipated these contributions seem, based on the assertions of those like Bryson, and how thrilling!

Patriarchy: "Masculine Empire"

In perhaps the very first piece I ever read about Mary Astell, Dale Spender wrote that Astell "helped to bring the concept of patriarchy into existence" centuries before it was more famously "reformulate[d] . . . for a new

138   Feminist Interpretations of Mary Astell

generation" by radical feminists (1982, 53–54). Yet, as I have written about elsewhere, I am repeatedly astonished and disappointed by how little use contemporary feminists make of our history (Weiss 2009), so this is an exciting chance to explore Spender's claim. What *was* Astell's understanding of patriarchy? What do her ideas about patriarchy reveal about her analysis of power? What makes patriarchy illegitimate? Dangerous? What role does each sex play in sustaining it? It is worth remembering as we study Astell's views on patriarchy, which "we have come to use and accept as a reality today, [that] her contribution must not be underestimated. It is not an easy task to describe the world in terms that have not been part of the culture and not learned" (Fricker 2007). "Some linguists state that it is impossible" (Spender 2009, 51). Astell's exemplary work, and surely that of many others, provide evidence that such analyses nonetheless exist, if we unearth and reconstruct them.

Patriarchy, for Astell, is most generally a "cruel and unjust" (*SP I*, 80) social system that grants men more authority than women, including authority over women. Both the "cruelty" and the "injustice" (*SP I*, 80) of systematic sexual inequality are precisely detailed despite being multifaceted and, alternatively, either silenced or misrepresented. Astell charges men with "despising Women, and keeping them in Ignorance and Slavery" (*SP I*, 28). Her links to tyranny and slavery as ways of capturing the situation of sexual inequality are characteristic of more recent understandings of patriarchy. Like other modern thinkers, including Locke, she sees "being subject to the inconstant, uncertain, unknown, arbitrary Will of Men, [as] the perfect Condition of Slavery" (*RM*, 18–19); unlike Locke, however, she applies this understanding not only to subjects and rulers, but also to the unequal and gendered power relations between the sexes that permeate society. "Men are possess'd of all Places of Power, Trust and Profit, they make Laws and exercise the magistracy, not only the sharpest Sword, but even all the Swords and Blunderbusses are theirs, which by the strongest Logic in the World, gives them the best Title to every thing they please to claim as their Prerogative; who shall contend with them?" (*RM*, 29). That "Men are possess'd of all Places of Power" means patriarchy is a "Tyranny" that regularly prevents "women from acting in the world, or doing any thing considerable" (*RM*, 23). As we will see, a limitless variety of social mechanisms are used to express and maintain male dominance.[4] Patriarchy infiltrates and organizes the supposedly separate public and private, the male and the female, attitudes as well as institutions.

The distribution of power in patriarchy does not, however, take the form of men possessing all forms and types of power, and women none. As

Astell as Analyst of Power   139

Johnson argues, male domination "doesn't mean that all men are powerful or all women are powerless—only that the most powerful roles in most sectors of society are held predominantly by men, and the least powerful roles are held predominantly by women" (2000). Astell agrees, further, that those with less power are not powerless. Like her, they can (and should) still "see with their own eyes, judge with their own understanding." And "tho' the Order of the World requires an Outward Respect and obedience from some to others, yet the Mind is free, nothing but Reason can oblige it, 'tis out of thee reach of the most absolute Tyrant" (*RM*, 56). Thus, despite the power of patriarchal arrangements, resistance is realistic, reasonable, thinkable, and doable. Feminists today, as well, reckon with the actual and potential powers of the weak and supposedly powerless (Carroll 1972; Janeway 1981).

Astell studies the starkly different valuing of the sexes; she compares "that Superior Genius which Men as Men lay claim to" (*RM*, 9) with the "Natural Inferiority of our Sex, which our Masters lay down as a Self-Evident and Fundamental Truth" (*RM*, 8). Characteristic of patriarchy, men determine the value of both themselves and women, and convincingly manage to pass their self-interested judgment off as indisputable, objective, and eternal "truth" or "fact." Women, and whatever work, events, values, etc., are strongly associated with them, are devalued in patriarchy, just as that which is connected with the male is overrated.

Such warped and groundless assessments of women's abilities and contributions confirm that misogyny is essential to patriarchy. Alan Johnson argues that misogyny "is a central part of sexist prejudice and ideology and, as such, is an important basis for the oppression of females in male-dominated societies. Misogyny is manifested in many different ways, from jokes to pornography to violence to the self-contempt women may be taught to feel for their own bodies" (2000, 197). Astonishingly, ridicule, sexual submission, violence against women, and their low self-esteem are also all subjects tackled by Astell. Over three hundred years ago, Astell recognized the hatred of all things female that is (part of) patriarchy, and the practices it leads to and requires. This description of its essence goes deeper than legal inequities and unequal opportunities, even as it perpetuates these and other injustices. "We must recognize the important place that the hatred of women has had in Western culture. . . . [F]eminism is rooted in a response to this kind of hatred" (Lister 2004, 72). As elsewhere, Astell sees this dynamic to be true not only in male-female relationships, but in most unequal relationships: the powerful often despise those they govern (*RM*, 84). "Power does naturally puff up, and he who finds himself

140   Feminist Interpretations of Mary Astell

exalted, seldom fails to think he *ought* to be so" (*RM*, 55). She laments that "Superiors indeed are too apt to forget the common Privileges of Mankind" (*RM*, 56). This loathing has concrete consequences, and these are perhaps what make unequal power so dangerous, so corrupting. For according to Astell, if one could have more power and also be virtuous and caring toward those with less power, then greater power could be used for the good of those with less.[5] General disdain for the female sex trickles down to the level of the individual, where actions are even more unchecked: "how can a Man respect his Wife when he has a contemptible Opinion of her and her Sex?" (*RM*, 57). Astell draws out what it means for women to live with men who feel disrespect and disdain for them, and the consequences are both wide-ranging and dire. Astell challenges patriarchy at its core when she declares, by contrast, "I love my Sex" (*RM*, 29). What deeper rejection can there be of patriarchy, what fuller embracing of the grounds for an alternative vision?

Complicating matters a bit, Morgan-Curtis notes that "though most common in men, misogyny also exists in and is practiced by women against other women or even themselves. . . . [Women have] internalized their role as societal scapegoats, influenced in the twenty-first century by multimedia objectification of women with its culturally sanctioned self-loathing and fixations on plastic surgery, anorexia and bulimia" (Morgan-Curtis 2006, 443). This internalization is, according to Astell, common and devastating. The "fixation" on beauty receives a great deal of her attention; in fact, it frames and forms the opening rounds of *A Serious Proposal*. She notes that women think too humbly of themselves (*SP I*, 54), are "insensible of their own worth" (*SP I*, 59), and believe the lies told them about their nature and capacities. Unfortunately, they respond to the devaluation in a self-defeating way, putting even more time into "improving" their physical appearance and trying to please men not worth the trouble of pleasing. But they understand that much is at stake in pleasing those who hold power in one's daily life.

Further, Astell understands that patriarchal rules for women are such that to follow them is actually to risk reinforcing the inequality that injures them, while to break them is to risk bringing forth negative consequences ranging from ridicule to physical punishment. An example of such a rule is how it is "thought a Wife's Duty to suffer everything without Complaint" (*RM*, 18). When followed, this silences women and leaves injustice unchallenged; when opposed, women are at well-documented risk of censure or retaliation. Qualities defined as virtues for women are also practices, temperaments, and values that perpetuate their subordination. For example, humility and modesty make it difficult or inappropriate to speak up, or to challenge the status quo. Consequently, revealing the self-preserving nature of the system, those qualities required to free or elevate oneself are deemed inappropriate for women. Such prerequisites might include "a few hours Solitude, a little Meditation and Watchfulness" (*SP II*, 133) or, later, a room of one's own, if we anticipate Virginia Woolf's attraction to Astell. Astell also understands that in a patriarchy, women are often blamed for having "by nature" those weaknesses and defects that are in fact the *product* of inequality. "Women are from their very Infancy debar'd those Advantages, with the want of which, they are afterwards reproached, and nursed up in those Vices which will hereafter be upbraided to them" (*SP I*, 60). These "reproaches" and "upbraidings" are self-serving to those with more power; ultimately, they function to justify men being "elevated in the social structure . . . and women devalued for their supposed lack of control—women are assumed to need men's supervision, protection, or control" (Johnson 2005, 47) . This is quintessential patriarchy in action: a trait/function associated with women is defined as a problem or inadequacy, its existence is attributed to their nature, and the "solution" is male power over women. Feminism, by contrast, questions the existence of the problem, interrogates possible causes, and seeks solutions consistent with diverse women's human dignity and self-respect. And these are precisely Astell's strategies and projects, even as we might differ over some of the items on her lists.

Astell does not suggest as a solution to sexual inequality that women strive to act as men have acted, as if the male model of behavior is unproblematic. While she comes down hard on women, variously described as "cheap and contemptible" (*SP I*, 51) and "a burden and nuisance to all about them" (*SP I*, 59), she suggests that men "are very often guilty of greater faults, and such as considering the advantages they enjoy, are much more inexcusable" (*SP I*, 56). Her rejection of the male model (of behavior, education, etc.), as well as her analysis of misogyny, vice/virtue, and unequal power just discussed, confirms Spender's association of Astell with contemporary radical feminism, as does her understanding of patriarchy as illegitimate and undesirable dominance over diminished and subordinated women, and her reevaluation of the "feminine." Fascinatingly, Sharrock shows that this rejection of the male model finds expression even in Astell's writing.

In trying to circumvent masculine author-ity, Astell has not also been contending for its feminization. . . . [She] specifically rejects the

142   Feminist Interpretations of Mary Astell

title of "Author." . . . [She] links the being an "Author" with the concept of "Authority." . . . [She also] distances herself from "Authority"
by being about to write against what is "Authorize[d]." . . . The Astell
who only "reflects," like the Astell of A *Serious Proposal to the Ladies*
who only "proposes," cuts herself off from author-ity and its dual significance. It is at this point that the dynamic exchange between an
author who authorizes and an authority that commands, linguisti-
cally bonded in the text and context of authority, most evidently
admit to their guilty partnership. Rather than feminizing author-ity,
Astell presents the concept of author-ity as being detrimental to the
interests of women (1992, 112–14).

Astell manages to capture many other aspects of patriarchy that I can
only sketch here. She sees the range and depth of what is affected, from
institutional arrangements to personal psychology: woman "puts her Fortune and Person entirely in his Powers; nay even *the very desires of her
Heart* according to some learned Casuists, so as that it is not lawful to
Will or Desire any thing but what he approves and allows" (RM, 48, my
emphasis). She also recognizes that while sexual inequality is often
defended as merely reflecting the nature of things, in fact it is constantly
enforced: "A Woman will not want being admonish'd of her Duty, the
custom of the World, Economy, every thing almost reminds her of it.
Governors do not often suffer their Subjects to forget obedience through
their want of demanding it" (RM, 53–54). Further, Astell is determined to
unveil the hidden truths behind the lies of patriarchy, "to disabuse women
of their illusions about marriage" and "to decipher the deceptions men use
to seduce and ruin women for their own pleasure" (Lister 2004, 63, 61).
She shows how great inequalities survive through ordinary rituals, giving
amazing analyses of practices like courtship and flattery. "She must be a
Fool with a witness, who can believe a Man, proud and vain as he is, will
lay his boasted Authority, the Dignity and Prerogative of his Sex, one
Moment at her Feet, but in prospect of taking it up again to more advantage; he may call himself her Slave a few days but it is only in order to
make her his all the rest of his Life" (RM, 44). By contrast, Astell refuses
to offer the ladies "Fustian Complements and Fulsome Flatteries" (SP I,
52). She insists that "the deceitful Flatteries of those who under pretence
of loving and admiring you, really served their own base ends" (SP I, 74)
offers evidence of the workings of patriarchy, the "thousand seductions"
(SP I, 77) of daily life and the vulnerability to them associated with the
feminine.

Overall, then, in her treatment of patriarchy we learn that systems of political power are not limited to the governmental, or only to visible or acknowledged structures and practices. More specifically, tyranny is not limited to state despots or dictators, for male dominance satisfies all the criteria of tyrannical rule: it is a cruel, unjust, self-interested, and arbitrary system of power over women, exercised for the most part with impunity and against the interests of most individuals and the community. Power is enforced, and constantly reinforced, in this case through systems of law and custom as well as in daily rituals and practices. Power is privilege, in this instance male privilege (Astell's "Prerogative"). Power can penetrate or dissolve supposed walls between the public and private, social and individual, for a system like patriarchy infiltrates and affects both. Those theoretical boundaries may in fact make the realities of oppression harder to grapple with and oppose. Beliefs that sustain the more powerful are often internalized by the less powerful, to their detriment. But inferior power leads to a need to please those with more, which diminishes and distracts those on the bottom, and brings them closer to what the despot says they are "by nature." The effects of tyrannical rule in the household rival those more commonly objected to in political prisons and ghettos. So reveals Mary Astell, early modern theorist of power.

Epistemological Effects of Unequal Power: "Wretched Incogitancy"

Astell begins her critique of the epistemological effects of unequal power with a description of the patriarchal norm for women, which especially notes the hidden nature and misdirected use of women's knowledge. "Indeed an affected Ignorance, a humourous delicacy and niceness which will not speculate a notion for fear of spoiling a look, nor think a serious thought lest she should damp the gaiety of her humour; she who is so top full of her outward excellencies, so careful that every look, every motion, every thing about her wou'd appear in Form, as she employs her Thoughts to a very pitiful use" (SP I, 125). Women are willingly supposed to sacrifice their intellectual potential, "serious thought," for the sake of their physical beauty, social success, and conformity to feminine norms of being entertaining, nice, and attractive. Specifically, they do not take epistemological risks—"speculation"—but direct their intellect to "safe" topics and "appropriate" ends. Patriarchy rewards (at least pretended) ignorance in women, and punishes (even the appearance of) intelligence.

144   Feminist Interpretations of Mary Astell

Women knowingly practice deception, since their ignorance is "affected"; as a consequence, they misrepresent or limit their capacities and interests to things approved of by men, whose attention they desire, and thus support further disingenuous social relations. These actions also reinforce sexual inequality. As stated earlier, acts and behaviors determined to be appropriate and virtuous for women also tend to perpetuate their subordination. Further, the ends to which their knowledge may be acceptably employed are deemed "pitiful," by which Astell means they are less spiritual, inspiring, elevating, and challenging than they need to and should be. A further social consequence of the epistemological undermining of women is that this "Tyrannous Domination . . . render[s] useless if not hurtful, the Industry and Understanding of half Mankind!" (RM, 31). As if we could ever spare all that intellectual energy and insight! But clearly, advocates of inequality must be willing to sacrifice things like merit and knowledge. For different reasons, both sexes lose out on opportunities to learn—women through exclusion and suspicion of their ideas, men because they refuse to learn from their "inferiors" or about whatever content may threaten their superior social status, which is always in need of reinforcement.

Women's sacrifice is based on two assumptions that Astell will challenge: that female intellect is inherently compromised and that intellectual development is incompatible with that which is feminine and desirable. A compromised intellect implies that men's intellectual guidance is necessary for women's very survival; hence, women must attract the men they need. Further, the argument is that any intellectual sacrifice on women's part is ultimately worth it—that less intellectually and spiritually developed women are better cared for, appreciated, and cherished.

Men, on the other hand, pretend competence and wisdom where they possess neither, as these traits are associated with masculinity and authority. They pay little attention and devote little time to matters deemed the domain of women, and thus remain ignorant in these areas. Their actions reinforce their power, but also contribute to the real divorce between knowledge and power. They, too, sometimes knowingly practice deception, but have more at stake than do women in believing the lies. While both sexes contribute to the maintenance of this arrangement, men have the major role in and motive for enforcing it, since they do not try to please women but serve as judges of women's "outward excellencies."

Astell knows that women's decisions and behaviors do not emerge from nowhere. She names, and then challenges, a "secret Maxim" that women have no reason, or are "little more than Brutes" (RM, 29). Men look "down on them as void of Understanding, and full of Ignorance and Passion, so that Folly and a Woman are equivalent Terms with him" (RM, 57). Fricker explores the epistemological consequences of these phenomena, emphasizing that someone on the bottom "may lose confidence in his belief, or in his justification for it, so that he ceases to satisfy the conditions for knowledge; or, alternatively, someone with a background experience of persistent testimonial injustice may lose confidence in her general intellectual abilities to such an extent that she is genuinely hindered in her educational or other intellectual development" (2007, 47–48). This line of thought explains why Astell speaks of the need for women to overcome the belief that their "improvement" is "impossible," a belief she, like Fricker centuries later, calls a "prejudice" that functions to dissuade and undermine women. In the face of these prejudices, "my Arguments what ever they may be in themselves, are weak and impertinent to you, because you make them useless and defeat them of the End they aim at" (SP I, 121). The epistemological consequence of being on the bottom is a lack of confidence in one's own intellectual capacities, a lack that, not coincidentally, reduces the chances of resistance. Oppression works most efficiently when subjects agree with their governors' opinions of them, and fail to see the worth of their voice. Astell thus has to push the point that women "have a greater share of sense, whatever some Men affirm, than to be content to be kept any longer under their Tyranny in Ignorance and Folly" (SP I, 121).

The next assumption Astell tackles is that making these choices pays off for women. Familiar advice to women includes "Let them not by any means aspire at being Women of Understanding, because no Man can endure a Woman of Superior Sense, or wou'd treat a reasonable Woman civilly" (RM, 30). Such messages present a stark and revealing set of alternatives: women's (feigned and/or real) ignorance bolstered by civil treatment by men, or women's intellectual development at the price of men's civility. What Astell reveals is that both alternatives express contempt for women, and each threatens aspects of her well-being. Neither is acceptable. To be associated with the reason of "Brutes" is the first step of dehumanization, while association with the reason of "men" results, at best, with being a social oddity, a masculinized woman.

It is, in fact, precisely in their relationships with men that the different epistemological positions of men and women bear their most poisonous fruit—not benefits—for women. Women come to know that men think themselves too good to learn anything from a woman. The prejudice, the assumption, is that women have nothing intellectual to offer to men and are, in fact, dependent on the good sense of men. Men "are, or at least *think*

146   Feminist Interpretations of Mary Astell

themselves too wise to receive Instruction from a Womans Pen" (SP I, 56). The insult to women is deep and unmistakable, cruel and humiliating. Looked at as an epistemological community, women are on the very margins, not treated equally as givers or receivers of knowledge. Their voice is automatically muted, questioned, without the authority of men's. Like other groups deemed more "Learned," men in this epistemological community will "continue wedded to their own Opinions, because they will not take the trouble of examining what is contrary to their receiv'd doctrines" (RM, 22).

Power is connected to credibility. Those with more power have the ability to legitimize abuses (RM, 69) and to label as enemies those who tell certain truths. Some can tell truths and be labeled liars or traitors, while others can tell lies and have them accepted. The association of credibility and epistemic authority with power is an important phenomenon, with consequences that range from the psychological (self-esteem) to the social (practice of exclusion). This association especially troubles Astell. Credibility should accompany reasonableness, not power. In response, Astell often ridicules the reasons of the powerful, as when she contrasts her well-defended positions with "masculine understandings" (RM, 9) and, more implicitly, her sarcasm with "manly jests" (RM, 58). "To be wronged in one's capacity as a knower is to be wronged in a capacity essential to human value. . . . No wonder, then, that being insulted, undermined, or otherwise wronged in one's capacity as a giver of knowledge is something that can cut deep. No wonder too that in contexts of oppression the powerful will be sure to undermine the powerless in just that capacity, for it provides a direct route to undermining them in their very humanity" (Fricker 2007, 44).

Astell resists the epistemological effects by moderating the claims of those who "know more." She asserts, for example, that "Knowledge is at best defective, and always progressive, so that she who knows the most has only this advantage, that she has made a little more speed than her Neighbours" (SP I, 125). This realization makes male claims to superiority less convincing. "But where is the shame of being taught? for who is there that does not need it?" (SP I, 125). Unfortunately for us all, those in power are not necessarily smarter, or even smart, even about seemingly straightforward matters like what is in their interest.

Astell argues that far from "unnecessary" or even actively destructive, "for Women to have Knowledge, [is of] . . . very great use, . . . not only in the Conduct of her own Soul but in the management of her Family, in the Conversation of her Neighbours and in all the Concerns of Life" (SP II,

202). In addition, women's miseducation contributes to the diminishment of men, leading all farther away from fulfilling their potential in what matters most, an absolutely abominable state of affairs to Astell.

Resistance: "Can You Be in Love with Servitude and Folly"?

"Far be it from her to stir up Sedition of any sort, none can abhor it more" (RM, 8). This quote is frequently seen as evidence that Astell does not endorse far-reaching change in practice. But "sedition," crucially, implies resistance to or insurrection against lawful authority, while Astell's pen is directed against authority—like patriarchal authority—that is contrary to natural law, to justice, to reason, to God's word. To support resistance to patriarchy, then, she has to show that sexual equality and women's authority are not intrinsically unjustifiable, and that the authority of men over women has been assumed to be legitimate when it is not.

It may not be as clear as one supposes, Astell argues, who the "good guys" are and who the "bad guys." From the first page of *Reflections* she usefully confronts the distinction between friend and enemy, putting forth the idea that those advocates of greater equality for the sexes who are seen as threats may in fact be the truth-tellers, most truly concerned with "the publick Good" (RM, 8), and thus the most genuine of friends. Astell asserts that "Covenants betwixt Husband and Wife, like Laws in an Arbitrary Government, are of little Force, the Will of the Sovereign is all" (RM, 52), implying that women's resistance to male authority is not sedition, is not insurrection against "lawful authority" or against the acts of "an equitable or honest Man" (RM, 52), but more akin to legitimate action against "Arbitrary Government." In her analysis of scripture, Astell praises Rebecca for paying "greater deference [than does Isaac] to the Divine Revelation, and for this Reason at least, ha[ving] a Right to oppose her Husband's Design" (RM, 23). More generally, she claims that "the Sovereignty of a Woman is not contrary to the Law of Nature; for the Law of Nature is the Law of God . . . who Inspir'd and Approv'd that great Woman" Deborah (RM, 24). While certainly most unsympathetic with, even condemning toward, some resistance to some legitimate authority, Astell sees women's resistance to sexual inequality, especially when grounded in reason and faith, as more just and a greater expression of devotion than is men's arbitrary authority over women.

Astell herself employs numerous tactics of resistance in both her life (which I will not go into here) and her writing (which I will). She published

148   Feminist Interpretations of Mary Astell

Reflections anonymously "for very good Reasons," including that "Bold Truths may pass while the Speaker is Incognito" (RM, 7), showing her awareness of prejudice in the form of deference to arbitrary and customary authority, and her willingness—nay, her determination—to find a way around it. She redefines who is destructive, undermining, seditious, and traitorous, as well as who is a good citizen and a friend of the public good. She reasons for herself and sets herself up as her own authority, very consciously setting aside (and thus challenging the status of) those already determined by others to deserve deference, saying she "neither advis'd with Friends, nor turn'd over Ancient or Modern Authors, nor prudently submitted to the Correction of such as are, or such as think they are good Judges" (RM, 8). She ridicules the arguments of her opponents, slyly, revealingly, referring to them as examples of "masculine wisdom" (RM, 66). She makes a philosophical argument against complaisance and for individual thought. She rips away the numerous protective layers surrounding male authority, showing not only the inconsistencies of their interpretations of scripture, for example, but ridiculing their tendency to hide behind scripture to avoid argument, attacking their exclusive right to translate and interpret it, pointing out the self-interested results of their "tricks," and limiting the subjects on which scripture is authoritative. She tears apart the "logic" of every defense of women's silence, lack of education, and deficiency of reason. She redefines terms (subjection does not equal natural inferiority, and is for the benefit of the subordinated) and changes the framework (the personal will sometimes be judged by criteria used by others only in the political, and vice versa). She challenges what counts as usurpation and what does not, insisting that women's "govern[ance] in their families . . . is not usurpation" (RM, 26), but that much male authority over women is. She constantly undermines the force and worth of tradition, custom, and habit, from diverse vantage points, including the fallibility of our ancestors (SP II, 136) and the need to honor reason more than habit.

Astell's critique of the status quo is that we sacrifice ridiculously for "a Yoke of Impertinent Customs" (SP I, 28). Both *Serious Proposal* and *Reflections* simply overflow with pleas and arguments to understand just what is at stake in resistance: "our Liberty" (SP I, 120), our "own interest" (SP I, 121), the chance "to brighten and enlarge your Soul" (SP I, 122), "tranquility of mind" (SP I, 123), happiness, "*inward* Beauty" (SP I, 51), and the possibility of nurturing "that particle of Divinity within you" (SP I, 53). Not only does Astell model resistance, she encourages others to follow suit, urging women not to "be content to be kept any longer under

Astell as Analyst of Power   149

. . . [men's] Tyranny in Ignorance and Folly," and offering assurance that "it is in your Power to regain your Freedom, if you please but t'endeavour it" (SP I, 121).

She discusses at length some of what stops people, or leads them to follow the injurious and self-defeating status quo; thus she addresses the question of how and why we are able to resist. Analyzing first at the more general level, she asserts that resistance requires being "above unjust Censures," being "too steady and well resolv'd to be sham'd from her Duty by the empty Laughter of such as have nothing but airy Noise and Confidence to recommend them" (SP I, 120) But on the other hand, Astell insists that "Firmness and strength of Mind will carry us thro all these little persecutions, which may create in us some uneasiness for a while, but will afterwards end in our Glory and Triumph" (SP I, 121). Her reference to "little persecutions" is a brilliant insight into the everyday and repetitious nature of acts of domination that refuses to regard them or their influence as beneath notice. Likewise, her focus on eventual "Glory and Triumph" wisely emphasizes that the real and important choice is between freedom and enslavement, not between approval and disapproval.

Astell's thoughts on immunity to "unjust Censures" and the "empty Laughter" of overconfident and noisy persecutors lead to a more general critique of women's extreme dependence on the approval of others, and the central role male validation plays in their subordination. She recognizes the very real power of "other peoples Eyes and Sentiments." The theme of "Laughter" in particular recurs throughout history, with being "laughable" astutely understood as a weapon to keep subjugated people in line. The Declaration of Sentiments, passed at the first women's rights convention in 1848, closes by acknowledging this obstacle: "We anticipate no small amount of misconception, misrepresentation, and ridicule." This prediction turned out to be spot on, as the participants and their vision of equality were subjected to a torrent of laughter and ridicule. Elizabeth Cady Stanton wrote at some length on this subject. Women need, she said, "to buckle on the armor that can best resist the keenest weapons of the enemy—contempt and ridicule." Astell learned much of this first hand, 150 years before Seneca Falls. A Serious Proposal "was the cause of her great notoriety, only increased by the publication of Some Reflections upon Marriage in 1700. For her pains Astell was pilloried on the stage, lampooned in the press, and publicly debated by some of the greatest wits of the land" (Springborg 1996, 9). After the negative response to Proposal I, she practiced what she preached about being "very indifferent [to] what the Critics say (SP I, 119).

150   Feminist Interpretations of Mary Astell

Astell admits that resistance is work. But she asks us to compare this effort with "the Labour and Cost . . . Money [and] Pains t'obtain a gay outside" (*SP I*, 121). Her first tactic, then, is to make visible the amount of work we do to maintain the status quo, to suggest that we stop supporting that, which has costs that range from misspent money to a misspent life, and instead "Labour . . . after [what] is Beautiful and Desireable" (*SP I*, 121). Again, women's happiness, tranquility, liberty, soul, and true interest are at stake.

What to resist, as already hinted at, is tyranny, arbitrary custom, that which turns upside down the values of the world that should rank intellect above body, the spiritual over the physical, the eternal over the ephemeral, etc. Astell speaks in the harshest of terms when describing the status quo to which she objects, at times seeming to come down harder on women than do the misogynists, but not sparing men, either. A "useless wretched Life" is, like our "chains," all we really risk losing (*SP I*, 121).

Astell understands why many people put up with unequal power. Her explanations range from "Laziness and Idleness" to "Pride and Conceitedness" (*SP II*, 135–36), from ignorance of male designs to misreadings of religious texts. Men are more likely than women to resist equality, not only because they perceive inequality as in their interest, shallowly and ultimately mistakenly, but also because as the dominant sex they are more conceited than women, whom she characterizes as "preposterously humble" (*SP I*, 54).

Astell does place some limits on resistance. "But when I speak of the little deference that is to be given to Names, Authorities, and receiv'd Opinions, I extend it no farther than to matters purely Philosophical to mere Humane Truths, and do not design any Prejudice to the Authority of the Church which is of different consideration" (*SP II*, 138). But even here, she accepts that one can "draw Conclusion, contrary to what has been already determin'd by the Catholick Church, or even by that particular Church of which he is a Member, . . . [if] it does plainly and evidently contradict that sense of Holy Scripture which has been receiv'd by the Church Universal" (*SP II*, 138). And then she summarizes this in a way that makes the deference indeed seem quite modest:

> So that to acquiesce in the Authority of the Church, so far as it is here pleaded for is no more than this, The calling in to our assistance the Judgment and Advice of those whom GOD hath set over us, and consequently whom he assists in a more especial manner to discharge that Function to which he has call'd them; and, in such disputable

points as we're not able to determine for our selves, a quiet submission to the Voice of our Guides, whom Modesty will us to think have greater Abilities and Assistances, as well as more Time and Opportunity to find out the Truth than we. (*SP II*, 139)

Illegitimate, injurious, and unjust power can and should be resisted. We need both knowledge and courage in order to resist effectively. Because of the invisibility of much of the work done to maintain the status quo, resistance seems like work while going along with and supporting inequality does not, but is. Similarly, because of the invisibility of some costs of unequal power, resisting inequality requires unveiling these truths, hearing the silenced voices, and reassessing the damages, if people are going to be motivated to change. Resistance can take place, just like the exercise of power, in public and private, in personal relations and in institutions, and the effects of change in one reverberate to the others.

Conclusion

To study the powerful is not autocratic. It is simply reasonable. . . . There is, I think, a serious flaw in this analytical economy, and in the common research strategy that flows from it. It presumes that margins, silences, and bottom rungs are so naturally marginal, silent, and far from power that exactly how they are kept there could not possible be of interest to the reasoning, reasonable explainer. A consequence of this presumption is that the actual amount and the amazing variety of power that are required to keep the voices on the margins from having the right language and enough volume to be heard at the center in ways that might send shivers up and down the ladder are never fully tallied. Power, of course, only exists within a relationship. So omitting myriad strands of power amounts to exaggerating the simplicity of the entire political system.

—Cynthia Enloe, *The Curious Feminist*

What counts as "an analysis of power"? Who needs to know what, according to whom, for what purposes? Such questions mark the intellectual borders of theories of power, determine what practices fall within the scope of discussion and which are beyond it, and reveal whose experiences are used as material and guides. Astell should indeed be considered an analyst of power, one who represented significant marginalized voices and experiences routinely ignored by other political thinkers, including most in the canon. With agility, learnedness, and spirit, she expands our understanding of the tyrannical, the structures that maintain oppression, and the dire

152   Feminist Interpretations of Mary Astell

consequences of domination for all parties and for the social fabric. Certainly Enloe would qualify as a disciple of Astell, in that Enloe, like Astell, expands "the common research strategy," focuses on both the power and the perspectives of the marginalized, tallies the resources devoted to the maintenance of unequal power, and complicates the political system. Bryson notwithstanding, Astell does indeed have "an analysis of power relations." It is an analysis that helps us see both micro and macro, intersecting systems of power, the forms it can take, the costs we absorb, the mirage of benefits, the deceptions it depends upon, the web of effects it has, the possibilities and challenges of resistance.

Abbreviations

RM   Mary Astell, *Reflections upon Marriage* (1996)
SP I   Mary Astell, *A Serious Proposal to the Ladies, Part I* (1997)
SP II   Mary Astell, *A Serious Proposal to the Ladies, Part II* (1997)

Notes

1. As Springborg notes (RM, 40n5), the Oxford English Dictionary defines "ruel" as "A bedroom, where ladies of fashion in the seventeenth and eighteenth centuries, especially in France, held a morning reception for persons of distinction; hence, a reception of this kind." I have never seen the aspect of women's education deemed "Affliction," and thus referred to in the quote above, really analyzed or linked with Woolf's "poverty" and "derision."

2. We might ask, as Adrienne Rich does nearly three centuries later, "What does a woman need to know?" (1979, 240). Like Rich, Astell almost offers an epistemology for/of the oppressed, and asks both "What do the subordinated need to know?" and "What does an educated woman need to know?"

3. Not always or necessarily, of course. Her analysis of the behavior of the Duchess of Mazarine, and her recommendations that oppressed women turn toward the spiritual, show that she knows women frequently choose what she clearly sees as less desirable, less constructive paths.

4. Astell is aware of the infinity of forms of mechanisms that sustain dominance. She opens A Fair Way with a list of tools and tactics that people bring to their battles. Among them: "Rudeness, Ill-manners, Opprobrious Language, Bitter Scurrilous Invectives, Rallying and Bullying, Barbarus Designs, Fools Coat, Knaves Coat and Traitors Coat . . . Lampooning, Insolent Behaviour, Gallows and Galleys, Essences of Persecution, Gall not a little and prejudice to Extremity, Positive Untruths . . . [and] Lies" (Astell 1996a, 88). Quite a list, by quite an observant analyst.

5. Whether she is assuming that those with less power are inferior in other ways—that they need "improving" in a way the more dominant do not—is a question for another day.

9

Mary Astell's Feminism

A Rhetorical Perspective

Christine Mason Sutherland

My interest in Mary Astell comes out of my work as a historian of rhetoric, in particular women's rhetoric—the art of communication—in which she was both a theorist and a practitioner. Instruction in rhetoric forms an important part of the advice she gives her readers to assist them in educating themselves. She hoped that by educating the women of her time she could help them to lead happier and more useful lives. The women she addressed were the "ladies": that is, women of the upper or genteel classes. Her first concern was with the unmarried, who were often scantily provided for, if at all, by their families, and unable to find employment; but later she addressed the troubles of the married, who she believed were often subject to abuse of various kinds. As I hope to show, training in rhetoric could, she thought, alleviate the troubles of both these groups.

154   Feminist Interpretations of Mary Astell

But first it will be useful to say something about the rhetorical tradition and women's relationship with it. The formal study of the practice of rhetoric began in the fifth century B.C. with Plato, who theorized it in broad outline, and Aristotle, who developed the theory, with modifications, in much more detail. Isocrates, contemporary with Plato, founded a school of rhetoric, and it was this educational tradition that survived the fall of Athens and was eventually taken up by republican Rome. Here it served as the foundation of the educational system. Essentially this rhetoric was the art of public speaking—though its principles were extended to include certain kinds of writing as well as speech—and it was designed to be used in the courts of law and in the political assembly, with arguments on both sides of a particular issue and a judge or jury or audience to decide the outcome. Hence it was known as contentio, a public battle of words. Such rhetoric functioned best under the democracy of ancient Athens or the republic in pre-imperial Rome. Without such political systems it often went into decline and underwent various transformations, but it was revived in something like its classical form in the Renaissance, when it again became of the first importance in education.

Since in classical Greece and Rome women were normally excluded from public debate in political assemblies and the law courts, they were not usually educated in rhetoric, though there were some exceptions (Cape 1997). Again, in the Renaissance, rhetoric was thought to be an unsuitable study for women, but during the sixteenth century some upper-class women were trained in it, although for the most part they did not participate in the public oral exercise of it. The great exception is, of course, Queen Elizabeth I of England. But although women were normally excluded from this mainstream rhetoric—contentio—there was another form of it, recognized by Cicero, sermo: the private or semipublic rhetoric of social conversation and letters. This too had its importance both in the practice of Cicero and in the Renaissance, when treatises often took the form of letters. Although they almost certainly did not see themselves as practicing a form of rhetoric, women naturally engaged in conversation and in letter writing. In certain situations, indeed, women have been not only allowed but also expected to participate in it. In the home, and in particular in the education of children, conversation has always been of the first importance. The greatest Roman teacher of rhetoric, Quintilian, recognized the significant part played by women's conversation in early childhood education (1989, 21–23). Moreover, it has often been the responsibility of women to spread family news and maintain family relationships by writing letters. It is this kind of rhetoric, sermo, that Mary Astell attempted to upgrade, theorize, and recommend to her audience of women in *A Serious Proposal to the Ladies, Part II.*

Astell's theory not only draws upon the ancient authorities, but also owes much to philosophers and rhetoricians who were closer to her own day. Among English thinkers, especially important were the Cambridge Platonists: Ralph Cudworth, the most celebrated of them, had influenced her uncle, Ralph Astell, the Anglican priest who gave her early instruction. However, the Cambridge Platonist who most strongly influenced her was John Norris of Bemerton, with whom she engaged in a long correspondence, later published as *Letters Concerning the Love of God.* Her relationship with John Locke (who was not a Cambridge Platonist) was more complicated: in spite of disagreeing radically with his latitudinarianism, she respected his ideas about style and recommended them to her ladies (*SP II*, 139).

Most of the important contemporary influences on Astell, however, were French. Petrus Ramus (1515–1572), for example, was at the forefront of the movement treating logic and rhetoric as separate disciplines, and his ideas were particularly influential in England: thus Astell's own treatment of logic precedes her discussion of rhetoric. She was also influenced by Descartes and by Poulain de la Barre, the latter of whom applied Cartesian philosophical principles to his discussion of women's rhetoric. And we know that Astell admired other French writers closer to her own time, especially Malebranche and Madeleine de Scudéry. Above all, she draws extensively on Antoine Arnauld and Pierre Nicole, and Bernard Lamy, whom she cites (along with Locke) in *A Serious Proposal, Part II.* I discuss some of these writers below.

Astell believed that the women she addressed were seriously undereducated, and she wrote the second part of her *Serious Proposal* to help them begin the project of educating themselves, until such time as the Protestant monastery she had proposed in *Part I* should be founded. The education she outlines in *A Serious Proposal, Part II* is designed to improve the lot of the ladies themselves, but also to enable them to be useful in their world. It was therefore important that she should teach them rhetoric, the art of effective communication, and this she does in chapter 3 of *A Serious Proposal, Part II.*

Astell precedes her discussion of rhetoric by a long discussion of logic, which is to be seen as an essential preliminary; authorities in rhetoric held that there must be wisdom as well as eloquence—res as well as verba: eloquence without wisdom, they held, is empty and valueless; wisdom without eloquence is ineffective. The relationship between rhetoric and logic, or dialectic, is an ancient one: Aristotle sees rhetoric as the counterpart of dialectic. Traditionally dialectic, or logic, dealt with general universal

156   Feminist Interpretations of Mary Astell

propositions; it was the business of rhetoric to apply such principles to specific contexts and situations. Much closer to Astell's time, Francis Bacon had made a similar distinction: "logic handleth reason exact and in truth, and rhetoric handleth it as it is planted in popular opinions and manners . . . for the proofs and demonstrations of logic are toward all men indifferent and the same; but the proofs and persuasions of rhetoric ought to differ according to the auditors" (1974, 141).

Because a grounding in logic was essential to the proper practice of rhetoric, Astell discusses it at length. The logic she recommends is drawn not from traditional sources but from the (then) new principles of Descartes. She does not name him, referring to him instead as "a Celebrated Author" (*SP II*, 123), but a comparison between his principles as set forth in *Discourse on Method* and Astell's in *A Serious Proposal, Part II* shows how far she was indebted to him.

Descartes's four rules are as follows:

> I believed that the following four rules would be sufficient for me, provided I made a firm and constant resolution not even once to fail to observe them:
> The first was never to accept anything as true that I did not plainly know to be such; that is to say, carefully to avoid hasty judgment and prejudice; and to include nothing more in my judgments than what presented itself to my mind so clearly and so distinctly that I had no occasion to call it in doubt.
> The second, to divide each of the difficulties I would examine into as many parts as possible and as was required in order better to resolve them.
> The third, to conduct my thoughts in an orderly fashion, by commencing with those objects that are simplest and easiest to know, in order to ascend little by little, as by degrees, to the knowledge of the most composite things, and by supposing an order even among those things that do not naturally precede one another.
> And last, everywhere to make enumerations so complete and reviews so general that I was assured of having omitted nothing. (*DM*, 11)

Here are Mary Astell's six rules:

> Rule I Acquaint our selves thoroughly with the State of the Question, have a Distinct Notion of our Subject whatever it be, and of Terms we make use of, Knowing precisely what it is we drive at.

Rule II Cut off all needless Ideas and whatever has not a necessary connexion to the matter under Consideration.

Rule III To conduct our Thoughts by order, beginning with the most Simple and Easie Objects, and ascending by Degrees to the Knowledge of the most Compos'd.

Rule IV Not to leave any part of our Subject unexamin'd. . . . To this Rule belongs that of Dividing the Subject of our Meditations into as many parts as we can, and as may be requisite to Understand it perfectly.

Rule V Always keep our Subject Directly in our Eye, and Closely pursue it thro all our Progress.

Rule VI To judge no further than we Perceive, and not to take any thing for Truth, which we do not evidently Know to be so. (*SP II*, 128)

It is immediately apparent that Astell's rules of logic have been inspired by Descartes, but she accommodates his directions to her primary audience of women. Since they are less well educated than the audience for which he wrote, and their position in the world is different, she adds advice that she believes they especially need to follow. In particular, the women need to guard against hastiness and lack of focus. For example, in her commentary on Rule II, she warns them about "those Causeless Digressions, tedious Parentheses and Impertinent Remarques, which we meet with in some authors. For, as when our Sight is diffus'd and extended to many objects at once, we see none of them Distinctly; so when the Mind grasps at every Idea that presents it self [or] rambles after such as relate not to its present Business, it loses its hold and retains a very feeble Apprehension of that which it shou'd Attend" (*SP II*, 126). It appears that Astell sees digression as a particular danger for her audience. She remarks on other rules too. Especially interesting is her comment on Rule IV, derived from Descartes's Rule IV, for here she feeds in ideas of decorum: "A Moral Action may in some Circumstance be not only Fit but Necessary, which in others, where Time and Place and the like have made an alteration, wou'd be most Improper; so that if we venture to Act on the former Judgment, we may easily do amiss, if we wou'd Act as we ought, we must view its New Face, and see with what Aspect that looks on us" (*SP II*, 127). Here we have a particularly good example of Astell's accommodation of Descartes's ideas to her own audience, for obviously propriety is of great concern in rhetoric, and it was especially so to her highborn ladies, as it was to Astell herself. Completeness for Astell and her audience includes, as it does not for Descartes, a study of the rhetorical situation: a change in time and place will

158   Feminist Interpretations of Mary Astell

involve a reconsideration of the facts, a different selection from them, perhaps, and a new presentation.

Rule V adds to those given by Descartes, and it is again apparent that Astell sees her audience as needing this particular piece of advice. As with Rule II, there is a danger of wandering attention, distraction, inattention to detail, so that the thinking becomes superficial, logically disconnected. Having directed her readers to keep the subject in view, she goes on, "there being no better Sign of a good Understanding than Thinking Closely and Pertinently, and Reasoning dependently, so as to make the former part of our Discourse a support to the Latter, and *This* an Illustration of *That*, carrying Light and Evidence in ev'ry step we take" (*SP II*, 127). This instruction in the process of logical argumentation is particularly necessary for her audience of women, who would be far more comfortable with a narrative than with an argumentative approach.

Astell's rules for thinking are combined with instructions for arrangement. Thus, Rule III is "to conduct our Thoughts by Order, beginning with the most Simple and Easie Objects," and Rule IV stresses the importance of recapitulation and the drawing of conclusions at the end of each part of the discourse. She reiterates and extends this advice in her later discussion of rhetoric. In fact, she finds it ultimately impossible to separate the method of thinking from organization, and organization from style. Thus, in her praise of clearness in style, she speaks of the importance of "Exactness of Method," which leads to "putting every thing in its proper place with due Order and Connexion," such that "the Readers Mind is gently led where the Writer wou'd have it" (*SP II*, 138).

The passage on logic in *A Serious Proposal, Part II* is followed by a much shorter one on rhetoric. In her advice on logic Astell has used the (to her) modern ideas of Descartes, but in her instruction on rhetoric she is almost certainly influenced by an ancient authority, Cicero (Herberg 1999). Here, though she does not cite him, she appears to be drawing on a passage in his *De Officiis*, where he recognizes sermo, semipublic and private communication—conversation and letters—as a legitimate form of rhetoric:

> The power of speech . . . is great, and its function is twofold: the first is oratory; the second, conversation. Oratory is the kind of discourse to be employed in pleadings in court and speeches in popular assemblies and in the senate; conversation should find its natural place in social gatherings, in informal discussions, and in intercourse with friends; it should also seek admission at dinners. There are rules for

Astell's Feminism   159

oratory laid down by rhetoricians; there are none for conversation; and yet I do not know why there should not be. (1913, 135)

Cicero goes on to specify the particular characteristics of sermo: it should be "easy and not dogmatic" (1913, 137)—that is, unlike contentio, it should not be confrontational. Cicero mentions courtesy and consideration as its important features: one should be careful not to hurt the feelings of others, avoiding anything that might give them offence. One should above all avoid boastfulness and a rude taking-over of the conversation: others must be allowed to speak. Extreme emotion, especially anger, should be avoided, and if reproof becomes necessary it should be offered tactfully and without the use of offensive language; and the voice should be clear and musical. In short, sermo belongs to our private, or semi-public, social life, and engages the same virtues as social behavior.

The similarities between Cicero's discussion and Astell's advice on rhetoric to the ladies are so strong as to suggest that she had read Cicero. Here are some of the similarities:

1. The importance of a musical voice (Cicero 1913, 135): Astell acknowledges this, reassuring her audience that "Nature does for the most part furnish 'em [women] with such a Musical Tone, Perswasive Air and winning Address as renders their Discourse sufficiently agreeable in Private Conversation" (*SP II*, 143).
2. The avoidance of dogmatism (Cicero 1913, 137). Astell: "Truth when Dogmatically dictated is apt to offend our Readers and make them imagine their Liberty's impos'd on, so far is Positiveness from bringing any body over to our Sentiments" (*SP II*, 141).
3. The importance of courtesy and consideration for others (Cicero 1913, 139). Astell: "we should therefore be careful that nothing pass from us which upbraids our Neighbours ignorance, but study to remove't without appearing to take notice of it" (*SP II*, 141).
4. The avoidance of boasting (Cicero 1913, 141). Astell: "Whence come those sharp Reflections, those imagin'd strains of Wit, not to be endur'd among Christians, and which serve not to convince but to provoke, whence come they but from Ill-nature or revenge, from a Contempt of others and a desire to set forth our own Wit? Did we write less for our selves we should sooner gain our Readers, who are many times disgusted with a well writ Discourse if it carries a tange of Ostentation" (*SP II*, 143).

160   Feminist Interpretations of Mary Astell

However, apparent as her debt to Cicero is, Astell is writing not from a classical but from a Christian perspective: she consistently relates faults in writing to moral deficiencies such as pride, vanity, and self-regard. And she concludes that "the way to be good Orators [she means communicators] is to be good Christians, the Practice of Religion will both instruct us in the Theory, and most powerfully enforce what we say of it. . . . Besides, by being True Christians we have Really that Love for others which all who have a desire to perswade must pretend to; we've that *Probity* and *Prudence*, that *Civility* and *Modesty* which the Masters of this Art say a good Orator must be endow'd with" (*SP II*, 142).

What Astell has done, then, is to redeploy the precepts of ancient Rome from a Christian point of view; and in this melding of classical advice with the precepts of Christian morality, she draws upon the work of Bernard Lamy, the seventeenth-century French philosopher, who also brought classical and Christian rhetorical precepts together, and whose *L'art de parler* she cites. Like Astell in the passage quoted above, Lamy believes that the guiding principle should be love. Both see pride as inhibiting communication; nothing (according to Lamy) "is so invincible an obstacle to perswasion as arrogancy and boldness" ([1675] 1986, 333). Astell makes the same point: "There's nothing more improper than Pride and Positiveness" (*SP II*, 141). Both see that the audience must not be humiliated: Lamy recommends that effective persuaders should "with such art conceal their triumph, that the vanquish't person is scarce sensible of his defeat, but rather thinks himself victorious over that error to which he was before a slave" ([1675] 1986, 355). We can hear echoes of Lamy in Astell when she makes the same point: "And since many would yield to the Clear Light of Truth wer't not for the shame of being overcome, we should Convince but not Triumph, and rather Conceal our Conquest than publish it" (*SP II*, 140).

What is especially noticeable in her use of Lamy, however, is how she adapts his masculine rhetoric to her own purpose and her own audience of women. For example, she takes a very different attitude to the relationship between speech and writing. He thinks they have little in common; she, on the other hand, like that classical authority on rhetoric, Quintilian, believes that there is a mutually supportive relationship: "I have made no distinction in what has been said between Speaking and Writing, because tho they are talents which do not always meet, yet there is no material difference between'em. They write best, perhaps, who do't with the gentile and easy aire of Conversation; and they Talk best who mingle Solidity of Thought with th'agreeableness of a ready Wit" (*SP II*, 143). Moreover, she has an altogether more optimistic view of human nature. Lamy is not entirely convinced that people have a natural appetite for the truth. Astell, on the other hand, is: "Truth is so very attractive, there's . . . a natural agreement between our Minds and it" (360). In particular, she eschews the model of warfare that he uses in chapter 4, where he makes a comparison between a soldier fighting and an orator speaking. He, of course, is addressing young men and instructing them in the principles of contentio; Astell is concerned, in her rhetorical theory, with her audience of women and with sermo.

How did Astell hope to benefit women by this instruction in rhetoric? We must bear in mind that when she wrote the second part of her *Proposal*, she was still hoping that the Protestant monastery she had promoted in the first part would be built. The residents in this institution would be upper-class who for whatever reason—lack of dowry, lack of opportunity—failed to enter the only career open to them, marriage. The foundation would provide education for the women themselves—in itself, a great benefit in Astell's estimation—and also prepare them to teach young girls. They would therefore need to know how to think and how to communicate. The instruction in rhetoric—thinking and communicating—was devised as an interim measure until the foundation could be established. Astell wanted to improve the material situation of the ladies in poverty, but she also wanted to address the morals of the rich. In her view, many upper-class women wasted their time in frivolous pursuits when as fully rational human beings they could use their minds for their own benefit and that of their community. Knowing how to use their minds and how to transmit their thoughts would, Astell believed, improve their behavior and greatly add to their happiness.

Though making her original proposal on behalf of unmarried women, Astell later saw the necessity to intervene on behalf of abused wives. Here, too, instruction in rhetoric might serve women well, especially instruction in how to think. In her view, women often made bad marriages because they had not been taught how to make a good choice of husband. She develops this idea at length in *Reflections upon Marriage*: "If a woman were duly Principled and Taught to know the World, especially the true Sentiments that Men have of her, and the Traps they lay for her under so many gilded Compliments, and such a seemingly great Respect, that disgrace wou'd be prevented which is brought upon too many Families, and Women would Marry more discreetly, and demean themselves better in a Married State than some People say they do" (RM, 74). The absolute necessity of the women's learning to think for themselves she stresses again in *The Christian Religion*: "If GOD had not intended that Women shou'd use their

162   Feminist Interpretations of Mary Astell

Reason, He wou'd not have given them any, for He does nothing in vain" (CR, 6). Women must know not only how they ought to live, but also why: most of the "Follies and Vices that Women are subject to . . . are owing to our paying too great a deference to other Peoples judgments, and too little to our own, in suffering others to judge for us, when GOD has not only allow'd, but requir'd us to judge for our selves" (CR, 36).

One result of the instruction in logic, then, should be the ability of women to choose suitable husbands. They will be able to see through the self-serving flattery of immoral gentlemen and know how to identify and value true goodness. But such protection against false suitors was not the only result of her teaching that Mary Astell hoped for. Although in A Serious Proposal, Part II she excludes women from speaking in Parliament, the courts of law, and the Church, she sees that they can, and ought, nevertheless, to make a contribution to the public good: "the true Christian seeks a Reputation from Vertues of a Public, not of a Private Nature" (CR, 325). Astell believed that because of the leisure they enjoyed, women could potentially make a contribution to scholarship: "And since it is allow'd on all hands, that the Mens Business is without Doors, and their's is an Active Life; Women who ought to be Retir'd, are for this reason design'd by providence for Speculation: Providence, which allots every one an Employment, never intended that anyone shou'd give themselves up to Idlenes and Unprofitable amusements. And I make no question but that great Improvements might be made in the Sciences, were not Women enviously excluded from this their proper Business" (CR, 296).

Such writing would probably take the form of letters. The writing of letters is particularly important in the history of women's rhetoric. It was originally a private form, and therefore women were not only free to engage in it but often were positively encouraged by their men folk to do so. In the fifteenth century, "men both tolerated and positively expected women to partake in letter-writing" (Truelove 2001, 44). It was letter-writing that opened up possibilities for women to escape from the sphere of private rhetoric into the public domain. Though originally a private form, it had very early been taken over for public discourse. Cicero himself had used it in this way. And his letters had been used as a model by some scholars of the Renaissance (Henderson 1983). It was this ambiguous characteristic of the letter that could be exploited by women to preserve decorum by writing in an ostensibly private form, but with a public readership in view. It was also the protection of the anonymity of print that allowed women to move into the public arena (Hiscock 1997, 411). Like most upper-class women of her time, Astell believed that it was indecent, that is, inappropriate, for women to draw attention to themselves. The man, according to the cultural values of the time, might promote himself and establish, as best he could, his personal reputation. But it was not proper for a woman to do so. The writing of letters, because it was a private form, and because it allowed the practice of anonymity, was an acceptable vehicle for women's engagement in rhetoric. Yet in the above quotation Astell suggests that scholarly research was an activity from which women were debarred. They were thus debarred because of considerations that went beyond decorum: they were held to be lacking in *ethos*, that is, the credibility of the writer. And since Astell did not believe in concealing the gender of the writer, this was a serious problem.

Ethos, in rhetoric, is one of the three means of persuasion identified by Aristotle, the other two being logos, the appeal to reason, and pathos, the appeal to the emotions. Ethos covers everything that is persuasive about the source of the message—the speaker or writer. Classical rhetoricians perceived three elements in ethos: intelligence, integrity, and goodwill. Intelligence includes the authority of the speaker to discuss this particular topic. Integrity is moral reliability: is the speaker honest and trustworthy? Goodwill refers to the relationship with the particular audience addressed, the extent to which the speaker has their interests at heart. If all three elements are satisfactorily present, the audience should respond by paying attention, by being receptive to the message, and by extending in their turn goodwill to the speaker. Ethos is of two kinds: intrinsic and extrinsic. Intrinsic ethos is the appeal of the writer or speaker in the text, or in the process of delivery—that is, how he or she "comes across." Extrinsic ethos concerns the reputation of the speaker, what we would now call his or her image.

Ethos has always been a problem for a woman. As Tita Baumlin has said, "Any use of public language risked the destruction of both her public image and her private virtues" (Baumlin 1994, 230). Thus, in drawing upon her ethos in order to communicate in public, a woman destroyed it. Two principles underlay this denial of standing in ethos to women: one, as we have seen, was the issue of decorum. This problem could be handled by publishing anonymously. But there remained another, much deeper problem, not social but philosophical: women were thought to be deficient in reason, and therefore also in morals. Because it was held that reason controlled the emotions and therefore moral behavior, if women were indeed to engage in scholarship, this false perception of their powers had to be corrected.

Yet Astell refers to this problem only once and then indirectly. Owing no doubt at least in part to her recognition of the weakness of women's

164   Feminist Interpretations of Mary Astell

ethos, she attempts to discount its importance. Her own view of ethos was similar to that of Plato: the truth should carry its own conviction. "If any is so needlessly curious as to enquire from what Hand they [the *Reflections*] come, they may please to know, that it is not good manners to ask, since the Title-Page does not tell them" (RM, 7). Like Plato, she believes that the source of the message should be irrelevant: "'Tis a very great Fault rather to regard who it is that Speaks, than what is Spoken, and either to submit to Authority, when we should only yield to Reason; or if Reason press too hard, to think to ward it off by Personal Objections and Reflections" (RM, 7).

However, Astell does indeed address the question of women's rationality, though she does not explicitly connect it with ethos. Her most extended discussion of it comes in the lengthy preface to the 1706 edition of *Some Reflections upon Marriage*. Responding to the criticism the book has received, she gives a full-scale defense of women's rationality. In maintaining as she does that women's reason is equal to men's, Astell was informed and supported by some of the intellectual developments of the seventeenth century. One of these was Cambridge Platonism, of which Astell was an adherent. Plato himself had a higher view of women than Aristotle, believing that those women who were to become guardians should receive the same education as men. To this Platonic position the Cambridge Platonists had added principles deriving from Christianity, especially the theology of St. Augustine of Hippo, who believed that although women might be inferior to men by nature, by grace they were their equals (Schiebinger 1989, 169), and that in the mind "there is no sex" (Harth 1992, 3). And the philosophy of Descartes encouraged women to seek their identity in the mind, not the body, which was dominated by the emotions. The liberating effect of Cartesian philosophy was, according to Ruth Perry, a key influence upon Astell: "Cartesian rationalism," she claims, "was the very cornerstone of her feminism" (Perry 1985, 491).

In her defense of woman's rationality, then, Astell argues as a Christian Platonist and also as a Cartesian. Though Descartes himself did not directly address the question of women's rationality, his disciple Poullain de la Barre did, contending that in rhetoric especially women are not only the equals of men but in some respects their superiors. Ruth Perry believes that Poullain's writings were a strong influence on Mary Astell. His work *The Equality of the Two Sexes* had been translated into English in 1677 and was published as *The Woman as Good as the Man*. And a French edition published in 1690 aroused considerable interest: "it caused quite a stir in Paris, and in 1692 and 1693, parts of it were exported to London by a

French Huguenot, named Pierre Monteux. Astell may well have read these in *The Gentlemen's Journal* or *The Ladies Journal*" (Perry 1986, 482).

Thus encouraged, Astell proceeded to argue cogently for the full rationality of women, basing her position also on common experience and on the authority of scripture. Part of her strategy is to make distinctions. One of these concerns the difference between nature and office: "we do not find that any Man thinks the worse of his own Understanding because another has superior Power, or conclude himself less capable of a Post of Honour because he is not Prefer'd to it" (RM, 16). In the hierarchical scheme (in which Astell fully believed), some people enjoyed more authority because of the office in which they served; but that did not mean that they were inherently more intelligent. She believes that women are by nature equal to men; she is, she says, "Ignorant of the *Natural Inferiority* of our Sex, which our Masters lay down as a Self-Evident and Fundamental Truth" (RM, 9), and she sees "nothing in the Reason of Things to make this either a Principle or a Conclusion, but much to the contrary" (RM, 9). The subjection of women she acknowledges as an inescapable fact, "but the Right can no more be prov'd from the Fact, than the Predominancy of Vice can justifie it" (RM, 10).

Astell makes another distinction, important at the time, between women and wives. Here she draws on her considerable knowledge of scripture and her theological expertise:

> [S]cripture commands wives to submit themselves to their own husbands; True, for which St Paul gives a mystical reason (Eph. 5.22) and St Peter a Prudential and Charitable one (I St Peter 3) but neither of them derive that subjection from the Law of Nature. Nay, St Paul, as if he foresaw and meant to prevent this Plea, giving Directions for their Conduct to Women in general (I Tim. 2), when he comes to speak of Subjection, he changes his Phrase from Women, which denotes the whole Sex, to Woman, which in the New Testament is appropriated to a Wife. (RM, 20)

In arguing for the full rationality of women, and thus establishing their ethos, even if she does not directly address their lack of it, Astell is helping to open to them the possibility of entering into the world of letters. This brings us to another point I wish to make about the feminism of Mary Astell's rhetoric: the model she provided for other women wishing to publish. For Astell herself moved from the private letter—her correspondence with John Norris—to the fully public tract, her political pamphlets. She did so by degrees. Her correspondence with Norris was not intended for publication, and in fact was not published until after *A Serious Proposal to the Ladies*. But it was begun before she wrote the proposal, and gave her her first experience of writing. In fact, as I have argued elsewhere, I believe her correspondence with Norris gave her important training as a rhetorician (Sutherland 2005, 45). When she came to write the *Proposal*, she again used the form of a letter, this time addressed to a wider audience, the ladies, though there is no doubt that she hoped her proposal would find a reader-ship beyond the upper-class women formally addressed. *A Serious Proposal, Part II* is again addressed to the ladies, though she arguably had a much wider audience in mind, including, according to Patricia Springborg, Dam-aris Masham and John Locke (Springborg 1997, xix). In *Some Reflections upon Marriage*, first published in 1700, she does not use the convention of the letter, nor is her proposed audience restricted to a single person or group of people: the audience to whom she directs the discourse is not restricted to her own sex but specifically to those who oppress women—that is, of course, what we now call the patriarchy. With this move into a more fully public arena, Astell abandons some of the principles of sermo. In her letters to Norris she shows due deference, and in her proposals to the ladies she treats her readers with tact and tenderness, herself using that gentleness and consideration she recommends to them in their practice of sermo. But in *Reflections* she moves into contentio—the battle of words—and she is unsparing in her attack upon the opposition. Although she never recommends to her ladies that they should participate in such battles, her own practice provides a model for them to follow if they should choose to do so.

Astell, then, improved women's standing in rhetorical ethos in a number of ways. She gave strong arguments for women's full rationality, and these arguments were strengthened immeasurably by her own example. By pub-lishing anonymously she conformed to the social demands of her day, not offending propriety. But although she concealed her name, she never con-cealed her sex; rather she proclaimed it. But whatever her position on ethos, since she did not conceal her sex, the credit she received for the brilliance of her own writing could not but contribute to the acceptance of women's abilities as thinkers and writers. This, and the path she forged in her achievements as a philosopher and polemicist, not only furthered the repu-tation of women in general, thus building for them a positive ethos, but also encouraged other women to follow her example.

In conclusion, then, we should consider the consequences for women of Mary Astell's achievements in rhetoric in her own time. In opening up its principles to her audience of ladies, in setting them an example by her own practice and in her arguments for their full acceptance as the intellectual equals of men, she served her own time well. It is known that she acted as a model for women in the early eighteenth century, women such as Mary Lady Chudleigh and Elizabeth Elstob, who were influenced and inspired by her (Sutherland 2005, 160). And she drew the attention of men as well: some of them admired her for her intellectual powers and her eloquence; others violently disagreed with her. Either way, she was recognized, indeed celebrated, and her success could not but have an influence on the way women were perceived. Mary Astell is an important figure in both the history of rhetoric and the history of feminism.

Abbreviations

CR   Mary Astell, *The Christian Religion, as Profess'd by a Daughter of the Church of England* (1705) (cited by page number)
DM   René Descartes, *Discourse on Method and Meditations on First Philosophy* (1980)
L   Mary Astell, *Letters Concerning the Love of God* (2005)
RM   Mary Astell, *Reflections upon Marriage* (1996)
SP II   Mary Astell, *A Serious Proposal to the Ladies, Part II* (1997)

10

Mary Astell on the Existence and Nature of God

Marcy P. Lascano

Mary Astell's philosophical theology has been largely ignored. However, there is a new modern edition of her major work in this field, *The Christian Religion*, and with it the hope of new interest in her work in this area (Astell 2013).[1] This essay will be the first to consider Astell's philosophical theology in its own right, without consideration of how her views relate to her overall political or feminist views. Here, I am concerned to show that

---

I would like to thank the participants at Women, Philosophy, and History: A Conference in Celebration of Eileen O'Neill and Her Work at Barnard College in 2009, and the 2009 "Oxford Seminar in Early Modern Philosophy, for helpful comments on earlier drafts of this essay. Many thanks must go to Martha Bolton, Don Garrett, and especially Tad Schmaltz for sharing his work on Descartes on self-existence. I would also like to thank the editors of this volume for many helpful comments and clarifications.

Astell was both active in the philosophical debates of her time concerning God's existence and nature and that she made interesting and original contributions to these philosophical subjects.

Mary Astell claims we cannot fully comprehend the nature of God "nor can any similitudes drawn from natural things, of which there are several, help us to a proper and worthy idea of the Divine Nature, tho' they may give us a faint resemblance of it" (CR, 62). In this chapter, I examine and evaluate Astell's arguments for the existence of God, and her views concerning God's attributes in her works, A Serious Proposal to the Ladies, Part II (1697) and The Christian Religion, as Profess'd by a Daughter of the Church of England (1705). I maintain that Astell's arguments for God's existence are a blend of ontological and cosmological arguments.[2] Although Astell's arguments begin with the claim that we have a natural notion of God as a being who has all the perfections, Astell does more than merely assert that this perfection entails God's existence. Astell wants to provide an argument that shows God as the sole source of perfection and existence in the world. It is only by giving a "first cause" argument that Astell can go on to show that our moral duties lie exclusively in the love of, and obedience to, God, who is the source of all happiness and life. In this section, I will demonstrate the unique features of Astell's arguments in contrast with those of her contemporaries.

Next, I consider some potential problems with her arguments and try to defend Astell against the charge of circularity and the failure to secure the unity of God. I also consider Astell's use of "Self-Existence" with respect to God. I argue that Astell follows Descartes's use of this term as meaning "having no outside cause" rather than "being uncaused." Finally, I address Astell's use of the notion of a perfection, which she maintains we cannot fully understand.

In the second part of the chapter, I explore Astell's views on the nature of God. While Astell does not think that we can comprehend the full nature of God's infinite perfections, she does think that we can have a robust enough conception of God to understand our obligations to him. Here, I discuss her views on God's goodness and perfection, omnipotence, and sovereignty.

The Existence of God

Astell, a devout Anglican and High Church Tory, thought that the love of God was the proper aim and duty of all people. As a supporter of women's

170   Feminist Interpretations of Mary Astell

education, she used theological arguments to argue for both the metaphysical and moral equality of men and women. In the second *Proposal*, Astell proffers a method for the improvement of women's understandings. The method, which is derived from Descartes's *Rules for the Direction of the Mind* (AT X, 359–472; CSM I, 9–78) and Arnauld and Nicole's *The Art of Thinking*, is given in order to help women approach learning in order to attain truth—both metaphysical and moral. In *The Christian Religion*, she encourages all people, but especially women, since she believes them to have been discouraged from contemplation, to improve their understanding of God and their place and duties in relation to him. In both these works, Astell promotes the perfection of the mind as the way to understand God, the world, and morality. Astell argues that in perfecting one's mind, one participates more fully in the perfection of God. It is through this manifestation of perfection that the world achieves its divine purpose. It is not surprising, then, that in both works, she should produce an argument for the existence of God.

Astell maintains that even a person who has had no training in divinity, by the mere use of reason, would find herself asking the questions "What am I? and from whence had I my Being?" (CR, 10). These questions are natural and fitting for creatures with reason and understanding, who are naturally inclined toward such philosophical questions, and will lead to the knowledge of their creator. In the second *Proposal*, Astell writes, "But if it be made a Question whether there is a God, or a Being Infinitely Perfect? We are then to Examin the Agreement between our Idea of God and that of Existence" (*SP II*, 180). In *The Christian Religion*, Astell notes, "If I had been admitted to converse among my Fellow-Creatures, the next thought must have been, certainly I do not owe my Being to those who are as weak, as precarious as I am; Mankind must have had a Beginning, and there must be a last resort to a Self-existing Being. And this Being which is so liberal in its communications, must needs possess in the utmost Perfection all that good which it bestows" (CR, 10).

Astell claims that even a woman, who has not be educated in theology, can use her reason to know that God exists, and to understand that he must be a perfect being. God has endowed all persons with reason in order that they may know him, come to love him, and obey his commands. She writes, "Reason is that light which God himself has set up in my mind to lead me to Him, I will therefore follow it so far as it can conduct me" (CR, 6).

Astell's arguments for the existence of God in *A Serious Proposal, Part II* and *The Christian Religion*, although they differ somewhat, combine onto-

Astell on the Existence and Nature of God   171

logical and cosmological arguments (CR, 62). Her arguments bear some resemblance to the arguments of John Locke and René Descartes. For instance, Astell favors the Lockean causal principle, *ex nihilo, nihil fit*, rather than the Cartesian containment principle *If an idea exists, then the cause of that idea must exist, too, and the cause must have at least as much formal reality as the idea has objective reality.*[3] In *The Christian Religion*, Astell begins the section concerning the existence of God as follows: "And when I think of God, I can't possibly think Him to be any other than the most Perfect Being; a Being Infinite in all Perfections" (CR, 7). These perfections include the attributes of wisdom, justice, holiness, omnipresence, and omnipotence. This idea of God also includes the idea of self-existence. She claims that self-existence "is the most remarkable, as being the original and basis of all the rest" (CR, 7). With these claims in hand, it would seem that her argument was complete. But, rather than argue that since God has all the perfections, and self-existence is a perfection, therefore God must exist (as Descartes's ontological argument runs), Astell provides a causal argument for God's self-existence and perfection. The argument she produces begins like an ontological argument, but proceeds via a causal principle to show that the collection of contingent beings must have a self-existent and perfect cause of their existence.

In the second *Proposal*, Astell says that when we ask "whether there is a God, or a being infinitely perfect," we must consider the agreement between the idea of God and the idea of existence (SP II, 180).[4] Here, Astell claims that we can know via intuition that these ideas agree. Astell argues that it is by examining our ideas, searching for the agreement or disagreement between them, that we can see that perfection contains the idea, or notion, of existence. For we see that the notion of a perfect being must contain the notion of existence as a part. This is true, she argues, for "tho the Idea of Existence is not Adequate to that of Perfection, yet the Idea of Perfection includes that of Existence" (SP II, 180). She maintains that existence is the foundation of all the other perfections, "since that which has no Being cannot be suppos'd to have any Perfection" (SP II, 180). That is, a being must have existence in order for a perfection to inhere in it. Thus, existence is the ground of all perfection.

The second portion of each of Astell's arguments is cosmological. In the second *Proposal*, she signals the change with new questions: "Why is it necessary that All Perfection shou'd be Centered in One Being, is't not enough that it be parcel'd out amongst many? And tho it be true that that Being who has all Perfection must needs Exist, yet where's the Necessity of an All-Perfect Being?" (SP II, 180).[5] Astell tells us that in order to answer

172   Feminist Interpretations of Mary Astell

this question, we must "look about for Proofs and Intermediate Ideas." Astell claims that "the Objection it self will furnish us with one" (*SP II*, 180). She goes on to argue that the many particular ideas of perfections which one might compound to make an idea of one all perfect being are the ideas of creatures. Creatures must be created, and so the intermediate idea of creature will lead us to their creator. She writes, "Now this idea [of Creature] naturally suggests to us that of Creation, or a Power of giving Being to that which before the exerting of that Power had none, which Idea if we use it as a Medium, will serve to discover to us that necessity of an All-Perfect Being" (*SP II*, 181).

Astell then proceeds to argue that whatever has any perfection must either get it from itself or from another. Creatures have perfections, but they cannot give them to themselves, for they cannot give themselves existence (which Astell thinks is the basis for all other perfections). In addition, they cannot receive their perfection from other creatures because, as Astell writes, "For tho some Particular Beings may seem to be the Cause of the Perfections of others, as the Watch-maker may be said to be the Cause of the Regular Motions of the Watch, yet trace it a little farther, and you'l find this very Cause shall need another, and so without End, till you come to the Foundation-head, to that All-Perfect Being, who is the last resort of your Thoughts, and in whom they Naturally and Necessarily rest and terminate" (*SP II*, 181).

In *The Christian Religion*, Astell notes that if God does not receive his existence from himself, then there must be something greater and more perfect than him from whom he gets his existence and perfections. However, this is impossible. For by supposition, in order for something to be God, it must have all the perfections. God is the perfect being (there is no greater being). She proceeds by showing that contingent beings cannot be the cause of themselves. She writes, "That there is a self-existing being is evident to the meanest understanding, for without it there could have been no men, no world, no being at all. Since that which once was not, could never have made itself; nor can any being communicate that to another which it has not itself. Therefore the self-existing being must contain all other perfections; therefore, it must be an intelligent being, and therefore, it must be God" (*CR*, 8).

Astell's argument might be formalized as follows:

1. If God is not self-existent, then he must be caused by something else.
2. No being can communicate that to another that which it lacks (for if it did, then something would come from nothing).

3. Therefore, if God is not self-existent, then there must be a being more perfect than him.
4. It is not possible that there be a being more perfect than God (for by supposition God is simply the being that contains all the perfections).
5. Therefore, God is self-existent and all perfect.
6. That which once was not can never be self-existent (for then something would come from nothing).
7. Man, the world, and all beings once were not.
8. Therefore, man, the world, and all beings are not self-existent.
9. Man, the world, and all other beings must be caused by something that is self-existent (otherwise something would have had to come from nothing).
10. That self-existent being which caused man, the world, and all other beings must contain all the perfections found in the things it causes.
11. Therefore, that self-existent being which created all things must be all perfect.
12. Therefore, that self-existent being which created all things is the all perfect God.

One might wonder why Astell does not rest content with the ontological portion of the argument. But we must bear in mind Astell's larger theological and moral concerns. Astell wants to show not only that God exists, but also our relation to him. Thus, it is necessary that she provide an argument that shows him as the creator of all things in order to establish our absolute dependence on God.

Although Astell's arguments bear some resemblance to those of Descartes, they are different in several important aspects. First, Astell's methodology differs from Descartes's in that she is concerned to show the relations of our ideas. Second, her arguments use a different, and perhaps more reasonable, causal principle—*ex nihilo, nihil fit*. Instead of assuming that existence is a property that must belong to a perfect being, as in some ontological arguments, she argues that if self-existence were not a predicate of such a being, we would have a violation of the *ex nihilo* principle. Likewise, Astell argues that a perfect being must exist in order to create all the attributes that are exhibited in the world; otherwise, something would come from nothing. She utilizes the *ex nihilo* principle in order to generate the causal principle that *a cause must have the perfections that it communicates to the effect.* She argues that if an effect could have some attribute or

174   Feminist Interpretations of Mary Astell

perfection that the cause lacks, then those perfections would have to come from nothing. It is clear from her discussion of the attributes of God that the cause of an effect must have the perfections it communicates in at least an equal or greater degree than the effect, but it need not contain the perfections in the same manner in which they are manifested in the effect. Here she seems to follow Descartes in thinking that a being with more overall perfection is capable of producing any of the effects found in lesser beings.

Objections

The first charge that one might level against the argument is that of apparent circularity. After all, Astell does begin her argument for the existence of God by claiming that God is a being who must contain all the perfections. If one is trying to prove the existence of a perfect being, then it seems that beginning with the premise that God is a perfect being is not appropriate. Circularity is a common charge against the ontological argument, for it seems that such arguments attempt to define God into existence. However, while Astell does claim that God is a being with all the perfections, we should read her as arguing that *if* God exists, then he must be a being with all the perfections. If there is no being with all the perfections, then there is no God. She argues it is necessary, given the existence of the perfections we see in the world, that a most perfect being exists.

The second problem that one might notice with the argument is that it seems that Astell has failed to show that there is only one self-existent being. This is a common difficulty in cosmological arguments that employ the causal principle *ex nihilo, nihil fit*. Locke, whose argument utilizes this principle, is accused by Leibniz of making the same mistake (Leibniz 1981, IV.x.6, 436). While the principle may guarantee that there must be some cause, it is not strong enough to show that there must be only one. Locke, when pressed in his correspondence with van Limborch on this matter, provided additional arguments for the claim that there can be only one omnipotent being (Locke 1981, vol. 6, 789). Astell proposes the question "Why is it necessary that All Perfection shou'd be Centered in One Being, is't not enough that it be parcel'd out amongst many?" (*SP II*, 180). Her answer is that when we imagine that perfection can be dispersed through a number of beings, we are actually imagining his creation, which is just that—the distribution of perfection into multiple beings. However, Astell argues that it is just this distribution of perfection that is in need of

Astell on the Existence and Nature of God   175

explanation and that will lead us to the inevitable idea of a single self-existent perfect being. In doing so, she turns this standard objection on its head. She writes, "For those Many whose Particular Ideas it wou'd have joyn'd together to make a Compound one of All Perfection, are no other than Creatures, as will appear if we consider our Idea of a Particular Being and of Creature, which are so far from having any thing to distinguish 'em, that in all Points they resemble each other" (*SP II*, 181).

Third, one might object to Astell's contention that God is *self-caused.* Some of Astell's contemporaries held that since God is an eternal and immutable being, God is simply uncaused. In Aristotelian terms, he is the "uncaused cause" or "unmoved mover." The notion of self-existence or self-causation was one that many philosophers and theologians resisted because they held that a cause must always precede its effect. This renders the notion of self-causation nonsensical since it is impossible for something to exist prior to causing its own existence. In addition, it was deemed somehow unfitting to speak of God as having any cause at all—even if it was himself. Descartes met with much resistance from Arnauld after claiming, in reply to Caterus's objections to the *Meditations,* "There is no need to say that God is the efficient cause of himself, for this might give rise to a verbal dispute. But the fact that God derives his existence from himself, or has no cause apart from himself, depends not on nothing but on the real immensity of his power; hence, when we perceive this, we are quite entitled to think that in a sense he stands in the same relation to himself as an efficient cause does to its effect" (AT VII, 111; CSM II, 80).

Here, Descartes maintains that there is a positive reason for God's existence, which is found in God's immense power. However, Arnauld rejected the idea that God's existence has any efficient cause, on the ground that nothing can stand in the proper relation to itself to be an efficient cause of itself. Arnauld claimed that God requires no cause of his existence because his existence is identical to his essence. Indeed, Descartes conceded this point in the Fourth Replies to the *Meditations.* However, Descartes maintains that in order to posit a cosmological argument for God's existence, we must be able to ask of anything, including God, what is the cause of its existence. If we exclude God from causal consideration before proving his existence, then we beg the question. If we understand *causa sui,* or self-existence, as being without a cause, then we undermine the causal principle used to generate the argument, namely, that since nothing can come from nothing, all things must have a cause or reason for their existence.

Descartes goes on to maintain that God's immense power is closer to the Aristotelian "formal cause." That is, God's power is not itself an efficient

176   Feminist Interpretations of Mary Astell

cause, but it does provide the reason or cause of there being no such efficient cause.[6]

Astell too seems to equate being self-existent with being without any outside cause rather than being simply uncaused. Astell writes of self-existence, "For if God deriv'd His Being from any but Himself, there must be something Greater and more Perfect than God, which is absurd, since God is by the supposition the most Perfect Being, and consequently Self-existing. Because there can be no Absolute and Infinite Perfection but where there is Self-existence; for from whence shall it be derived? And Self-existence is such a Perfection as necessarily includes all other Perfections" (CR, 8).

In the second *Proposal*, Astell explicitly states that she does not take God to be self-caused, but that he must exist by virtue of his nature. Astell writes,

> If to this it be Objected that we as good as affirm that this All-Perfect Being is his own Maker, by saying that he is Self-Existent, and so we fall into the same Absurdity which we imputed to that Opinion which supposes that Creatures were their own Maker. The reply is easie, That we do not say he Made him self, we only affirm that his Nature is such, that tho we can't sufficiently Explain because we can't comprehend it, yet thus much we can discern, that if he did not Exist of himself no other Being could ever have Existed. (SP II, 181)

Astell's argument for God's existence is based on the causation of perfections. In order for the argument to justify stopping at God as the first and sole cause of all perfections, she must explain how God's perfections come into existence. Here, I believe that, like Descartes, Astell sees God's nature as a positive cause or reason for his perfections.[7] She does not hold that God is the efficient cause of his perfections, for she seems to believe that efficient causes must precede their effects. Thus, we must understand her not as saying that God is the efficient cause of himself, but rather that God's nature is the ground of all existence, including his own.

Finally, Astell herself considers the objection that we cannot have the idea of a perfect being because we cannot, as limited and imperfect beings, understand what would constitute perfection. She asserts, however, that we do not need to have a precise idea of perfection. She writes, "We need not be told wherein Perfection consists, for let us be ever so skeptical, we must needs acknowledge, that Wisdom and Goodness, Justice and Holiness, are Perfections, and indeed the greatest Perfections, so that an intelligent Nature defective in these can't be perfect, but destitute of them must needs be miserable. Knowledge and Power without them wou'd not be beauties but blemishes; nor can a Being be infinitely Wise and Good, Just and Holy, unless He be also Omnipresent and Omnipotent" (CR, 7).

It is sufficient for having the idea of a perfect being to know that he must have certain attributes—those that if any intelligent being were to lack them, it would be miserable. In other words, we can know by experience what the good-making qualities of beings are. According to Astell, we first observe the "excellencies," or perfections, in created beings. These are generally moral attributes, like goodness and mercy. These moral attributes are connected to metaphysical attributes such as wisdom and power. Thus, our understanding of the metaphysical perfections is derived from our observation of moral perfection. Astell holds that a perfect being must possess the moral virtues since they are inseparable from knowledge and power. An all-knowing and all-powerful being without the moral virtues would be an object of fear rather than love, and one's justice and goodness is lessened if one does not have the knowledge and power to act in accordance with them. Since the intellectual and moral attributes must coincide in every moral agent, we can deduce that they must coincide in the most perfect being. Astell writes, "tho' Moral and Intellectual improvements may be consider'd apart, they can't really be separated, at least not in a Christian sense" (CR, 296).

Knowledge of God's Nature

Even though Astell believes that we can come to know that God must possess certain attributes by simply examining what is good for a rational human being, she cautions us that the ideas of attributes which we draw from our experience must not be taken as indicative of the divine nature. We can only infer that the positive qualities we see in nature bear some "faint resemblance" to those of God. However, we can know that some resemblance holds because we cannot conceive of properties being in the world without also being contained somehow in its cause.

Moreover, Astell cautions against philosophical discourses that deny certain attributes predicated of God in Holy Scripture or known through reason. She claims that these discourses are due to unbridled "pride" and show "contempt" for God. She writes,

> The other Contempt for God which I was to take notice of, is what
> Ladies I hope are but little, if at all concern'd in, that is, those bold
> Discourses about the Nature and Attributes of God, wherein Men

178   Feminist Interpretations of Mary Astell

take upon them to deny not only what He has declar'd of Himself in His Word, but even what Natural Reason teaches; which plainly proves, That if there be a God, He must needs be infinitely Wise and Good, Just and Holy; and that to deny Him to be Infinite in all Perfections, either Directly or by Consequence, is in some respects worse than to deny His Existence. (CR, 181)

Astell claims that these sorts of inquiries into the nature of God are beyond our rational capacities and are not necessary for this life. However, it is clear that some knowledge of God is necessary. She writes,

By the knowledge of God and of our Selves, which I take to be the proper aim of all our Contemplations, I do not mean a curious research into the Divine Nature, which being hid from us in inaccessible Light, we shou'd humbly Adore and not subtilly dispute about; nor a Physical Disquisition of our own Nature, since God by denying us an Idea of our Souls, signifies that this is not our present business. But I understand a Knowledge of the Relation we stand in to our God, and of the Obligations arising from it. (CR, 306)

Here, Astell claims that we cannot have a complete conception of ourselves as intelligent souls, let alone a conception of God's nature. Rather, we should content ourselves with the knowledge that we are completely dependent upon God and that we owe our love and servitude to him alone. Our meditations allow us to achieve the amount of knowledge about the nature of God necessary in order to understand our subordinate position and duty to him.

Astell tells us in the second *Proposal* exactly why it is that we should be careful in our meditations on the nature of God. Paraphrasing Descartes's *Principles of Philosophy*, she defines a clear idea as that "which is Present and Manifest to an attentive Mind," and a distinct idea as that "which is so Clear, Particular, and Different from all other things, that it contains not any thing in it self which appears not manifestly to him who considers it as he ought" (*SP II*, 172).[8] She proceeds to say that we have a clear, but not a distinct, idea of God because as finite minds we cannot distinctly perceive that which is infinite. She then argues that where we have merely clear ideas, we cannot argue beyond our incomplete ideas and claim that there is something contradictory in the concept. She writes, "Now where our knowledge is Distinct, we may boldly deny of a subject, all that which after a careful Examination we find not in it: But where our Knowledge is only

Clear, and not Distinct, tho' we may safely Affirm what we see, yet we can't without a hardy Presumption Deny of it what we see not" (*SP II*, 172–73).

The methods for coming to understand God are through our "natural notion" of God and through revelation. A natural notion of God is not simply an innate idea; rather, Astell defines our natural notion as "that which mere reason will help us to" (*CR*, 97). She claims that reason cannot completely comprehend God, but is a type of "natural and universal revelation" (*CR*, 22). Moreover, she claims that all that we discover about God via the use of proper reason is knowledge, while revelation, which gives us particular notions about God not attainable through reason (such as the tripartite nature of God), produces faith.

In the remainder of the chapter, I will focus on Astell's discussion of several of the attributes of God, and how these attributes are manifested in his creation. I will begin with a discussion of her views concerning God's goodness and perfection.

God's Attributes: Goodness, Moral, and Metaphysical Perfection

Astell argues that God's nature is the ground of divine will and action. God's actions must be the direct result of his divine nature (his wisdom and goodness). Astell writes,

> Now not to be too Metaphysical, or tedious in the Enquiry, I take the Glory of God to be the greatest Good. . . . By the Glory of God, I understand the Manifestation of the Divine Attributes, according to the Eternal Reason of things; which some call the Rule of Order. Now this rule is nothing else, but that Way which the Wisdom and Perfection of the Divine Nature oblige God to Act, whenever He thinks fit to exert his Power and shew forth His Glory. And because His Goodness is over all His Works, He is pleas'd to take the greatest Glory in the display of this Attribute. (*CR*, 201)

Astell argues that God's glory and goodness are proven from the beauty and variety, as well as the perfection, of his creation. She writes, "Cou'd there have been a more excellent End than the Glory of God, that had been the End of Creation, (which is not a mere empty show and noise like human Glory, but which consists in the Beauty and Perfection of His Works and Ways) being the best Design, all things were created for this purpose" (*CR*, 109).

180   Feminist Interpretations of Mary Astell

Astell maintains that it is God's goodness that prompts him to create the best. She writes, "God always does what most becomes Him, and it is the Perfection of His Nature to do always, and freely, that which is absolutely and entirely the Best" (CR, 21). Astell holds that God creates by means of communicating his goodness, or perfections, into finite forms. She describes God as a "communicative being" and claims that a being "which is so liberal in its communications, must needs possess in the utmost Perfection all that good which it bestows" (CR, 10). The view that God creates by an act of communicating his perfections can be traced back to Plato, the idea being that goodness needs to be exemplified in order to be maximal. St. Thomas Aquinas also held this view, and he also held that God communicated his goodness to his creation in every possible way.[9] Since God communicates his infinite goodness in every way possible, we should expect to see a variety of things in the world, each bearing its own unique perfection. Astell writes, "Yet all the Works of God are Perfect in their kind, tho' all of them do not possess the same degree of Perfection, for this wou'd not consist with the Perfection of the Whole, which arises from the order and symmetry of the several parts; among which there wou'd be little or no beauty if there were no distinctions, no different degrees of Glory" (CR, 109). Astell notes that some of the various created beings are free. She writes, "We know that the excellency of a work appears by that variety of Beauties that are in it: What makes the Universe so Beautiful but its innumerable varieties? And you who are such loves of Variety can have nothing to say against it. Was it then unfit for God to adorn His Creatures with all imaginable Ranks and Degrees of Being, consequently with Free Agents which is a very noble Order?" (CR, 91).

The metaphysical perfection of the world consists in the manifestation of God's perfections in a created universe that contains great variety and order. It is through God's moral and metaphysical perfection that the universe gains its metaphysical perfection. It is then the duty and obligation of each created being to achieve the greatest perfection of which it is capable in order to glorify God. Astell writes,

> But in whatever Degree of Being a Creature is plac'd, whether it be a Free or Necessary Agent, there must be a certain measure of Perfection belonging to its Rank, which it cannot attain but by some certain and stated Progressions or Methods, suitable to the Nature that God has given it, and in the same manner as a Seed becomes a Plant, or a Plant a Tree. Some actions therefore do naturally and necessarily

Astell on the Existence and Nature of God   181

tend to the Perfection of Mankind, and others as naturally and necessarily drag us down into Misery. (CR, 92)

The obligation to perfect one's nature, for human beings, is the duty to understand and obey God's will. Each individual contributes to the moral perfection of the world insofar as he does his duty to God. The perfection of a rational human being consists in the perfection of reason. The more a person's actions are guided by reason, the more they will conform to God's will. Astell writes,

> We have already seen that there is a God; consequently we who are His Creatures and who depend upon Him entirely owe Him the utmost Duty and Service. It has also been prov'd, That God, has Reveal'd his Will to us, hence it follows, that it is our Duty and Wisdom to apply the most exact Obedience to His Reveal'd Will, even tho there were no Sanctions annext to it. . . . [I]t is our highest Interest to be Obedient, and we can't transgress without the greatest Folly and Madness, as well as the most notorious Injustice, Ingratitude, and Wickedness. (CR, 89)

Astell defines "good" as that which glorifies God, and "evil" as that which offends God (CR, 201). To glorify God is to perfect oneself by properly manifesting the attributes that are suited to your rank of being, as was said above. According to Astell, what offends God is the "hinderences which Rational and Free Agents put in their own, and in each others way, towards the attainment of that Happiness which the Wisdom and Goodness of God originally design'd for them" (CR, 201). By which, Astell means to imply that sin, which is a barrier to eternal life, is offensive to God.

Astell addresses some aspects of the problem of evil as well. It might seem inconsistent with God's goodness that we suffer. However, Astell maintains that these conditions give us opportunity to improve our virtue. She also claims that since no temporal good is our true good, earthly suffering does not really cost us. The pain and suffering is always, however unlikely it may seem, to our own benefit. She writes, "So that a true Christian rejoyces evermore, in all Circumstances; he gives thanks always for all things; For all things that God sends without exception, for Poverty, Afflictions, Persecutions, and what Men account most Calamitous. And good Reason, since these are only Exercises of his Vertue, and opportunities to encrease his Reward; since they deprive him of no real Good, but

182   Feminist Interpretations of Mary Astell

bring him much, fortifying his Mind with such a Joy as no Man can take from him" (CR, 192).[10]

Astell maintains that God's goodness prevents him from deceiving us, or from positing pain as mere torture. Instead, we can know that pleasure and pain are instruments by which we can learn what is harmful and helpful to us. She states, in several passages, that all things in the world tend toward the good, and in fact, the best. Our inability to understand how these things tend toward the good is no barrier to them being so. However, Astell does not address the question of whether some lives are so miserable that it would be better had they not lived at all. We can assume that she would reply that the life of the body is not our concern, rather it is the well-being of the soul that matters and that will result in our everlasting happiness. Still, since Astell maintains that all pain is used instructionally, one might wonder if God uses some earthly creatures' lives as a mere means to bringing about this knowledge.

In addition, one might object that eternal damnation is not just punishment for a finite sin. However, Astell tells us that vengeance is necessary for God's justice, and that eternal damnation is a fitting punishment for offending God. Since we owe God for our existence, we have a duty to obey and serve him. Moreover, only the most severe punishment will be an effective deterrent to sin. She writes,

> And since we find in Fact that the severest Threatening, even Inconceivable and Eternal Misery, does not deter Mankind from Sinning, from doing that which naturally and necessarily tends to their own hurt, it is not to be imagin'd that lower motives wou'd have any effect upon them. So that God has appointed a Hell for the Wicked in mere Goodness to Mankind, since this or nothing will work upon the most disingenuous Tempers, and stir them up to qualify themselves for that Heaven which He is desirous to bestow on them. (CR, 93)

Justice and vengeance are for our own well-being and prepare us for our future reward. However, Astell assures us that mercy is also part of God's justice. Having created the human mind, God understands its limitations, and makes some allowances for them. It is willful disobedience that justly merits the punishment of eternal misery. Astell does not think that God is in any way responsible for our tendency to sin. He has given us enough reason to gain knowledge of our true good. Nor does he give us any temptations that are impossible for us to resist. Astell claims that sin and evil are due to intellectual errors, namely, to mistaking worldly goods for our true

Astell on the Existence and Nature of God   183

good. She writes, "For the irregularity of our Wills proceeds from the error of our understandings, from calling Good Evil, and Evil Good" (CR, 154).[11] Astell's works are, at least in part, designed to provide a method for avoiding error and sin by increasing our knowledge of God and our obligations to him.

God's Omnipotence and Sovereignty

Astell argues that a perfect being must be omnipotent. And though she follows Descartes in many respects, Astell does not seem to hold Cartesian views with respect to God's omnipotence. Some commentators suggest that Descartes held that God's omnipotence entails the ability to do absolutely anything, even make contradictions true.[12] Descartes holds that God controls all truths and is absolutely sovereign. There is nothing that is not dependent on God's will. However, in connection with her criticisms of Locke on thinking matter, Astell argues that God cannot make contradictions true, nor can he act in a way that is inconsistent with his nature. In her discussion of Locke, she recounts Descartes's Sixth Meditation arguments for mind and body distinction. She concurs with Descartes's conclusion that since she is essentially a thinking thing and clearly and distinctly perceives that she can exist without her body, it is impossible for thought to belong to matter. However, Astell does add one caveat: "Unless God has been pleas'd to Reveal that it is possible to His Omnipotency, for if so, I must conclude that I only imagine and don't indeed perceive that Repugnancy" (CR, 268).

Astell no doubt wants to leave room for the seemingly contradictory claim in scripture that God is both three persons and is one. We might think that she would say that this is not a truth about God's nature that we could come to via reason. The tripartite nature of God is a revealed truth, and thus an article of faith, not reason. However, in the second *Proposal*, Astell claims that we merely lack the requisite ideas to understand the compatibility of the truth of the proposition *that there is only one God*, and the proposition *that there are three persons in the godhead*. Instead of claiming that we should accept the trinity as a mere article of faith, she seems to argue that the claim of God being both one and three is not contrary to reason, although we presently cannot know it. She writes,

> Revelation which is but an exaltation and improvement of reason has told us, that the Father is God, the Son is God, and the Holy Ghost

is God, and our idea of the godhead of any one of these persons, is as clear as our idea of any of the other. Both reason and revelation assures us that God is one simple essence, undivided, and infinite in all perfections, this is the natural idea which we have of God. How then can the Father be God, the Son God, and the Holy Ghost God, when yet there is but one God? That these two propositions are true we are certain, both because God who cannot lie has revealed them, and because we have as clear an idea of them as it is possible a finite mind should have of an infinite nature. But we cannot find out how this should be, by the bare consideration of these two ideas without the help of a third by which to compare them. This God has not thought fit to impart to us, the prospect it would have given us would have been too dazzling, too bright for mortality to bear, and we ought to acquiesce in the divine will. So then, we are assured that these two propositions are true, There is but one God; and, there are three persons in the godhead: but we know not the manner how these things are. Nor can our acquiescence be thought unreasonable, nor the doctrine we subscribe to be run down as absurd and contradictory. (*SP II*, 147–48)

This passage seems to be a good indication that Astell did not see omnipotence to entail the ability to make contradictions true. She could claim that God's power is beyond our conception. For it would be easy, given her belief that there are matters which are confined to the realm of revelation and faith alone, to say that the seemingly contradictory nature of the trinity is one such matter. However, as the quote above shows, she refrains from taking this line on the trinity.

If Astell did not believe that God's omnipotence implies he could make contradictions hold, then it seems likely that her views on God's relation to the necessary, or eternal, truths was quite different from Descartes's views. It seems likely that Astell held that God is sovereign over all created things, but that he does not create the necessary truths.

Further evidence that Astell thought that God cannot change the eternal truths is her contention that God's power is constrained by his nature. Astell claims that God always does what is fitting. She holds that when we speak of God as not being able to do something, we are claiming that certain aspects of God's nature constrain his ability to will or do certain acts. She writes, "The same natural Notions do also assure us, That the Essential Rectitude of the Divine Nature, will not permit Him to use His

Power and Lawful Authority otherwise than is just and fit" (CR, 98). So, although Astell maintains that God, in principle, has the power to do many things that he does not in fact do, other aspects of his nature, his goodness and justice, make it impossible that he will or bring about those actions.

Indivisibility, Incorruptibility, and Immateriality

Astell argues that the human soul is immortal because it is indivisible and incorruptible. The argument is, in part, based on the fact that God is immaterial rather than material and extended. The discussion takes place in *The Christian Religion* in a section where Astell argues against John Locke's claim that God could superadd thought to matter. Locke claims that it is not contradictory that God should make a material extended thing think. However, Astell holds the Cartesian view that matter, or body, is essentially extended and that mind is essentially thoughtful, and that the two are distinct substances. She claims that if it were possible for body or matter to think, then since we know that God is a thinking being, it would have to be the case that God is possibly extended. However, whatever is extended is capable of division. And whatever is capable of division is capable of corruption. It is inconsistent with the nature of an all-perfect being to be corruptible. Astell writes,

> But we are sure, that God who is All Perfection Thinks, and that He is not Extended, for to be Extended, and for this reason Divisible, is a great Imperfection, and not consistent with His Eternity. And since the First Intelligence the Father of Spirits, is not, cannot be Extended, this is a strong Presumption at least, if it is not a Proof, That Body is incapable of Thought, and that Creatures form'd after His own Image are Immaterial, and consequently in their own Nature, and not barely by Positive Institution, Immortal. (CR, 261)

Astell adds that if thought belonged to both body and mind, then perhaps God would not need to be extended to think. However, Astell claims that if thought belonged to both body and mind, there would be no distinction between them. So that wherever thought occurs, we would have both body and mind. This would again imply that God must be extended if thinking, which is impossible.

186   Feminist Interpretations of Mary Astell

Conclusion

In *A Serious Proposal to the Ladies, Part II* and *The Christian Religion*, Astell actively engages in the debates regarding God's existence and nature. In doing so, she provides unique arguments for the existence of God. Like many of the philosophers writing on these topics, her arguments bear some resemblance to those that others proposed.[13] However, her arguments do succeed in pushing the debates forward and answering objections to previous versions. Astell produces these arguments in order to lay the foundation for Christian belief and moral duties. In addition, she discusses a number of God's attributes, drawing from our experience of the world, our natural notion of God, and scripture to do so. Astell maintains that our ability to understand the nature of God is limited, and that we should not enter into philosophical discourses that can result in the denial of aspects of God known via our natural notion of God or from revelation. However, she does believe that we can have a clear idea of God's nature, if not a distinct one, and that this idea is robust enough to satisfy the questions that we have regarding our creator and our obligations to him.

Abbreviations

AT   René Descartes, *Oeuvres de Descartes*, vols. I–XII (1996) (cited by volume and page number)
CR   Mary Astell, *The Christian Religion, as Profess'd by a Daughter of the Church of England* (1705) (cited by section number)
CSM   René Descartes, *The Philosophical Writings of Descartes*, vols. I–II (1985) (cited by volume and page number)
CSMK   René Descartes, *The Philosophical Writings of Descartes*, vol. III (1991) (cited by page number)
L   Mary Astell, *Letters Concerning the Love of God* (2005)
SP I   Mary Astell, *A Serious Proposal to the Ladies, Part I* (2002)
SP II Mary Astell, *A Serious Proposal to the Ladies, Part II* (2002)

Notes

1. Unfortunately, the new edition did not appear before the writing of this essay, so citations are to the 1705 edition. See the references for more information.

2. Although there are many versions of the ontological and cosmological arguments, in general, ontological arguments attempt to derive the existence of God from premises known a priori (prior to experience) or by reason alone. Cosmological arguments argue from facts about the world to the existence of God as the unique first cause. For examples of ontological arguments, see Anselm (2001), Descartes (AT, VII 63–71; CSM II, 44–49). For examples of the cosmological argument, see Aquinas (1950, Prima Pars, Question 2, Article 3), Descartes (AT VII, 34–52; CSM II, 24–36), Locke (1975, bk. 4, chap. 10), Clarke (1998), and Leibniz (1989, 149–50).

Astell on the Existence and Nature of God   187

3. See Descartes (AT VII, 40; CSM II, 28). Locke's principle, which translates as *from nothing, nothing comes*, was also accepted by Descartes, and it has been argued that Descartes's cosmological argument relies only on the *ex nihilo* principle and not the stronger containment principle. See Nolan and Nelson (2006, 104–21).

4. The phrase "being infinitely perfect" is used by both Nicolas Malebranche and John Norris. Astell likely adopted it from Norris—see Astell and Norris (2005, 72) and Norris (1701, 158). However, I am not here concerned with the phrase, but with her methodology for discerning the relationship between existence and being.

5. Springborg notes that Locke and Stillingfleet discuss these issues in their famous "Correspondence." In the correspondence, Locke defends his stance that we can know that God, a substance, exists because the existence of properties requires a substance in which they can inhere. I do agree that Astell's arguments were affected by a portion of this debate. However, it seems to me that this particular portion of Astell's argument is mainly concerned, not with whether we can infer a substance from its attributes, but with what sort of thing is required in order to create the perfections we see in the world.

6. For more on Descartes's understanding of God as *causa sui*, see Schmaltz (2011, 2014).

7. This notion was "in the air" at the time. Samuel Clarke makes a similar point in his Boyle Lecture of 1704 on the "Nature and Attributes of God." Astell names this work as the sort of inquiry into God's nature that is "contempt" for God.

8. Astell paraphrases Descartes's *Principles of Philosophy* pt. I §45, see Descartes (AT VIIIA, 22; CSM I, 207–6).

9. For a wonderful discussion of Aquinas's views on creation and communication, see Kretzman (1991).

10. Astell quotes John 16:22.

11. Here, Astell follows Descartes's account of error and sin, and she recommends his method for guarding against intellectual error, as well as a thorough understanding of God as our sole good, as the remedy.

12. On this reading of Descartes, Descartes holds that for any proposition P, possibly P is true. Some commentators argue that Descartes holds a more limited view. In the limited view, Descartes denies that for any proposition P, possibly P is true. However, possibly possibly P is true. For more on Descartes in relation to the eternal truths, see Curley (1984), Kaufman (2003, 2005), Pessin (2010), Plantinga (1980), and Walski (2003).

13. Purely original arguments for the existence of God are quite rare. Descartes's cosmological argument for the existence of God in the Third Meditation might be one. In addition, Leibniz's argument based on pre-established harmony, and Malebranche's argument from "mere sight," might be unique. What these arguments have in common is that they are based on each philosopher's unique metaphysical commitments. It should be noted that many of these philosophers (including Locke, Berkeley, and Spinoza) produce versions of arguments for the existence of God that are refinements of ontological, cosmological, and design arguments which date back to Plato and Aristotle. When dealing with arguments with such a long and distinguished lineage, we see that originality comes from innovation.

11

The Emerging Picture of Mary Astell's Views

Alice Sowaal

Introduction

The Re-Reading the Canon series has the stated goal of focusing on "writings of major figures in the Western philosophical tradition," with volumes devoted to individual philosophers, "covering the full range of the philosopher's thought and representing the diversity of approaches now being used by feminist critics" (see the description of the series). That is, by and large, it has been a series devoted to feminist examination of the writings of

I thank Kathleen Ahearn, Jacqueline Broad, Nona Caspers, Karen Detlefsen, Susan Patterson Glover, Amy Parsons, Ruth Sheldon, Christine Sutherland, Penny A. Weiss, Shelley Wilcox, and students at San Francisco State University for reading and commenting on earlier drafts of this essay.

The Emerging Picture of Astell's Views   189

figures canonical to the history of philosophy. With this volume on Astell, however, the series extends its compass, taking on an examination of a philosopher whom many would argue is not a canonical figure and perhaps not even a "major figure." Why, then, should the series include a volume on Astell?

Different answers lie in how we frame the question of the history of philosophy. One approach to re-reading the philosophical canon is this: for what reasons do understudied thinkers belong to the collection of figures and texts that we consider foundational to the discipline of philosophy? This question statically fixes the collection of figures and texts we regard as "the canon" and skeptically interrogates the newcomers and their writings, putting the burden of proof on them as we examine their place with respect to our well-established heroes and beloved volumes. A more neutral approach would be: how do we know that we have the canon right until we have fully examined the works of the understudied philosophers? This question invites an open-ended investigation into these new candidates, and it allows for the opportunity to open our hallowed canon to the full story of our history of philosophy. A third, more historical, and perhaps the most liberating approach circumvents the issue entirely: does it even make sense to talk about a canon, or rather, can we just examine excellent work done in a specific period? These last two questions invite open-ended investigation into new candidates and their writings, thereby allowing for the opportunity to construct a fuller history of philosophy.

Regardless of which of these three approaches drives our study, there is a specific problem involved in producing research on such understudied figures. The problem—on which, in this volume, much headway on Astell is made—is this: without generations of scholarship on their writings, we have neither standard interpretations of their philosophical views nor frameworks to understand what led them to philosophize in the first place. For example, in contrast to research on Mary Astell, we have over 350 years of continuous philosophical scholarship on René Descartes, and scholars throughout the academy are familiar with the details of his views and with the many approaches to interpreting his goal of offering a general philosophical ground for the scientific revolution.

Scholarship on Descartes continues in part by evaluating and developing those interpretations and in part by reconceiving his project, which lately has been framed in terms of his views of the passions and his specific innovations with respect to the life sciences. All of these interpretations are done, however, against the backdrop of the existing research. But for Astell, though her work was well known at the time, even the details of her

190   Feminist Interpretations of Mary Astell

immediate reception have been almost entirely forgotten. This means that although there now exist a handful of philosophical articles on her ideas, scholars working on Astell do so without general agreement on what overarching goals she exercised in developing her philosophical works. In other words, whereas researchers have drawn a picture regarding who Descartes was and what he was up to philosophically, we are still working on how to represent Astell's overall project.

In this conclusion, I will suggest that this volume draws such a picture. Though the contributors are of diverse disciplinary backgrounds and have primarily worked independently from one another, they focus on common themes in a way that can be interpreted as coalescing to reveal both Astell's impetus to philosophize and some of the views that she develops as a result of her endeavors.

The picture they draw shows that Astell recognizes women as being in a specific predicament and thus as needing a specific remedy. The predicament is that, in addition to the biblical Fall (which Astell understood as affecting all humans, regardless of gender), women are subject to what we today call patriarchal aspects of social institutions and customs; together, these gravely affect women's embodiment, psychology, virtue, and behavior. For Astell, the remedy is a form of education that brings about new ways to understand oneself, to use ethos to communicate with others, to form friendships with other women and spouses, to develop virtue, and to discharge one's moral duties. According to Astell, new forms of education, friendship, and marriage all increase the human ability to develop rationality, to exercise freedom, and to realize women's metaphysical equality with men. In explaining how this can manifest, Astell grounds her conceptions of rationality, freedom, and equality in a system of metaphysics, epistemology, and ethics, which has deep roots in Cartesian philosophy.

Thus a case is made for Astell's strong contribution to both the history of philosophy and the history of feminism. Of course, this volume is meant neither as the last proper attempt at approaching and situating Astell's feminism nor as an exhaustive account of Astell's motives to philosophize. There is still much room for new scholarship on Astell. These new interpretations will develop in conversation with the earlier ones as we continue to examine her views with respect to our own current concerns.

However, what we find in this volume, and what I tease out in this conclusion, is one way in which these contributors may be seen as working together on a collection of common themes that show how Astell pursues the project of systematically and coherently theorizing traditional philosophical questions as they arise in analyzing both women's daily lives and the societies in which they live. Thus, this conclusion serves as a sketch of

The Emerging Picture of Astell's Views   191

the emerging picture of Mary Astell's views as it is developed in this volume. After that sketch, I offer a description of how these scholars contribute new ways of understanding Astell as a feminist, and I close with some remarks about a further area of study on Astell that has not been explored to its full potential and to which more attention could be paid so that we, as twenty-first-century feminists, can stay true to our developing ideals.

Education, Friendship, and Marriage

Astell's own education in rationalist philosophy—led perhaps by her uncle, Ralph Astell, who studied with the Cambridge Platonists—was unique. In seventeenth-century England, women of the upper ranks were educated with an eye toward their marriage prospects. In order to attract potential suitors, such women would read in English and French, speak some French, study geography, and know how to dance, play music, and do needlework. According to Astell, the extent of women's education was sorely lacking. She argues that women in this condition are in need of a special kind of education that addressed all levels of their condition, from the metaphysical to the political. This means they should study the Bible and works of important and timely philosophers, for example, Plato, Aristotle, Descartes, Malebranche, and Scudéry, and do so in their original languages (*SP I*, 79–83). In this section, I discuss how the authors in this volume present Astell's account of the need for education and how she grasps the relations among education, friendship, marriage, equality, and rationality.

The biblical Fall, according to Astell, explains the general need to educate all people: All human rational and moral capacities are affected by the Fall, and thus all are in need of improvement (Sowaal, 58ff.; Broad, 22; Detlefsen, 80–81). To improve, people must learn how to develop their rational capacities and develop virtue such that they can discharge their spiritual duties, which will prepare them for eternity—duties to God, self, and other (Broad, 20; Glover, 95, 101; Lascano, 178–82). The focus of education, then, must be on fields—philosophy, theology, and rhetoric—that specifically teach these abilities. The Fall brought about a moral impediment, and education must remedy this with moral improvement.

But while everyone is in need of moral improvement, not everyone receives it. It is hard to overstate Astell's dismay at the lack of women's moral education, which she sees as the result of sexual inequality at the political and social levels. Such inequalities are perpetuated by both governmental inequality and "everyday and repetitious" acts of domination (Weiss, 149; see also Hedrick Moser, throughout, on the tyrannical husband).

192 Feminist Interpretations of Mary Astell

These acts of domination themselves lead to additional moral impediments that also call for further remedy.

At the extreme, when sexual inequality manifests as psychological and physical violence—as Astell thinks it can, especially in marriages—it prompts psychological trauma in women (Hedrick Moser, 116). But even in cases when women do not experience such forms of violent abuse, social inequality can have lasting effects. That is, in addition to psychological trauma, there can be epistemic impediments, like ignorance, whether feigned or real. On this point, Weiss writes, "Women knowingly practice deception, since their ignorance is 'affected'; as a consequence, they misrepresent or limit their capacities and interests to things approved of by men, whose attention they desire, and thus support further disingenuous social relations. These actions also reinforce sexual inequality" (144).

Though some women may practice deception about their rational capacities, others are ignorant about themselves. They may not even be able to conceptualize themselves as the kind of beings that have intellectual capacities; that is, they may hold the "Woman's Defective Nature Prejudice" (Sowaal, 60–61). Thus, social inequality can lead women to live with the kind of self-doubt that manifests as a concern about the goodness of their intellectual nature. Ahearn maintains that self-doubt further affects women's self-esteem and that it also promotes the view that women were made merely to admire and serve men as opposed to God (49). This lack of knowledge is not limited to the self, however; women may also be ignorant about the true nature of human relationships—including that of marriage (Detlefsen, 81–83)—and they may be unclear about how to best communicate with others (Sutherland). Thus, women need improvement at all levels of their being. Astell maintains that such improvement best develops within community.

Hedrick Moser helps explain why community is important to Astell. Because of the "damaging effects of trauma," which "shatters human faith in the goodness of life, of the divine, and of human relationships" (120), a new self needs to be forged. This new self must be forged within community because women must establish a renewed sense of safety and trust in human relationships, and they must place their suffering within a spiritual narrative (124; see also Ahearn, 53, on community and the cultivation of self-esteem). The "Religious Retirement," the name for the academy that Astell proposes in *Serious Proposal I*, can meet these needs. This ideal is a separated community where women, within the context of friendships, escape the inequality and domination of their current society and are able to pursue moral education by studying philosophy, theology, and rhetoric.

The Emerging Picture of Astell's Views   193

Sutherland explains that training in rhetoric is important because a part of the development of one's rational capacity is training in how to properly organize one's thoughts and communicate them to others. This training can lift the troubles of two groups of women in "upper or genteel classes": unmarried women who cannot find employment and are without family support, and married women who are subject to abuses (153). Once these women learn the rhetorical skills of sermo—"the private or semi-public rhetoric of social conversation and letters"—they can improve their abilities to effectively communicate (Sutherland, 154).

But the goal of such learning is not merely to retain or improve one's social standing. Rather, according to Astell, a central aspect of this teaching is that love should be the guiding principle of all communication and that rationality should ultimately be in service not only to oneself, but also to one's community and friends. Further, she maintains that if this goal is successfully reached, it will ultimately lead to happiness (Sutherland, 161).

Friendship is an issue central to Astell's views on moral improvement. Broad explains that, for Astell, within communities like the Religious Retirement, women have a special opportunity to develop the kind of friendship that is integral to their education and improvement, namely "character friendship." This is the kind of friendship that focuses on bringing about moral improvement, and it is best known from Aristotle's writings. This form of friendship is rooted in the kind of love characterized by benevolence, in familiarity with each other's character, and in the mutual desire to develop each other's moral perfection (Broad, 22ff.; Ahearn, 36ff.).

Detlefsen points out that, for Astell, friends' mutual cultivation of rational capacities ultimately serves the higher goal of together honoring and serving God (87–90). Though one always has the self-regarding duty to improve one's own rational capacities, once in a character friendship, this self-regarding duty extends to one's friend as an other-regarding duty. Friends not only develop their own rational capacities, but also help each other in doing so. This idea connects with a point made by Lascano, who explains that all improvement by created beings ultimately serves to bring about God's "glory and goodness[, which] are proven from the beauty and variety, as well as the perfection of his creation" (179).

Astell maintains that the friendships established in the Religious Retirement do not need to be limited to a time behind closed walls or kept separate from society in general. Rather, she uses this model of friendship to discuss the potential of another form of relationship as well, namely marriage (Detlefsen, 88–89). As can women in the Religious Retirement, wives and husbands can also be character friends. In being so, they have

194   Feminist Interpretations of Mary Astell

the same duties of friendship that are present between other character friends. Prior to entering into this kind of friendship, each spouse-to-be has the duty to perfect her or his own rational capacities, for each is a rational being created by God. During marriage, this self-regarding duty extends to one's spouse as an other-regarding duty. That is, the wife and husband each have not only the duty to perfect their own rational capacities (a duty each had before the marriage), but also the additional duty to support the development of the other's rational capacities (Detlefsen, 88).

As she did in her earlier discussion of education, Astell, when addressing marriage, employs the lens of the Fall. She maintains that, though women and men are metaphysically equal after the Fall and before marriage, once a woman marries a man, an inequality is created. However, this inequality is social, not metaphysical. Following St. Paul, Astell gives a theological justification for this point by distinguishing between women and wives: whereas women (in general) need not submit to men (in general), a wife must submit to her husband (Sutherland, 165; Detlefsen, 81; for related issues, see Glover, 105). Though the wife does not lose her metaphysical equality with her husband (for both are rational beings), she does lose her claim to social equality with her husband, to whom she must now submit.

Though Astell thinks this kind of social inequality does not affect metaphysical equality, she holds that social inequality does have a metaphysical basis. This is because the kind of social submission involved in marriage is intertwined with issues involved in the ontological status of marriage. Astell understands marriage in a way very different from how most secular people think of it today. Today, many think of marriage—both the ceremony *and* the institution—as based in custom; however, for Astell, marriage is a biblical institution, divinely instituted and grasped by faith (Detlefsen, 83; Glover, 105). That is, for Astell, God, not society, sanctions marriage. This view of marriage as a divine institution, not a civil one, affects Astell's understanding of equality between wives and husbands. That is, though the husband-wife relationship is not intrinsic to the nature of any individual woman or man, once a woman and man enter into a marriage, "husbands (as husbands) are superior to wives (as wives)" (Detlefsen, 82). The view that marriage was not merely sanctioned by society but by God is not idiosyncratic to Astell. The opening of the solemnization of matrimony in the *Book of Common Prayer* states clearly that marriage was "instituted of God in the time of mans innocency" (Howell and Howell 1734). Glover discusses how Sarah Chapone, a feminist thinker of the next generation, also maintained this belief shared by Christians (Glover, 107).

The framework of character friendship allows Astell to articulate the differences between happy and unhappy marriages. A marriage is happy when each spouse both develops their own rational capacities and supports their spouse in doing the same; otherwise, the spouses take on conflicting roles, and the marriage is not happy (Detlefsen, 82). Astell was familiar with ways in which marriages can go dreadfully wrong when spouses take on conflicting roles. Again, she sees education as a solution. Astell describes the nascent form of some marital problems as they surface during the "perils of courtship" (Ahearn, 52). When a young woman lacks education, she lacks an understanding of her true perfections (an understanding of her nature) and their origin (in God). Without such understanding, she is more liable to develop vices such as imprudence, vanity, and pride. If she enters courtship with such vices, she may not be able to distinguish between flattery and true regard, which could lead her to accept a flattering suitor who will later discourage her from developing her rational capacities (Sowaal, 68–69). Such a young woman, when entering a marriage without a sense of her rational capacities, will not support her husband or encourage him to develop his capacities (Detlefsen, 82). Astell maintains that such a young woman may bind herself in an unhappy marriage between conflicting spouses.

For Astell, given that marriage is a divine institution, it cannot be undone. In other words, Astell, in keeping with the views of her time, holds that divorce is not a true solution for an unhappy marriage (Detlefsen, 83; Glover, 105). Further, the young woman who finds herself in such an unhappy marriage is responsible for her prison, for she has agreed to it. However, Astell also maintains that her suitor and onlookers—her family and "friends"—also hold responsibility here. These others are also to blame, for they have allowed her to develop without the kind of education and character friendship that would have led her to exercise prudence and other virtues in the context of courtship (Sowaal, 68). Further, her suitor has double the guilt for ruining himself and his wife (Hedrick Moser, 123).

Astell gives rich descriptions of unhappy marriages. Hedrick Moser explains that, according to Astell, in those marriages where the husband does not develop his rational capacities, there develops a "state of tyranny where all, or even randomly selected, impulses of the wife are cut at the roots by the husband, where desires are quashed and their destruction gives pleasure to the tyrant" (Hedrick Moser, 114). Hedrick Moser and Weiss explain that here the wife experiences epistemic consequences of being repeatedly discounted in this manner: The wife's one essential human value as a rational being is undermined as is her sense of her own humanity

196   Feminist Interpretations of Mary Astell

(Hedrick Moser, 116; Weiss, 146). This holds not only in a marriage, but also in the company of men in a misogynist society (Hedrick Moser, 118–19; see also Weiss, 138ff.).

As wretched as these relationships can be, there are benefits of an unhappy marriage. Detlefsen writes about Astell's view: "[N]o matter how badly treated a wife might be, if she has cultivated her God-given rationality through excellent education before entering into that bond, she can continue to develop and find comfort in her rational, contemplative nature even within that bond. . . . [T]his marriage can become] an excellent testing ground for Christian virtues" (83). In other words, as in any terrible situation that life presents, there is religious potential in a bad marriage: the wife can use it as a refining fire to further develop her spiritual condition and further strengthen her focus on God's love.

According to Astell, though wives should not leave bad marriages, women can avoid such marriages in the first place. That is, when a woman is educated in her capacity to achieve moral perfection—which happens when she understands her duties to God, herself, and others—she can enter marriage with an understanding of her duties in this context: to choose social submission, to continue developing her rational capacity, and to support her husband in developing his rational capacities. This moral training will also help the woman to make a better choice regarding which man she chooses as a husband in the first place.

Thus, Astell repeatedly refers to the themes of rationality and equality in articulating her interconnected views on education, friendship, and marriage. But what grounds Astell's positions on rationality and equality? It is one thing to claim that women and men are both rational and thus equal, but it is quite another thing to provide a philosophical justification for this position. As I will discuss in the next section, Astell, as a philosopher, presents such a justification.

Philosophical Foundation of Equality, Rationality, and Freedom

I will now turn to how the combined insights of the contributors in this volume reveal aspects of Astell's systematic philosophical justification for her views not only on equality and rationality, but also on related issues of freedom. I begin with her treatment of equality by focusing on her discussion of inherent sexual equality, which provides a natural segue to the other two topics. We find that, for Astell, humans are equal insofar as they are rational, and one effect of the cultivation of rationality is freedom. I

The Emerging Picture of Astell's Views   197

conclude by connecting this view with claims discussed earlier about education, friendship, and marriage.

Astell offers both theological and metaphysical justifications for her claim that women and men are equal. As Glover explains, in presenting the theological justification, Astell appeals to St. Paul's biblical writings. This is surprising, for Paul's teachings were seen as promoting the inferiority of wives to husbands. However, as Astell interprets them, Paul's writings hold that unmarried women are by no means inferior to men (Glover, 103).

In presenting her metaphysical justification for equality, Astell focuses primarily on giving an account of the mind and body as "really distinct" in the Cartesian sense. Lascano and Detlefsen focus on this part of Astell's project. In accounting for the real distinction between mind and body, Astell equates the mind with the immortal soul and argues that the soul is indivisible and incorruptible and thus different from the divisible and corruptible body (Lascano, 185). Astell realizes that "she is essentially a thinking thing and clearly and distinctly perceives that she can exist without her body" and that "it is impossible for thought to belong to matter" (Lascano, 183). That is, "sex attaches to bodies and not to souls" (Detlefsen, 76). Because sex attaches to bodies, the most important part of a human being—the soul—is equal to the most important part of every other human being—namely, to every other soul. Given this, women and men are equal (Detlefsen, 76). This is a natural, intrinsic equality, and it is rooted in "shared rationality" (Detlefsen, 82). This means that women's and men's ability to reason is due not to the sex of their bodies, but to their souls and to the rational capacity God has given each of them (Detlefsen, 76). In this way, the themes of equality and rationality connect with each other.

Astell also connects the themes of equality and rationality with another theme important to her philosophy—freedom. The kind of freedom under discussion here is psychological, an effect of the cultivation of one's rational capacity such that the mind can judge according to reason and without the distractions of sense, appetite, passion, or custom. For this reason, I will refer to it as a "rationally informed freedom."

Here a brief foray into Astell's epistemology is relevant. In presenting her epistemology, Astell gives an account of ideas, the abilities of the mind, and how such ideas and abilities can be perfected. Though the perfection of each of these abilities is important to Astell's overall project, in what follows, I focus on her account of the abilities of the mind and how the perfection of these rational capacities leads to freedom. (For more on Astell's account of ideas, see Lascano on clear and distinct perceptions

198   Feminist Interpretations of Mary Astell

[178]; for more on additional abilities of the mind, see Detlefsen on the differences between faith, science, and opinion [76–77, 83].)

As Sowaal discusses, one ability of the mind is judgment, which is made possible by the combined efforts of the understanding and the will, each of which has a "proper object": the proper object of the understanding is truth, which has being in God's ideas; the proper object of the will is the Good, which is God's will (Sowaal, 62). When a human's understanding and will function properly, she is able "to formulate clear, rational principles of behavior" and "to pursue those principles" (Detlefsen, 85); further, she is able to suspend judgment when appropriate (Broad, 22). A human who can do this is free (Detlefsen, 85). She is in the state of "true Liberty" (Broad, 22). With this proper exercise of the will, the human being can achieve the most important moral end—happiness (Broad, 21–24).

However, given the Fall, not everyone exercises this freedom. Because the Fall weakens the frame of the mind, the understanding becomes fettered by ignorance and the will becomes manacled by custom (Sowaal, 60; Broad, 22). Thus, the will becomes unruly. Taking direction from senses, appetites, passions, and custom, the will acts on blind faith and confused and obscure ideas (Broad, 22, 23, 29; Detlefsen, 85–86; Sowaal, 62). The will has a negative effect on judgment and the ability to be moral. Such an unruly will leads to the cultivation of vice, which is problematic for all people and especially so for the young woman in courtship, as discussed above (Sowaal, 68–69).

All people are in need of the kind of training that leads to the proper use of the understanding and the will (Sowaal, 41–45; Broad, 21ff.). This kind of training not only improves individual people, but also serves a higher purpose, namely God. God is the origin of our rationality and our rationally informed freedom. Developing our "God-given rationality" is "the means by which we attain our end of honoring and serving God" (Detlefsen, 78); when developing this kind of freedom, we literally partake in God's task of creating a world that manifests his perfections (Lascano, 179ff.).

Some lines of connection can now be drawn among a number of themes presented in this chapter—rationality, freedom, equality, education, friendship, and marriage. When one is perfectly rational, one is also perfectly free; insofar as everyone is metaphysically equal because they have shared rationality, everyone has the potential to cultivate rationally informed freedom. However, every human's God-given rational capacities are damaged by the Fall (this is the epistemic effect of the Fall, versus the moral effect, which is vice); women have the added burden of political and social oppression. So while all people can improve their rational capacities and

The Emerging Picture of Astell's Views   199

develop liberty, women need additional help. The space of the Religious Retirement can be useful for women to escape the social and political inequality in their society so that they can heal from trauma, develop character friendships, learn about the true natures of things, acquire skills in rhetoric, and develop liberty. These teachings will help women to discern whether their suitors are interested in developing their rational capacities and whether these men will encourage them to do the same. Ultimately, character friendships can be brought to marriages as well. In the event that the marriage goes awry for some unforeseeable reason, such a rationally engaged woman is prepared to mine the spiritual context of the marriage in order to cultivate her virtues, one of which is to align herself properly such that she loves God.

But this leaves hanging an important thread of Astell's thinking. When discussing the love of God and the development of our rational capacities, Astell uses the language of virtue and duty: she discusses friendship as a virtue, pride and vanity as vices; she maintains that we have duties to develop our rational capacities and to encourage our friends to do the same. How does she understand virtues and duties, both separately and in connection with each other? How are virtues cultivated and duties discharged? The contributors in this volume point to how Astell addresses these questions in her writings on ethics.

An Ethics of Virtues and Duties

Astell develops her ethics by drawing on two traditions—virtue theory and deontological ethics. In this section, I recapitulate some of the central points made by several essays in the volume that discuss how Astell uses the tools of these two traditions.

Broad argues that Astell's writings have much in common with the virtue tradition, according to which the character of the moral agent is of prime importance in evaluating ethical behavior. Arguing that Astell should not be considered a virtue *ethicist* in the strictest sense (for she does not hold the tenet that goodness is metaphysically prior to rightness), Broad maintains that we can think of Astell as a virtue *theorist* in a more general sense, for she writes about many themes central to this tradition: virtue, moral education, moral judgment, character, friendship, and the role of the passions in moral action (Broad, 20ff.).

Astell has much to say about what the passions are, how they can be regulated, cultivated, and educated such that the virtues (or vices) develop.

200   Feminist Interpretations of Mary Astell

The passions are the result of the union between the mind and body. This means that the human being—and thus the moral agent—is always the *embodied* being (Broad, 23). Though the moral agent is always embodied and always has bodily passions, women as women and men as men do not necessarily have different passions, virtues, or vices. Here Astell can be seen as arguing against a popular view of the time, namely that women naturally have "feminine vices," such as imprudence, vanity, and pride (Broad, 17; Sowaal, 60, 64). She does so by using a Cartesian theory of the passions to show how in both women *and* men the seeds of these virtues can degenerate into vices and unruly passions. That is, anyone with poor moral education can develop "feminine vices," and thus such vices are not natural or inherent features of the souls of women (Sowaal). In addition to prudence, pride, and vanity, other passions discussed in this volume are self-esteem (Ahearn), love (Broad, 23–24; Ahearn), generosity (Broad, 25–26; Ahearn, 46–49; Sowaal, 63–68), admiration (Broad, 23–24; Ahearn, 46), courage (Broad, 25–26), and tranquility (Ahearn, 39, 43).

For Astell, though the passions cannot be avoided, they can be properly directed such that they become dispositions "to feel, choose, or act in accordance with right reason toward the right ends" (Broad, 23). Such moral education allows passions to develop into virtues. Ahearn compares Astell's account of this training with that of Descartes. In doing so, she argues that while Descartes maintains that this training is a relatively easy process that anyone can properly engage, Astell claims that it is difficult and rarely successful (44). The difficulty she posits stems from epistemic impediments rooted in the Woman's Defective Nature Prejudice, which, as mentioned above, is the view that women are defective because they do not have intellectual natures that can be perfected (Ahearn, 49; Sowaal, 60–61).

Whereas the virtue tradition focuses on the character of the moral agent, the deontological tradition focuses on the duties of the moral agent, maintaining that actions are judged as moral insofar as relevant duties are discharged. Astell uses tools from this latter tradition when she gives accounts of duties to ourselves and to others, duties that involve the education of our own and others' rational capacities such that we can cultivate our rationally informed freedom, form friendships, and have happy marriages.

Lascano explains how Astell grounds these duties in an additional one, namely our duty to God. Like all created beings, we have the duty to obey and serve God, for God brought us into existence and he communicates to us his perfections of freedom and rationality (Lascano, 180). This duty is discharged by "properly manifesting the attributes that are suited to [our]

The Emerging Picture of Astell's Views   201

rank of being" (Lascano, 181), thereby contributing to the overall moral perfection of the world. As humans, we do this by developing our rational capacities such that we understand and obey God's will (Lascano, 181). Astell holds that by perfecting our minds—and by developing our freedom and rationality—we not only discharge our duty to God, but also literally *participate* in God to a greater degree (Lascano, 170). As we participate in God, we perfect and glorify God, and the two-way relationship that we have with God is complete. God creates us with specific abilities, and we perfect those abilities, thereby participating in, perfecting, and glorifying God.

In examining Astell's discussion of virtue and duty, we see Interconnections among her views. On the one hand, her ethics draws on her more general philosophy. That is, she needs her metaphysical account of humans as created by God to explain the origin of our ethical passions and duties; she needs her epistemological account of our rational capacities to show how we can improve our passions and fulfill our duties. On the other hand, her ethics also helps support her general philosophy in that her theory of vice shows that differences between the characters of women and men are not metaphysical ones; her ethical account of character friendship helps explain how metaphysical and epistemological perfection arises. Indeed, Astell is a systematic philosopher.

Astell and Feminism

There has been much recent disagreement about the degree to which Astell is a feminist, primarily because of her views about Cartesianism, Christian theology, and conservative Tory political hierarchy. Contributors to this volume are no exception. Several authors address these issues head on, shedding new light on her positions and revealing their feminist potential. These authors and others—even those who hesitate to call Astell a feminist—argue that Astell is of interest to twenty-first-century feminists insofar as she theorizes philosophical issues in ways akin to contemporary feminists. I will discuss in turn both of these approaches.

Contemporary feminists have viewed Descartes's philosophy with suspicion. One reason for concern relates to his dualism and its effects. It is claimed that he influenced people in the modern era to think in terms of two kind of things—minds and bodies—which he subsequently aligned with other pairs, some of which are: rational and material; active and passive; cultural and natural; dominant and subordinate; masculine and feminine; and European and other. Within this binary system, the mind is favored and is associated with what is rational, active, cultural, dominant, masculine, and European, whereas the body is denigrated and associated with what is material, passive, natural, subordinate, feminine, and other. Given this, it is thought that Cartesianism has led to the subordination of nature, women, and the "cultural other" (Bordo 1987; Merchant 1980; Tuana 1992; but also see Schmitter 2005). Given this interpretation of Descartes, it is not surprising that Astell—a Cartesian—has been viewed by such contemporary feminists as an unlikely source of feminism. However, research on Astell has troubled this reading of Descartes (Atherton 1993). This is at least partly because, according to Astell, Cartesian mind-body dualism works to serve (rather than to disrupt) two of her goals: arguing that women and men are equally rational and articulating a theory of the subordination of women.

Research efforts in this volume extend beyond an account of the surprising claim that Astell employs Cartesianism toward feminist ends. Instead, they examine different ways of assessing Astell's Cartesianism. On the one hand, scholars advance accounts of precise manners in which Astell's philosophy develops or diverges from the details of Descartes's philosophical views. Several contributors employ this approach: Ahearn (on generosity, self-esteem, and mastery of the passions); Broad (on generosity); Detlefsen (on method, human nature, and the origin of individual differences); Lascano (on the causal principle, the ontological argument, God's nature, the mind-body distinction, and the eternal truths); Sowaal (on method and generosity); and Sutherland (on method).

On the other hand, scholars also now work to defend theses regarding which part of Descartes's general system grounds Astell's feminism. Detlefsen puts forward an original view regarding this anchor. In doing so, she argues against an earlier view held by Broad, namely that Astell's feminism is most squarely rooted in her development of Descartes's moral theory (Broad 2007). Taking issue with this account, Detlefsen explores the potential of reading Astell's feminism as rooted in Cartesian epistemology (80).

Discussing Astell with respect to Descartes allows us to square Astell's contributions to feminism with what many contemporary readers may find an antiquated metaphysics, especially insofar as it is rooted in a theory of God's nature and involvement with the world. This latter point brings us to another concern about Astell's feminism, namely her commitment to a philosophical theology. On this issue, two major contributions are made in this volume: Lascano presents the details of Astell's philosophi-

The Emerging Picture of Astell's Views   203

cal theology, and Hedrick Moser addresses Astell's theology from the perspective of feminist theology and spirituality. Here I will focus on the latter contribution as it addresses the tensions between Astell's feminism and her Christianity.

While readers may be tempted to ignore Astell's theological writings, Hedrick Moser argues that this is a mistake. In doing so, she writes that "Astell's faith, rather than detracting from the power of her theories, or being a mere by-product of her time period, as some critics have argued, is integral to her prescription for survival and recovery within this traumatic system" (113). Further, she holds that "[i]f we attend to her feminist analysis of women's subordination and the damaging effects of tyranny in marriage without attending to her religious vision, then we receive the diagnosis and ignore the prescription for a cure" (126).

When women can connect their suffering with a spiritual narrative and focus on the eternal, their affliction "can be turned into spiritual energy" and their "suffering into virtue" such that they can prepare their souls for "communion with the divine" (122–23).

Religious frameworks—and the social hierarchies embedded in them—were not the only ones that Astell endorsed. She supported obedience to God's appointed authorities in the political sphere. However, as three contributors to this volume argue, Astell also had a well-developed theory of resistance to oppression and, for this reason, should not be seen as a naïve defender of a conservative system.

Weiss and Hedrick Moser discuss Astell's account of resistance at the institutional and personal levels. Weiss explains that though Astell writes that she abhors sedition, she implies that only sedition against lawful authority is problematic. When Astell shows that there is no metaphysical ground to the sexual inequality in society, she resists unlawful authority: "Astell's pen is directed against authority—like patriarchal authority—that is contrary to natural law, to justice, to reason, to God's word" (Weiss, 147). This kind of resistance, "especially when grounded in reason and faith," is "more just and [is] a greater expression of devotion than is men's arbitrary authority over women" (Weiss, 147). Hedrick Moser describes Astell as a "predecessor to modern feminists" because of her "implicit theorization of violence at the core of domestic relationships" and her account of trauma that emphasizes "the violent elements of Astell's analysis of tyrannical marriage" (113). Thus, though Astell subscribes to patriarchal systems, she also reveals their biases and effects, and she teaches others to do the same.

204   Feminist Interpretations of Mary Astell

Detlefsen's reading of Astell's view of the self can be seen as complementing these two accounts of resistance. According to Detlefsen, Astell presents a new account of the self in order to resist oppression. On this view, the self is not an isolated individual but rather is formed in communities of character friends such that women can resist oppression rooted in the patriarchal inequalities at the personal and institutional levels of society. This self has a kind of autonomy that is formed in community, and thus it is a nascent form of what some twenty-first-century feminists call "relational autonomy" (87). According to Detlefsen, however, there is still some doubt as to whether this is enough to categorize Astell as a feminist in contemporary terms. While Detlefsen reads Astell as developing some ideas that we today recognize as feminist, she still sees Astell as accepting the social status quo in a way that is troublesome to current-day feminists.

In these ways, several contributors to this volume assess the claim that Astell's adherence to Cartesianism, theology, and Tory politics pose stumbling blocks to categorizing her as a feminist. Further, these and other contributors connect Astell's theorizing to that of contemporary feminists. In addition to such connections that have been discussed above, we find that Astell fits Allison Jaggar's broad criteria for a feminist ethic (Broad, 30–31); argues against metaphysical essentialism (Sowaal, 70), and employs rhetoric that eschews such views (Sutherland, 164); constructs a psychological theory that has much in common with the contemporary trauma theory of Cathy Caruth and Judith Herman (Hedrick Moser, 113ff.); has a rich theory of embodiment (Ahearn, 40–41; Hedrick Moser, 117–19; Broad, 23); presents a view of the passions that involves the kind of movement of mind that allows for feminist consciousness raising (Broad, 32–33); has a theory of feminist friendship that compares with that of Marilyn Friedman (Broad, 32); develops accounts of self-referential preferences and of what Miranda Fricker calls "testimonial injustice" (Hedrick Moser, 115; Weiss, 145); and develops a theory of power that precedes that of Foucault and that includes discussion of patriarchy, misogyny, domination, incredulity, resistance, and epistemological community (Weiss, 131ff.). This approach to studying Astell through her alignment with contemporary feminist theorizing is both useful and straightforward, for it strives to show how Astell's systematic development of ideas may be fruitful for current conversations.

There is, though, a sense in which the approaches taken in this volume are out of step with important contemporary feminist projects. At

The Emerging Picture of Astell's Views   205

issue here is the emphasis on gender in isolation from other aspects of identity, for example, race, class, sexuality, and nation. In this regard, scholars here follow a trend in the examination of the early modern European philosophical canon that focuses primarily on women philosophers and, where relevant, on their views regarding gender and patriarchy. Contemporary social theorists—including feminist, critical race, queer, and postcolonial theorists—offer additional methodologies that may be used as tools in widening this focus. One is intersectional methodology, which explores the intricacies of identity and the complex connections among different systems of oppression (Crenshaw 1991; Hill Collins 1990). Another is standpoint theory, which examines how such aspects of identity are often tied to specific societal locations and thus carry unique epistemic advantages and disadvantages (Hartsock 1998; Mills 1997; Tuana 2004; Sullivan and Tuana 2007). It will be an exciting moment when philosophers begin to engage Astell—as well as the reformation of the philosophical canon—by widening their attention to include discussion of additional aspects of identity and systems of oppression over and above gender and patriarchy.

Conclusion

The contributions in this volume reveal that Astell's philosophical works contain all of the central features that one would expect of a systematic philosopher of the early modern period: a metaphysics, an epistemology, an ethics, and a social and political philosophy. Further, as was standard in the time, Astell was deeply influenced by traditional theological problems, and these are integral to her general theorizing. However, it is also revealed that she stands apart from many canonical philosophers of the period in that she helps usher in a new tradition of theorizing by employing issues of abstract philosophy—Cartesian ones, at that—in large part *because* they allow her to theorize many issues that concern women, issues that feminists still see as important today. These range from abstract issues (concerning God, the soul, and bodies) both to structural issues (about patriarchy and marriage) and to personal issues (regarding freedom, friendship, and love). That is, we find that Astell is the kind of intellectual who takes seriously philosophical, theological, and feminist concerns. May we continue to find ways to read and explore Astell's thoughts and writings such that we—and subsequent generations of philosophers and feminists—

gain a richer picture of our intellectual past and a more expansive vision of our future.

Abbreviations

SP I   Mary Astell, *A Serious Proposal to the Ladies, Part I* (1997)

References

Achinstein, Sharon. 2007. "Mary Astell, Religion, and Feminism: Texts in Motion." In *Mary Astell: Reason, Gender, Faith*, edited by William Kolbrener and Michal Michelson, 17–30. Burlington, Vt.: Ashgate.

Acworth, Richard. 1977. "Malebranche and His Heirs." *Journal of the History of Ideas* 38 (4): 673–76.

Allen, Amy. 2005. "Feminist Perspectives on Power." In *Stanford Encyclopedia of Philosophy*. Stanford University, 1997–. Accessed December 12, 2010. http://plato.stanford.edu/entries/feminist-power/.

Anselm. 2001. *Proslogion, with the Replies of Gaunilo and Anselm*. Edited and translated by Thomas Williams. Indianapolis: Hackett.

Apetrei, Sarah. 2008. "'Call No Man Master upon Earth': Mary Astell's Tory Feminism and an Unknown Correspondence." *Eighteenth-Century Studies* 41 (4): 507–23. Accessed December 15, 2013. doi:10.1353/ecs.0.0008.

Aquinas, Thomas. 1950. *Summa Theologiae*. Edited by P. Caramello. Turini: Marietti.

Arnauld, Antoine, and Pierre Nicole. 1693. *Logic, or The Art of Thinking*. London: Printed by T. B., to be sold by Randal Taylor near Stationers Hall.

———. 1996. *Logic, or The Art of Thinking: Containing, Besides Common Rules, Several New Observations Appropriate for Forming Judgment*. Edited and translated by Jill Vance Buroker. Cambridge: Cambridge University Press.

Astell, Mary. 1694. *A Serious Proposal to the Ladies, for the Advancement of Their True and Greatest Interest. By a Lover of Her Sex*. London: For R. Wilkin at the King's-Head in St Paul's Church-Yard.

———. 1697. *A Serious Proposal to the Ladies: Part II, Wherein a Method Is Offer'd for the Improvement of Their Minds*. London: Printed for Richard Wilkin.

———. 1700. *Some Reflections upon Marriage*. London: Stationer's Hall.

———. 1704a. *A Fair Way with the Dissenters and Their Patrons*. London: E. P. for Richard Wilkin.

———. 1704b. *An Impartial Enquiry into the Causes of Rebellion and Civil War in This Kingdom*. London: E. P. for Richard Wilkin.

———. 1704c. *Moderation Truly Stated: Or, A Review of a Late Pamphlet, Entitul'd, Moderation a Vertue*. London: J. L. for Rich. Wilkin.

———. 1705. *The Christian Religion, as Profess'd by a Daughter of the Church of England. In a Letter to the Right Honourable, T.L.CI*. London: S. H. for R. Wilkin.

———. 1709. *Bart'lemy Fair: Or, an Enquiry After Wit; in Which Due Respect Is Had to a Letter Concerning Enthusiasm, to My LORD ****. London: Richard Wilkin.

———. 1986. *The First English Feminist: Reflections upon Marriage and Other Writings by Mary Astell*. Edited by Bridget Hill. New York: St. Martin's Press.

———. 1996a. "A Fair Way with the Dissenters." In *Political Writings*, edited by Patricia Springborg, 81–127. Cambridge: Cambridge University Press.

208   References

———. 1996b. *Reflections upon Marriage*. In *Astell: Political Writings*, edited by Patricia Springborg, 1–80. Cambridge: Cambridge University Press.

———. 1997. *A Serious Proposal to the Ladies, Parts I and II* (1694, 1697). Edited by Patricia Springborg. London: Pickering and Chatto.

———. 2002. *A Serious Proposal to the Ladies, Parts I and II* (1694, 1697). Edited by Patricia Springborg. Orchard Park, N.Y.: Broadview Press.

Astell, Mary, and John Norris. 1695. *Letters Concerning the Love of God, Between the Author of the Proposal to the Ladies and Mr. John Norris: Wherein His Late Discourse, Shewing that It Ought to Be Intire and Exclusive of All Other Loves, Is Further Cleared and Justified*. London: J. Norris.

———. 2005. *Letters Concerning the Love of God*. Edited by E. Derek Taylor and Melvyn New. Aldershot, U.K.: Ashgate.

———. 2013. *The Christian Religion, as Professed by a Daughter of the Church of England*. Edited by Jacqueline Broad. Toronto: Centre for Reformation and Renaissance Studies and Iter Publishing.

Atherton, Margaret. 1993. "Cartesian Reason and Gendered Reason." In *A Mind of One's Own: Feminist Essays on Reason and Objectivity*, edited by Louise M. Antony and Charlotte Witt, 19–34. Boulder, Colo.: Westview Press.

Audi, Robert, ed. 1999. *The Cambridge Dictionary of Philosophy*. 4th ed. Cambridge: Cambridge University Press.

Bacon, Francis. 1974. *The Advancement of Learning and New Atlantis*. Oxford: Clarendon Press.

Bailey, Joanne. 2002. "Favoured or Oppressed? Married Women, Property, and 'Coverture' in England, 1660–1800." *Continuity and Change* 17 (3): 351–72. Accessed December 15, 2013. doi:10.1017/S0268416002004253.

Ballard, George. 1752. *Memoirs of Several Ladies of Great Britain, Who Have Been Celebrated for Their Writings or Skill in the Learned Languages, Arts, and Sciences*. Oxford: Printed by W. Jackson, for the author. Eighteenth Century Collections Online (CW101843422).

———. 1985. *Memoirs of Several Ladies of Great Britain, Who Have Been Celebrated for Their Writings or Skill in the Learned Languages, Arts, and Sciences*. Edited and introduced by Ruth Perry. Detroit: Wayne State University Press.

Ballard Manuscripts. Bodleian Library. University of Oxford. Vols. 41 and 43.

Baron and Feme: A Treatise of the Common Law Concerning Husbands and Wives. (1700) 1738. London: Printed by the assigns of Richard and Edward Atkyns . . . for John Walthoe.

Baumlin, James S., and Tita French Baumlin, eds. 1994. *Ethos: New Essays in Rhetorical and Critical Theory*. Dallas: Southern Methodist University Press.

Baumlin, Tita. 1994. "'A Good (Wo)man Skilled in Speaking': Ethos, Self-Fashioning, and Gender in Renaissance England." In *Ethos: New Essays in Rhetorical and Critical Theory*, edited by James S. Baumlin and Tita French Baumlin, 229–63. Dallas: Southern Methodist University Press.

Bechtold, Brigitte. 2000. "More Than a Room and Three Guineas: Understanding Virginia Woolf's Social Thought." *Journal of International Women's Studies* 1 (2): 1–11.

Blackstone, William. 1979. *Of Public Wrongs*. Vol. 4 of *Commentaries on the Laws of England: A Facsimile of the First Edition of 1765–1769*. Chicago: University of Chicago Press.

Bonfield, Lloyd. 1983. *Marriage Settlements, 1601–1740: The Adoption of the Strict Settlement*. Cambridge: Cambridge University Press.

Bordo, Susan. 1987. *The Flight to Objectivity: Essays on Cartesianism and Culture*. Albany: SUNY Press.

Bradshaw, Leah. 1991. "Political Rule, Prudence, and the 'Woman Question' in Aristotle." *Canadian Journal of Political Science* 24 (3): 557–73.

Broad, Jacqueline. 2002. *Women Philosophers of the Seventeenth Century*. Cambridge: Cambridge University Press.

———. 2003. "Adversaries or Allies? Occasional Thoughts on the Masham-Astell Exchange." *Eighteenth-Century Thought* 1:123–49.

———. 2007. "Astell, Cartesian Ethics, and the Critique of Custom." In *Mary Astell: Reason, Gender, Faith*, edited by William Kolbrener and Michal Michelson, 165–80. Burlington, Vt.: Ashgate.

———. 2009. "Mary Astell on Virtuous Friendship." *Parergon: Journal of the Australian and New Zealand Association for Medieval and Early Modern Studies* 26 (2): 65–86.

Broad, Jacqueline, and Karen Green. 2009. *A History of Women's Political Thought in Europe, 1400–1700*. Cambridge: Cambridge University Press.

Brown, Deborah. 2006. *Descartes and the Passionate Mind*. Cambridge: Cambridge University Press.

Brown, Deborah, and Calvin Normore. 2003. "Traces of the Body: Cartesian Passions." In *Passion and Virtue in Descartes*, edited by Byron Williston and Andre Gombay, 83–106. Amherst, N.Y.: Humanity Books.

Bryson, Cynthia. 1998. "Mary Astell: Defender of the Disembodied Mind." *Hypatia* 13 (4): 40–62.

Bryson, Valerie. 1992. *Feminist Political Theory: An Introduction*. New York: Paragon House.

Buickerood, James G. 2004. Introduction to *The Philosophical Works of Damaris, Lady Masham: A Discourse Concerning the Love of God; Occasional Thoughts in Reference to a Vertuous or Christian Life*, by Damaris Masham, edited by James Buickerood, v–xliv. Bristol, U.K.: Thoemmes Continuum.

Butler, Melissa A. 2009. Review of *Mary Astell: Theorist of Freedom from Domination*, by Patricia Springborg, and *Mary Astell: Reason, Gender, Faith*, edited by William Kolbrener and Michal Michelson. *A History of Political Thought* 30 (4): 733–36.

Cape, Robert W., Jr. 1997. "Roman Women in the History of Rhetoric and Oratory." In *Listening to Their Voices: The Rhetorical Activities of Historical Women*, edited by Molly Meijer Wertheimer, 112–32. Columbia: University of South Carolina Press.

Carroll, Berenice. 1972. "Peace Research: The Cult of Power." *Journal of Conflict Resolution* 16 (4): 585–616.

Caruth, Cathy. 1995. Introduction to *Trauma: Explorations in Memory*, edited by Cathy Caruth, 3–12. Baltimore: Johns Hopkins University Press.

———. 1996. *Unclaimed Experience: Trauma, Narrative, History*. Baltimore: Johns Hopkins University Press.

Castiglione, Baldesare. 1980. *The Book of the Courtier*. Translated by George Bull. New York: Penguin.

Chapone, Hester (née Mulso). 1807. *The Posthumous Works of Mrs. Chapone: Containing Her Correspondence with Mr. Richardson; A Series of Letters to Mrs. Elizabeth Carter, and Some Fugitive Pieces, Never Before Published; Together with an Account of Her Life and Character, Drawn Up by Her Own Family*. 2 vols. London: Printed for J. Murray.

Chapone, Sarah. 1735. *The Hardships of the English Laws in Relation to Wives*. London: Printed by W. Bowyer for J. Roberts. Eighteenth Century Collections Online (CW3324435887).

Chudleigh, Mary Lee. 1993. "To the Ladies." In *The Poems and Prose of Mary, Lady Chudleigh*, edited by Margaret J. M. Ezell, 83–84. New York: Oxford University Press.

Cicero, M. Tullius. 1913. *De Officiis*. Translated by Walter Miller. London: William Heinemann.

Clarke, Norma. 2005. "Elizabeth Elstob (1674–1752): England's First Professional Woman Historian?" *Gender and History* 17 (1): 210–20. Accessed December 15, 2013. doi:10.1111/j.0953-5233.2005.00378.x.

Clarke, Samuel. 1998. *A Demonstration of the Being and Attributes of God, and Other Writings*. Edited by Ezio Vailati. Cambridge: Cambridge University Press.

Cocking, Dean, and Jeanette Kennett. 2000. "Friendship and Moral Danger." *Journal of Philosophy* 97 (5): 278–96.

Coke, Edward. 1979. *The First Part of the Institutes of the Laws of England: 1628 Edition*. 2 vols. New York: Garland.

Coogan, Michael D., Marc Z. Brettler, Carol Newsom, and Pheme Perkins, eds. 2010. *The New Oxford Annotated Bible with the Apocrypha*. New Revised Standard Version. Oxford: Oxford University Press.

210   References

Cook, Blanche Wiesen. 1977. "Female Support Networks and Political Activism: 'Lillian Wald, Crystal Eastman, and Emma Goldman.'" *Chrysalis* 3 (Autumn): 43–61.

Cooper, John M. 1977. "Aristotle on the Forms of Friendship." *Review of Metaphysics* 30 (4): 619–48.

Cornett, Judy M. 1997. "Hoodwink'd by Custom: The Exclusion of Women from Juries in Eighteenth-Century English Law and Literature." *William and Mary Journal of Women and the Law* 4 (1): 1–89. Accessed December 15, 2013. http://scholarship.law.wm.edu/wmjowl/v014/iss1/2/.

Crenshaw, Kimberlé W. 1991. "Mapping the Margins: Intersectionality, Identity Politics, and Violence Against Women of Color." *Stanford Law Review* 43 (6): 1241–99.

Curley, E. M. 1984. "Descartes on the Creation of the Eternal Truths." *Philosophical Review* 93 (4): 569–97.

Dalmiya, Vrinda, and Linda Alcoff. 1993. "Are 'Old Wives' Tales' Justified?" In *Feminist Epistemologies*, edited by Linda Alcoff and Elizabeth Potter, 217–24. New York: Routledge.

Daybell, James, ed. 2001. *Early Modern Women's Letter Writing, 1450–1700*. Basingstoke, U.K.: Palgrave.

Delany, Mary. 1861. *The Autobiography and Correspondence of Mary Granville, Mrs. Delany: With Interesting Reminiscences of King George the Third and Queen Charlotte*. Edited by Lady Augusta Waddington Hall Llanover. Vol. 1. London: Richard Bentley.

Delany, Patrick. 1732. *Revelation Examined with Candour. Or, a Fair Enquiry into the Sense and Use of the Several Revelations Expressly Declared, or Sufficiently Implied*. Vol. 1. Dublin: Printed by S. Powell for George Grierson in Essex-street, George Risk, George Ewing, and William Smith, Booksellers in Dame's-street. Eighteenth Century Collections Online (CW3317610110).

Descartes, René. (1649) 1989. *The Passions of the Soul*. Translated by Stephen Voss. Cambridge: Hackett.

———. 1964–76. *Oeuvres de Descartes*. 12 vols. Edited by Charles Adam and Paul Tannery. Paris: Librairie Philosophique J. Vrin / CNRS.

———. 1980. *Discourse on Method and Meditations on First Philosophy*. Translated by Donald A. Cress. Indianapolis: Hackett.

———. 1985. *The Philosophical Writings of Descartes*. Vols. I–II. Translated by John Cottingham, Robert Stoothoff, and Dugald Murdoch. Cambridge: Cambridge University Press.

———. 1991. *The Philosophical Writings of Descartes*. Vol. III. Translated by John Cottingham, Robert Stoothoff, Dugald Murdoch, and Anthony Kenny. Cambridge: Cambridge University Press.

Detlefsen, Karen. 2013. "Margaret Cavendish and Thomas Hobbes on Freedom, Education, and Women." In *Feminist Interpretations of Thomas Hobbes*, edited by Nancy Hirschmann and Joanne Wright, 149–68. University Park: Pennsylvania State University Press.

Duran, Jane. 2000. "Mary Astell: A Pre-Humean Christian Empiricist and Feminist." In *Presenting Women Philosophers*, edited by Cecile T. Tougas and Sara Ebenreck, 147–54. Philadelphia: Temple University Press.

———. 2006. *Eight Women Philosophers: Theory, Politics, and Feminism*. Urbana: University of Illinois Press.

Ellenzweig, Sarah. 2003. "The Love of God and the Radical Enlightenment: Mary Astell's Brush with Spinoza." *Journal of the History of Ideas* 64 (3): 379–97.

Enloe, Cynthia. 2004. *The Curious Feminist: Searching for Women in a New Age of Empire*. Berkeley: University of California Press.

Erickson, Amy Louise. 1993. *Women and Property in Early Modern England*. London: Routledge.

———. 2007. "Possession—and the Other One-Tenth of the Law: Assessing Women's Ownership and Economic Roles in Early Modern England." *Women's History Review* 16 (3): 369–85. Accessed December 15, 2013. doi:10.1080/09612020601022261.

Ezell, Margaret J. M. 1987. *The Patriarch's Wife: Literary Evidence and the History of the Family*. Chapel Hill: University of North Carolina Press.

———. 1993. Introduction to *The Poems and Prose of Mary, Lady Chudleigh*, edited by Margaret J. M. Ezell, xvii–xxxvi. New York: Oxford University Press.

References   211

Frede, Michael. 1999. "On the Stoic Conception of the Good." In *Topics in Stoic Philosophy*, edited by Katerina Ierodiakonou, 71–94. Oxford: Clarendon Press.

Fricker, Miranda. 2007. *Epistemic Injustice: Power and the Ethics of Knowing*. Oxford: Oxford University Press.

Friedan, Betty. 1963. *The Feminine Mystique*. New York: W. W. Norton.

Friedman, Marilyn. 1993. *What Are Friends For? Feminist Perspectives on Personal Relationships and Moral Theory*. Ithaca: Cornell University Press.

Gill, Michael. 2006. *The British Moralists on Human Nature and the Birth of Secular Ethics*. Cambridge: Cambridge University Press.

Goldie, Mark. 2007. "Mary Astell and John Locke." In *Mary Astell: Reason, Gender, Faith*, edited by William Kolbrener and Michal Michelson, 17–30. Burlington, Vt.: Ashgate.

[Gould, Robert, and Thomas Brown]. 1682. *Love Given O're: Or, A Satyr Against the Pride, Lust, and Inconstancy, &c. of Woman*. London: Andrew Green.

Green, Karen. 2005. "On Translating Christine de Pizan as a Philosopher." In *Healing the Body Politic: The Political Thought of Christine de Pizan*, edited by Karen Green and Constant J. Mews, 117–37. Turnhout, Belgium: Brepols.

———. 2007. "*Phronesis* Feminised: Prudence from Christine de Pizan to Elizabeth I." In *Virtue, Liberty, and Toleration: Political Ideas of European Women, 1400–1800*, edited by Jacqueline Broad and Karen Green, 23–38. Dordrecht, Netherlands: Springer.

Green, V. H. H. 1961. *The Young Mr. Wesley: A Study of John Wesley and Oxford*. London: E. Arnold.

Greenberg, Lynne A. 2005. Introduction to *Legal Treatises: Essential Works for the Study of Early Modern Women*, pt. 1, vol. 3, lx–lxiii. 2nd ser. Aldershot, U.K.: Ashgate.

Harris, Jocelyn. 2012. "Philosophy and Sexual Politics in Mary Astell and Samuel Richardson." *Intellectual History Review* 22 (3): 445–63. Accessed December 15, 2013. doi:10.1080/1749697 7.2012.695198.

Harth, Erica. 1992. *Cartesian Women: Versions and Subversions of Rational Discourse in the Old Regime*. Ithaca: Cornell University Press.

Hartmann, Van C. 1998. "Tory Feminism in Mary Astell's *Bart'lemy Fair*." *Journal of Narrative Technique* 28 (3): 243–65.

Hartsock, Nancy C. M. 1998. *The Feminist Standpoint Revisited and Other Essays*. Boulder, Colo.: Westview Press.

Harwood, John T., ed. 1986. *The Rhetoric of Thomas Hobbes and Bernard Lamy*. Carbondale: Southern Illinois University Press.

Henderson, Judith Rice. 1983. "Erasmus on the Art of Letter-Writing." In *Renaissance Eloquence: Studies in the Theory and Practice of Renaissance Rhetoric*, edited by James J. Murphy, 331–55. Berkeley: University of California Press.

Herberg, Erin. 1999. "Mary Astell's Rhetorical Theory: A Woman's Viewpoint." In *The Changing Tradition: Women in the History of Rhetoric*, edited by Christine Mason Sutherland and Rebecca Sutcliffe, 147–57. Calgary: University of Calgary Press.

Herman, Judith Lewis. 1992. *Trauma and Recovery*. New York: Basic Books.

Hill Collins, Patricia. 1990. *Black Feminist Thought: Knowledge, Consciousness, and the Politics of Empowerment*. Boston: Unwin Hyman.

Hirschmann, Nancy. 2003. *The Subject of Liberty: Toward a Feminist Theory of Freedom*. Princeton: Princeton University Press.

———. 2007. *Gender, Class, and Freedom in Modern Political Thought*. Princeton: Princeton University Press.

Hiscock, Andrew. 1997. "'Here's No Design nor Plot, nor Any Ground': The Drama of Margaret Cavendish and the Disorderly Woman." *Women's Writing* 4 (3): 401–20.

Hoagland, Sarah Lucia. 1998. "Femininity, Resistance, and Sabotage." In *Women and Values: Readings in Recent Feminist Philosophy*, edited by Marilyn Pearsall, 78–86. 2nd ed. Belmont, Calif.: Wadsworth.

212   References

Hobbes, Thomas. 1994. *Leviathan*. Edited by Edwin Curley. Indianapolis: Hackett.
hooks, bell. 2004. "Understanding Patriarchy." No Borders. Accessed July 25, 2004. http://imag-inenoborders.org/pdf/zines/UnderstandingPatriarchy.pdf.
Horvitz, Deborah M. 2000. *Literary Trauma: Sadism, Memory, and Sexual Violence in American Women's Fiction*. Albany: SUNY Press.
Howell, William, and William Howell. 1734. "The Form of Solemnization of Matrimony." In *The Common-Prayer-Book, the Best Companion in the House and Closet, as Well as in the Temple, or, A Collection of Prayers out of the Liturgy of the Church of England: Most Needful Both for the Whole Family Together, and for Every Single Person Apart by Himself, with a Particular Office for the Sacrament*. London: Printed for J. J. and P. Knapton.
Hursthouse, Rosalind. 1999. *On Virtue Ethics*. Oxford: Oxford University Press.
Jaggar, Alison M. 1990. "Feminist Ethics: Projects, Problems, Prospects." In *Feminist Ethics*, edited by Claudia Card, 97–98. Lawrence: University Press of Kansas.
James, Susan. 2002. "The Passions and Philosophy." In *Feminism and the History of Philosophy*, edited by Genevieve Lloyd, 131–59. Oxford: Oxford University Press.
Janes, Regina. 1976. "Mary, Mary, Quite Contrary, or Mary Astell and Mary Wollstonecraft Compared." *Studies in Eighteenth-Century Culture* 5:121–39.
Janeway, Elizabeth. 1981. *Powers of the Weak*. New York: Knopf.
Johns, Alessa. 1996. "Mary Astell's 'Excited Needles': Theorizing Feminist Utopia in Seventeenth-Century England." *Utopian Studies* 7 (1): 60–74.
Johnson, Allan G. 2000. "Misogyny." In *The Blackwell Dictionary of Sociology: A User's Guide to Sociological Language*, 197. Oxford, U.K.: Blackwell.
———. 2005. *The Gender Knot: Unraveling Our Patriarchal Legacy*. Philadelphia: Temple University Press.
Kaufman, Daniel. 2003. "Divine Simplicity and the Eternal Truths in Descartes." *British Journal for the History of Philosophy* 11 (4): 553–79.
———. 2005. "God's Immutability and the Necessity of Descartes's Eternal Truths." *Journal of the History of Philosophy* 43 (1): 1–19.
Kinnaird, Joan K. 1979. "Mary Astell and the Conservative Contribution to English Feminism." *Journal of British Studies* 19 (1): 53–75.
Kolbrener, William. 2007. "Astell's 'Design of Friendship' in *Letters* and *A Serious Proposal, Part I*." In *Mary Astell: Reason, Gender, Faith*, edited by William Kolbrener and Michal Michelson, 49–64. Burlington, Vt.: Ashgate.
Kolbrener, William, and Michal Michelson, eds. 2007. *Mary Astell: Reason, Gender, Faith*. Burlington, Vt.: Ashgate.
Kremer, Elmar J. 2000. "Malebranche on Human Freedom." In *The Cambridge Companion to Malebranche*, edited by Steven M. Nadler, 190–219. Cambridge: Cambridge University Press.
Kretzmann, Norman. 1991. "A General Problem of Creation: Why Would God Create Anything at All?" In *Being and Goodness: The Concept of the Good in Metaphysics and Philosophical Theology*, edited by Scott Charles MacDonald, 208–28. Ithaca: Cornell University Press.
La Capra, Dominick. 2001. *Writing History, Writing Trauma*. Baltimore: Johns Hopkins University Press.
A Ladies Religion: In a Letter to the Honourable My Lady Howard. The Second Edition. With a Prefatory Epistle to the Same Lady, by a Lay-Gentleman. 1697. London: Tho Warren for Richard Baldwin at the Oxford-Arms in Warwick-lane.
Lamy, Bernard. (1675) 1986. "The Art of Speaking." In *The Rhetoric of Thomas Hobbes and Bernard Lamy*, edited by John T. Harwood, 165–377. Carbondale: Southern Illinois University Press.
Lascano, Marcy. Forthcoming. "Early Modern Women on the Cosmological Argument: A Case Study in Feminist History of Philosophy." In *Feminist History of Philosophy: The Recovery and Evaluation of Women's Philosophical Thought*, edited by Eileen O'Neill and Marcy Lascano. Dordrecht, Netherlands: Springer.

The Lawes Resolutions of Womens Rights. (1632) 2005. In Legal Treatises: Essential Works for the Study of Early Modern Women, edited by Lynne A. Greenberg, pt. 1, vol. 3, [i–xiv], 1–404. 3rd ser. Aldershot, U.K.: Ashgate.

Leibniz, Gottfried Wilhelm. 1981. New Essays on Human Understanding. Edited and translated by Peter Remnant and Jonathan Bennett. Cambridge: Cambridge University Press.

———. 1989. Philosophical Essays. Edited and translated by Roger Ariew and Daniel Garber. Indianapolis: Hackett.

Lister, Andrew. 2004. "Marriage and Misogyny: The Place of Mary Astell in the History of Political Thought." History of Political Thought 25 (1): 44–72.

Locke, John. 1695. The Reasonableness of Christianity, as Delivered in the Scriptures. London: Printed for Awnsham and John Churchil at the Black Swan in Pater-Noster Row.

———. 1884. "Deus." In The Life and Letters of John Locke: With Extracts from His Journals and Common-place Books, edited by Lord Peter King, 313–16. London: George Bell and Sons, York Street, Covent Garden.

———. 1975. An Essay Concerning Human Understanding. Edited by Peter H. Nidditch. Oxford: Clarendon Press.

———. 1981. Correspondence of John Locke. Edited by Esmond Samuel De Beer. Oxford: Clarendon Press.

———. 2003. "The Second Treatise of Government." In Locke: The Political Writings, edited by David Wootton, 261–386. Cambridge: Hackett.

London Jests. 1685. London: Dorman Newman.

Mackenzie, Catriona, and Natalie Stoljar. 2000. Introduction to Relational Autonomy: Feminist Perspectives on Autonomy, Agency, and the Social Self, edited by Catriona Mackenzie and Natalie Stoljar, 3–34. New York: Oxford University Press.

Macpherson, Sandra. 2010. Harm's Way: Tragic Responsibility and the Novel Form. Baltimore: Johns Hopkins University Press.

Mainardi, Pat. 1970. The Politics of Housework. Boston: New England Free Press.

Malebranche, Nicolas. (1674–75) 1980. The Search After Truth. Edited and translated by Thomas M. Lennon and Paul J. Olscamp. Columbus: Ohio State University Press.

McCrystal, John. 1992. "A Lady's Calling: Mary Astell's Notion of Women." Political Theory Newsletter 4:156–70.

McFarlane, Alexander C., and Bessel A. van der Kolk. 2007. "Trauma and Its Challenge to Society." In Traumatic Stress: The Effects of Overwhelming Experience on Mind, Body, and Society, edited by Bessel A. van der Kolk, Alexander C. McFarlane, and Lars Weisaeth, 24–46. New York: Guilford Press.

Merchant, Carolyn. 1980. The Death of Nature: Women, Ecology, and the Scientific Revolution. San Francisco: Harper and Row.

Miller, Shannon. 2008. Engendering the Fall: John Milton and Seventeenth-Century Women Writers. Philadelphia: University of Pennsylvania Press.

Mills, Charles W. 1997. The Racial Contract. Ithaca: Cornell University Press.

Mintz, Samuel. 1969. The Hunting of Leviathan: Seventeenth-Century Reactions to the Materialism and Moral Philosophy of Thomas Hobbes. Cambridge: Cambridge University Press.

More, Henry. (1653) 1969a. The Antidote Against Atheism. In Philosophical Writings of Henry More, edited by Flora Isabel MacKinnon, 3–53. New York: AMS Press.

———. (1659) 1969b. The Immortality of the Soul. In The Philosophical Writings of Henry More, edited by Flora Isabel MacKinnon, 57–180. New York: AMS Press.

———. (1690) 1997. An Account of Virtue, or Dr. Henry More's Abridgment of Morals Put into English. Facsimile edition, translated by Edward Southwell. Bristol, U.K.: Thoemmes Press.

———. 1930. Enchiridion Ethicum: The English Translation of 1690 Reproduced from the First Edition. Translated by Edward Southwell and Sterling P. Lamprecht. New York: Facsimile Text Society.

214   References

Morgan-Curtis, Samantha A. 2006. "Misogyny." In *International Encyclopedia of Men and Masculinities*, edited by Michael Flood, Judith Kegan Gardiner, Bob Pease, and Keith Pringle, 443. New York: Routledge.

Murphy, James J., ed. 1983. *Renaissance Eloquence: Studies in the Theory and Practice of Renaissance Rhetoric*. Berkeley: University of California Press.

Myers, Joanne E. 2012. "Enthusiastic Improvement: Mary Astell and Damaris Masham on Sociability." *Hypatia* 28 (3): 533–50.

Nelson, Alan. 1997. "Descartes's Ontology of Thought." *Topoi* 16 (2): 163–78.

———. 2005. "The Rationalist Impulse." In *A Companion to Rationalism*, edited by Alan Nelson, 3–11. Malden, Mass.: Blackwell.

Nolan, Lawrence, and Alan Nelson. 2006. "Proofs for the Existence of God." In *The Blackwell Guide to Descartes' Meditations*, edited by Stephen Gaukroger, 104–21. Malden, Mass.: Blackwell.

Norris, John. 1701. *An Essay Towards the Theory of the Ideal or Intelligible World*. London: Samuel Manship.

———. 1710. *A Treatise Concerning Christian Prudence*. London: Samuel Manship.

Oakley, Justin. 1996. "Varieties of Virtue Ethics." *Ratio* 9 (2): 128–52.

O'Neill, Eileen. 1998. "Disappearing Ink: Early Modern Women Philosophers and Their Fate in History." In *Philosophy in a Feminist Voice*, edited by Janet Kourany, 17–62. Princeton: Princeton University Press.

———. 1999. "Women Cartesians, 'Feminine Philosophy,' and Historical Exclusion." In *Feminist Interpretations of René Descartes*, edited by Susan Bordo, 232–57. University Park: Pennsylvania State University Press.

———. 2007. "Mary Astell on the Causation of Sensation." In *Mary Astell: Reason, Gender, Faith*, edited by William Kolbrener and Michal Michelson, 145–63. Burlington, Vt.: Ashgate.

Perry, Ruth. 1984. "Mary Astell's Response to the Enlightenment." In *Women and the Enlightenment*, edited by Margaret Hunt, Margaret Jacob, Phyllis Mack, and Ruth Perry, 13–40. New York: Haworth Press.

———. 1985. "Radical Doubt and the Liberation of Women." *Eighteenth-Century Studies* 18 (4): 472–93.

———. 1986. *The Celebrated Mary Astell: An Early English Feminist*. Chicago: University of Chicago Press.

———. 1990. "Mary Astell and the Feminist Critique of Possessive Individualism." *Eighteenth-Century Studies* 23 (4): 444–57.

Pessin, Andrew. 2010. "Divine Simplicity and the Eternal Truths: Descartes and the Scholastics." *Philosophia* 38 (1): 69–105.

Pickard, Claire. 2007. "'Great in Humilitie': A Consideration of Mary Astell's Poetry." In *Mary Astell: Reason, Gender, Faith*, edited by William Kolbrener and Michal Michelson, 115–26. Burlington, Vt.: Ashgate.

Plantinga, Alvin. 1980. *Does God Have a Nature?* Milwaukee: Marquette University Press.

Plato. 1973. *Phaedrus and Letters VII and VIII*. Translated by Walter Hamilton. Harmondsworth, U.K.: Penguin.

Porter, Jean. 2001. "Virtue Ethics." In *The Cambridge Companion to Christian Ethics*, edited by Robin Gill, 96–111. Cambridge: Cambridge University Press.

Poulain de La Barre, François. (1673) 1989. *The Equality of the Two Sexes*. Translated by Daniel Frankforter and Paul J. Mormon. Lewiston, N.Y.: Edwin Mellen.

———. (1677) 1988. *The Woman as Good as the Man, or The Equality of Both Sexes*. Translated by A. L. MacLean, edited by Gerald M. MacLean. Detroit: Wayne State University Press.

Quintilian, Marcus Fabius. 1989. *Institutio Oratoria*. Translated by H. E. Butler. Vol. 1. Cambridge: Harvard University Press.

Rabieh, Linda R. 2006. *Plato and the Virtue of Courage*. Baltimore: John Hopkins University Press.

Raftery, Deirdre. 1997. "'Whether a Maid May Be a Scholar': Defining the Female Intellectual Sphere [A Serious Proposal: Mary Astell and Education for Women]." In *Women and Learning in English Writing, 1600–1900*, 37–43. Portland: Four Courts.

Reiss, Timothy J. 2000. "Revising Descartes: On Subject and Community." In *Representations of the Self from the Renaissance to Romanticism*, edited by Patrick Coleman, Jayne Lewis, and Jill Kowalik, 16–38. Cambridge: Cambridge University Press.

Rich, Adrienne. 1979. "Toward a Woman-Centered University." In *On Lies, Secrets, and Silence: Selected Prose, 1966–1978*, 125–55. New York: W. W. Norton.

Richardson, Leslie. 2005. "Leaving Her Father's House: Astell, Locke, and Clarissa's Body Politic." *Studies in Eighteenth-Century Culture* 34:151–71. doi:10.1353/sec.2010.0026.

Richardson, Samuel. (1747–48) 1985. *Clarissa, or The History of a Young Lady*. Edited by Angus Ross. London: Penguin.

———. 1986. *The Papers of Samuel Richardson*. The Forster and Dyce Collections. Part 2: Eighteenth-Century Manuscripts. Reels 15 and 16. Brighton, U.K.: Harvester Press.

Scaltsas, Patricia Ward. 1990. "Women as Ends—Women as Means in the Enlightenment." In *Women's Rights and the Rights of Man*, edited by A. J. Arnaud and E. Kingdom, 138–48. Aberdeen: Aberdeen University Press.

Schiebinger, Londa. 1989. *The Mind Has No Sex? Women in the Origins of Modern Science*. Cambridge: Harvard University Press.

Schmaltz, Tad. 2011. "Causa Sui and Created Truth in Descartes." In *The Ultimate Why Question: Why Is There Anything at All Rather Than Nothing Whatsoever?* edited by J. Wippel, 109–24. Washington: Catholic University of America Press.

———. 2014. "Causation and Causal Axioms." In *Descartes' "Meditations": A Critical Guide*, edited by Karen Detflefsen, 82–100. Cambridge: Cambridge University Press.

Schmitter, Amy M. 2005. "The Passionate Intellect: Reading the (Non-)opposition of Reason and Emotions in Descartes." In *Persons and Passions*, edited by Joyce Jenkins, Jennifer Whiting, and Christopher Williams, 48–81. Notre Dame: University of Notre Dame Press.

Schwarz, Joan I. 1999. "Eighteenth-Century Abduction Law and Clarissa." In *Clarissa and Her Readers: New Essays for the Clarissa Project*, edited by Carol Houlihan Flynn and Edward Copeland, 269–308. New York: AMS Press.

Scott, David. 2002. *On Malebranche*. Belmont, Calif.: Wadsworth / Thomson Learning.

Shapiro, Lisa. 1999. "Cartesian Generosity." In *Norms and Modes of Thinking in Descartes*, edited by Tuomo Aho and Mikko Yrjonsuuri, 249–75. Acta Philosophica Fennica 64. Helsinki: Philosophical Society of Finland.

Sharrock, Catherine. 1992. "De-ciphering Women and De-scribing Authority: The Writings of Mary Astell." In *Women, Writing, History, 1640–1740*, edited by Isobel Grundy and Susan Wiseman, 109–24. Athens: University of Georgia Press.

Slote, Michael. 2010. "Justice as a Virtue." In *Stanford Encyclopedia of Philosophy*. Stanford University, 1997–. Accessed May 31, 2010. http://plato.stanford.edu/archives/fall2010/entries/justice-virtue/.

Smith, Florence M. (1916) 1966. *Mary Astell*. New York: AMS Press.

Smith, Hilda L. 1982a. " 'A New Path to Honor': English Feminists, 1690–1710." In *Reason's Disciples: Seventeenth-Century English Feminists*, 115–50. Urbana: University of Illinois Press.

———. 1982b. *Reason's Disciples: Seventeenth-Century English Feminists*. Urbana: University of Illinois Press.

———. 1998. "Introduction: Woman, Intellect, and Politics: Their Intersection in Seventeenth-Century England." In *Women Writers and the Early Modern British Political Tradition*, edited by Hilda L. Smith, 1–14. Cambridge: Cambridge University Press.

———. 2007. " 'Cry Up Liberty': The Political Context for Mary Astell's Feminism." In *Mary Astell: Reason, Gender, Faith*, edited by William Kolbrener and Michal Michelson, 193–204. Burlington, Vt.: Ashgate.

Snow, Nancy E. 2002. "Virtue and the Oppression of Women." In "Feminist Moral Philosophy," special issue, *Canadian Journal of Philosophy* 32:33–61.

Sowaal, Alice. 2005. "Mary Astell." In *Stanford Encyclopedia of Philosophy*. Stanford University, 1997–. Accessed December 12, 2006. http://plato.stanford.edu/archives/fall2005/entries/astell/.

216   References

———. 2007. "Mary Astell's *Serious Proposal*: Mind, Method, and Custom." *Philosophy Compass* 2 (2): 227–43. doi:10.1111/j.1747–9991.2007.00071.x.

———. 2011. "Descartes's Reply to Gassendi: How We Can Know All of God, All at Once, but Still Have More to Learn About Him." *British Journal for the History of Philosophy* 19 (3): 419–49.

Spender, Dale. 1982. *Women of Ideas and What Men Have Done to Them: From Aphra Behn to Adrienne Rich*. Boston: Routledge and Kegan Paul.

Spring, Eileen. 1993. *Law, Land, and Family: Aristocratic Inheritance in England, 1300 to 1800*. Chapel Hill: University of North Carolina Press.

Springborg, Patricia. 1995. "Mary Astell (1666–1731), Critic of Locke." *American Political Science Review* 89 (3): 621–33.

———, ed. 1996. *Astell: Political Writings*. Cambridge: Cambridge University Press.

———, ed. 1997. *A Serious Proposal to the Ladies, Parts I and II*. London: Pickering and Chatto.

———. 2002. Introduction to *A Serious Proposal to the Ladies, Parts I and II*, by Mary Astell, 9–41. Orchard Park, N.Y.: Broadview Press.

———. 2005. *Mary Astell: Theorist of Freedom from Domination*. Cambridge: Cambridge University Press.

Sprint, John. 1699. *The Bride-Womans Counseller: Being a Sermon Preach'd at a Wedding, May the 11th, 1699, at Sherbourn, in Dorsetshire*. London: H. Hills.

Squadrito, Kathleen M. 1991. "Mary Astell." In *A History of Women Philosophers: Modern Women Philosophers, 1600–1900*, edited by Mary Ellen Waithe, 87–99. Dordrecht, Netherlands: Kluwer Academic.

Staves, Susan. 1990. *Married Women's Separate Property in England, 1600–1833*. Cambridge: Harvard University Press.

Stimpson, Catharine. 1986. Preface to *The Celebrated Mary Astell: An Early English Feminist*, by Ruth Perry, xi–xii. Chicago: University of Chicago Press.

Stone, Lawrence, and Jeanne C. Fawtier Stone. 1984. *An Open Elite? England, 1540–1880*. Oxford: Clarendon Press.

Sullivan, Shannon, and Nancy Tuana. 2007. *Race and Epistemologies of Ignorance*. Albany: SUNY Press.

Sutherland, Christine Mason. 1995. "Mary Astell: Reclaiming Rhetorica in the Seventeenth Century." In *Reclaiming Rhetorica: Women in the Rhetorical Tradition*, edited by Andrea Lunsford, 93–116. Pittsburgh: University of Pittsburgh Press.

———. 2005. *The Eloquence of Mary Astell*. Calgary: University of Calgary Press.

Sutherland, Christine Mason, and Rebecca Sutcliffe, eds. 1999. *The Changing Tradition: Women in the History of Rhetoric*. Calgary: University of Calgary Press.

Swan, Beth. 1997. *Fictions of Law: An Investigation of the Law in Eighteenth-Century English Fiction*. Frankfurt am Main: P. Lang.

Syfers, Judy. 1971. *Why I Want a Wife*. Pittsburgh: Know.

Taylor, E. Derek. 2001. "Mary Astell's Ironic Assault on John Locke's Theory of Matter." *Journal of the History of Ideas* 62 (3): 505–22.

———. 2009. *Reason and Religion in "Clarissa": Samuel Richardson and "The Famous Mr. Norris, of Bemerton."* Farnham, U.K.: Ashgate.

Taylor, E. Derek, and Melvyn New, eds. 2005. Introduction to *Mary Astell and John Norris: Letters Concerning the Love of God*, 1–41. Aldershot, U.K.: Ashgate.

Thickstun, Margaret Olofson. 1991. " 'This Was a Woman That Taught': Feminist Scriptural Exegesis in the Seventeenth Century." *Studies in Eighteenth-Century Culture* 21:149–58.

Tietjens Meyers, Diane. 1997. "Personal Autonomy and the Paradox of Feminine Socialization." *Journal of Philosophy* 84:619–28.

Tilmouth, Christopher. 2007. "Generosity and the Utility of the Passions: Cartesian Ethics in Restoration England." *Seventeenth Century* 22 (1): 144–67.

Treatise of Feme Coverts: Or, The Lady's Law. Containing All the Laws and Statutes Relating to Women, *Under Several Heads.* 1732. In the Savoy [London]: Printed by E. and R. Nutt, and R. Gosling. Eighteenth Century Collections Online (CW3324473616).

Trianosky, Gregory. 1990. "What Is Virtue Ethics All About?" *American Philosophical Quarterly* 27 (4): 335–44.

Trill, Suzanne, Kate Chedgzoy, and Melanie Osborne, eds. 1997. *Lay By Your Needles Ladies, Take the Pen: Writing Women in England, 1500–1700.* London: Arnold.

Truelove, Alison. 2001. "Commanding Communications: The Fifteenth-Century Letters of the Stonor Women." In *Early Modern Women's Letter Writing, 1450–1700,* edited by James Daybell, 42–58. Basingstoke, U.K.: Palgrave.

Tuana, Nancy. 1992. *Women and the History of Philosophy.* St. Paul: Paragon House.

———. 2004. "Coming to Understand: Orgasm and the Epistemology of Ignorance." *Hypatia* 19 (1): 194–232.

Van der Kolk, Bessel A., and Alexander C. McFarlane. 2007. "The Black Hole of Trauma." In *Traumatic Stress: The Effects of Overwhelming Experience on Mind, Body, and Society,* edited by Bessel A. van der Kolk, Alexander C. McFarlane, and Lars Weisaeth, 3–23. New York: Guilford Press.

Van der Kolk, Bessel A., Alexander C. McFarlane, and Lars Weisaeth, eds. 2007. *Traumatic Stress: The Effects of Overwhelming Experience on Mind, Body, and Society.* New York: Guilford Press.

Van der Kolk, Bessel A., Lars Weisaeth, and Onno van der Hart. 2007. "History of Trauma in Psychiatry." In *Traumatic Stress: The Effects of Overwhelming Experience on Mind, Body, and Society,* edited by Bessel A. van der Kolk, Alexander C. McFarlane, and Lars Weisaeth, 47–76. New York: Guilford Press.

Walski, Gregory. 2003. "The Cartesian God and the Eternal Truths." In *Oxford Studies in Early Modern Philosophy,* edited by Daniel Garber and Steven Nadler, 1:23–44. Oxford: Oxford University Press.

Weiss, Penny A. 2004. "Mary Astell: Including Women's Voices in Political Theory." *Hypatia* 19 (3): 63–84.

———. 2009. *Canon Fodder: Historical Women Political Thinkers.* University Park: Pennsylvania State University Press.

Weiss, Penny A., and Loretta Kensinger. 2007. "Digging for Gold(man): What We Found." With Berenice Carroll. In *Feminist Interpretations of Emma Goldman,* edited by Penny A. Weiss and Loretta Kensinger, 3–18. University Park: Pennsylvania State University Press.

Wertheimer, Molly Meijer. 1997. *Listening to Their Voices: The Rhetorical Activities of Historical Women.* Columbia: University of South Carolina Press.

Wigelsworth, Jeffrey R. 2009. *Deism in Enlightenment England: Theology, Politics, and Newtonian Public Science.* Manchester: Manchester University Press.

Wilde, Cornelia. 2012. *Friendship, Love, and Letters: Ideals and Practices of Seraphic Friendship in Seventeenth-Century England.* Heidelberg: Universitatsverlag.

Wilson, Catherine. 2004. "Love of God and Love of Creatures: The Masham-Astell Debate." *History of Philosophy Quarterly* 21 (3): 281–98.

Woolf, Virginia. 1938. *Three Guineas.* New York: Harcourt Brace Jovanovich.

———. 2005. *Three Guineas.* Edited by Mark Hussey. London: Harcourt.

Zomchick, John P. 1993. *Family and the Law in Eighteenth-Century Fiction: The Public Conscience in the Private Sphere.* Cambridge: Cambridge University Press.

Zook, Malinda. 2007. "Religious Nonconformity and the Problem of Dissent in the Works of Aphra Behn and Mary Astell." In *Mary Astell: Reason, Gender, Faith,* edited by William Kolbrener and Michal Michelson, 99–113. Burlington, Vt.: Ashgate.

Contributors

Kathleen A. Ahearn is Lecturer in English at John Carroll University. Her publications on Astell and Cavendish have appeared in the journals *Appositions* and *Women's Writing*. She is currently working on a project that ties confession and male mentorship to Astell's style of philosophizing.

Jacqueline Broad is Australian Research Council Future Fellow in Philosophy at Monash University. She recently completed a modernized edition of Astell's *The Christian Religion, as Profess'd by a Daughter of the Church of England* (2013) and a monograph entitled *The Philosophy of Mary Astell* (2015). Her other publications include *Women Philosophers of the Seventeenth Century* (2002) and *A History of Women's Political Thought in Europe, 1400–1700* (coauthored with Karen Green, 2009). She has written numerous articles on Astell, Cavendish, van Helmont, Glanvill, Christine de Pizan, Malebranche, Masham, Locke, and Margaret Fell, which have been published in numerous volumes and in the journals *Studies in History and Philosophy of Science*, *Parergon*, *Journal of the History of Ideas*, *Eighteenth-Century Thought*, *Stanford Encyclopedia of Philosophy*, and *British Journal for the History of Philosophy*.

Karen Detlefsen is Associate Professor of Philosophy and Education at the University of Pennsylvania. She is the editor of *Descartes' Meditations: A Critical Guide* (2012). Her articles on Descartes, du Châtelet, Cavendish, Hobbes, Haller, Wolff, and Malebranche have been published in *Philosophy Compass*, *Archiv für Geschichte der Philosophie*, *Oxford Studies in Early Modern Philosophy*, *Perspectives on Science*, and volumes by Kluwer, Cambridge, and the Pennsylvania State University Press.

Susan Paterson Glover is Associate Professor of English at Laurentian University. Her primary area of research is the eighteenth-century English novel, with a particular interest in women and the law. She has published articles in *Ideas, Aesthetics, and Inquiries* and *Eighteenth-Century Fiction*, as well as in a volume by Wiley-Blackwell. She is also the author of *Engendering Legitimacy: Law, Property, and Early Eighteenth-Century Fiction* (2006) and is preparing an edition of Sarah Chapone's *The Hardships of the English Laws in Relation to Wives* (1735).

220   Contributors

Elisabeth Hedrick Moser received her doctorate in English at Saint Louis University, where she is now an instructor. Her dissertation, "Sustaining Practices: Autobiographical Responses to World War II in Stein, Woolf, and Doolittle," focuses on the civilian experience of war trauma through the angle of autobiography and maps out a paradigm for a dialectical relationship between acute trauma theory and political perceptions of violence. She has given presentations on writers and intellectuals such as Marilynne Robinson, Sigmund Freud, Gertrude Stein, and Lorine Niedecker.

Marcy P. Lascano is Associate Professor of Philosophy at California State University, Long Beach. She has published on Leibniz, Anne Conway, Damaris Masham, Émilie du Châtelet, and Princess Elisabeth of Bohemia and on cosmological arguments in *Philosophy Compass, Modern Schoolman, British Journal for the History of Philosophy, Leibniz Review,* and volumes published by Cambridge, Springer, and Routledge. She has coedited (with Eileen O'Neill) *Feminist History of Philosophy: The Recovery and Evaluation of Women's Philosophical Thought* (forthcoming, 2016).

Alice Sowaal is Associate Professor of Philosophy at San Francisco State University. She has published articles on Descartes and Astell in the *British Journal for the History of Philosophy, Canadian Journal of Philosophy, Philosophy Compass,* and *Stanford Encyclopedia of Philosophy,* as well as in volumes published by Blackwell and Cambridge.

Christine Mason Sutherland is the author of *The Eloquence of Mary Astell* (2005), as well as the coeditor (with Rebecca Sutcliffe) of *The Changing Tradition: Women in the History of Rhetoric* (1999) and (with Beverly Matson Rasporich) *Woman as Artist: Papers in Honour of Marsha Hanen* (1993). More recently, she coedited (with George Melnyk) *The Art of University Teaching* (2011). Her writing on the rhetoric of St. Augustine, on the early women writers Margaret Cavendish, Margaret Fell, and Mary Astell, and on feminist historiography has been published in several other collections. She has also published in the journals *Rhetorica, Rhetoric Society Quarterly,* and *Rhetor.*

Penny A. Weiss is Chair of Women's and Gender Studies and Professor of Political Science at Saint Louis University. She has authored *Gendered Community: Rousseau, Sex, and Politics* (1993), *Conversations with Feminism: Political Theory and Practice* (1998), and *Canon Fodder: Historical Women Political Thinkers* (2009), and coedited *Feminism and Community* (1995) and *Feminist Interpretations of Emma Goldman* (2007). In addition, she has written a number of book chapters and has published articles in the *Journal of Political Philosophy, Hypatia: A Journal of Feminist Philosophy, Feminist Teacher, Polity,* and *Political Theory.*

Index

Achinstein, Sharon, 50
Acworth, Richard, 38
Addams, Jane, 1
admiration, 19, 23–24, 30n10, 46, 124, 200
Ahearn, Kathleen, 9, 13–14, 200, 202
Allen, Amy, 129
Apetrei, Sarah, 110n31
Arendt, Hannah, 1, 129
Aristotle
    on character friendship, 27, 31
    influence of, 7, 8, 9
    on male domination, 31
    magnaminity, 70n3
    Nicomachean Ethics, 27
    on practical wisdom, 28
    rhetoric, 154, 156, 163, 164, 187n13
    virtue tradition and, 20
Arnauld, Antoine, 5, 97–98, 155, 170
Astell, Mary
    on access to supreme Good, 95
    as analyst of power, 10, chapter 8
    antifeminist views of, 83
    Bart'lemy Fair or an Enquiry After Wit, 4
    Cartesianism of, 70n5, 75–76, 80, 89, 164, 202
    Christian perspective of, 20, 160
    Cicero's influence on, 159–60
    conception of liberty, 55n11. *See also* will
    contemporary influences on, 155
    contradictions in views of, 108n1
    contribution to history of education, 11
    correspondence of, 3–4, 33n14, 37, 53, 94, 96, 110n31, 165–66
    Descartes' influence on, 33n11, 42, 43, 44, 157–58, 173–74
    educational theory of, 92n9, 191

education in rationalist philosophy, 191
as "enthusiast," 72n18
embodiment, views of, 23, 40–41, 117–19
epistemology and method of, 77, 79
A Fair Way with the Dissenters and Their Patrons, 4
on female monastery, 124, 127n13
in history of feminism, place of, 12–13, 75, 190–91, 201, 204
idea of academy, 53, 56n12
influence of, 4, 8, 15, 95–96, 108, 110n27
interpretations of works of, 14–15, 189–90
legacies, 3, 11–14
Letters Concerning the Love of God, 35
Moderation Truly Stated, 4
moral philosophy of, 7, 19–20, 30
More's influence on, 33n11
observation on minds and bodies, 39–40
pamphlets in defense of Anglicanism, 33n2
personal relationships, 4, 115
philosophical theology of, 168–69, 202–3
in philosophical tradition, 3, 5, 6, 10
poetry of, 92n15
as polemicist, 3, 38, 166
as predecessor of modern feminism, 112–13, 203
principles of arguments of, 173–74
on purpose of philosophy, 20
relatives of, 109n13
religious views, 70n1, 93–94, 126n3
in rhetorical tradition, 6–7, chapter 9
rules for thinking, 158
scepticism of men's ability to change, 90
scholarship on, 4–5
six rules of logic, 156–58

222   Index

Astell, Mary (*continued*)
  sources of information of life of, 105
  on status quo, critique of, 133, 141, 148–49,
    150, 151, 204
  on status quo, acceptance and submission to,
    30, 56, 84
  theory of virtue, 30–31
  theory of vice. *See* vice
  training as rhetorician, 166
  on true greatness, 72n20
  use of term "generosity" by, 70n3. *See also*
    generosity
  use of term "science" by, 76–77, 83, 91n6
  use of term "self-existence" with respect to
    God by, 169
  utopian vision of female society, 124–25
  as virtue theorist, 199
  on women's freedom, 22, 92n16. *See also* will
  writing on marriage, 104–5, 109n6
Astell, Ralph, 191
Atherton, Margaret, 6
Augustine, Saint, Bishop of Hippo, 164
authority
  concept of, 141–42
  of men over women, 148
  resistance to, 147, 203
autonomy. *See also* will
  conception of, 86–87
  theory of relational, 9, 12, 88–91, 204

Bacon, Francis, 135, 156
Ballard, George, 105, 106, 108, 110n32
Barclay, Linda, 16
Barksdale, Clement, 5
*Baron and Feme: A Treatise of the Common Law
  Concerning Husbands and Wives*, 97
Baumlin, Tita, 163
Beauvoir, Simone de, 1, 129
Bigelow, John, 16
Blackstone, William, 109n15
Bolton, Martha, 168
Boyle, Deborah, 67, 72n22
Broad, Jacqueline
  on Astell's Cartesian epistemology, 80
  on Astell's conception of liberty, 55n11
  on Astell's feminism, 13
  on Astell's passion for love, 9
  on Astell's refrain against custom, 78
  on Astell's theory of virtue, 199
  on Descartes's philosophy, 37
  interpretation of Astell's ethics, 84–85
  "Mary Astell and the Virtues," 7

  on wife's freedom, 110n24
  on women's intermix with their bodies, 40
Brown, Deborah, 41, 71n3
Bryson, Cynthia, 23, 128–29
Butler, Melissa, 91n1

Cartesian containment principle, 171
Cartesian generosity, 47, 48, 53
Cartesian self-esteem, 53, 61
Caruth, Cathy, 113, 127n11, 204
Chapone, John, 98, 110n29, 194
Chapone, Sarah
  Astell's influence on, 8, 104, 106
  on changes of status of women in marriage,
    103, 104
  circle of friends, 98
  correspondence of, 106–7
  on Deism, 104
  *The Hardships of the English Laws in Relation
    to Wives*, 96, 98–99, 104
  on ignorance of young women, 102
  on injustices in marriage, 100, 101, 103
  life of, 96, 98
  on obligations of men and women, 104
  polemic with Richardson, 107
  posthumous works, 106
  on submission to authority, 107
Christian Religion, The (Astell)
  on definition of freedom, 22. *See also* will
  editions, 33n4, 168
  on existence and nature of God, 170, 171, 186
  on extension of God, 185
  on importance of moral education, 21
  polemic with Locke, 185
  structure of, 20
  theory of virtue, 18
  on understanding of God, 170
  on women's education, 161–62
  on women's virtues, 25
Chudleigh, Lady Mary, 99, 167
Cicero
  on characteristics of sermo, 7, 154
  De Officiis, 158
  letter-writing of, 162
  on rhetoric, 158–59
  on virtues, 20
civility, 135–36
Clarissa (Richardson), 95, 106, 109n5, 110n30
Clarke, Norma, 105, 108
Clarke, Samuel, 187n7
Coke, Edward, 97
Collins, Anthony, 104

community
   intellectual, 124
   and cultivation of self-esteem, 53
   as vital aspect for recovery from trauma, 123, 192
Cooper, Anthony Ashley, 4, 5
consciousness raising, 32–33
courage, virtue of, 19, 20, 21, 25–27, 29, 30, 31–32
courtship, 52, 68
Coventry, Ann, 26, 33n13
credibility, 146
Cudworth, Ralph, 38, 59, 155
custom, 21, 22, 26, 32, 39, 43, 60, 61, 70n4, 94, 96, 103, 108n1, 132, 134, 143, 148, 150, 197, 198
customs, 78, 79, 82, 92n13, 190, 194

Daly, Mary, 1
D'Avenant, William, Sir, 5
Defoe, Daniel, 4, 5
deism, 110n22
Delany, Mary, 96, 98, 99, 106, 110n29
Delany, Patrick, 104, 110n21
Descartes, René
   Discourse on the Method, 61, 98
   on dualism of soul and body, 76, 183, 201
   on error and sin, 187n11
   on eternal truth, 187n12
   on existence of God, 171, 175, 187n3, 187n13
   failure to recognize special conditions of women's life, 91n3
   on free will, 43
   on generosity, 25, 33n12, 45–46, 47, 70n3
   influence of, 7, 8, 9, 12, 44, 155, 157–58, 202
   Jesuit education of, 54
   Method of doubt, 61
   method for judging, 45
   moral philosophy of, 37
   on omnipotence of God, 183
   on passion, 42, 43
   Passions of the Soul, 25, 41–42, 55n6, 61
   philosophical scholarship on, 189
   on power of God, 175–76
   on pride, 48
   on principles of logic, 156
   Principles of Philosophy, 178
   Rules for the Direction of the Mind, 170
   on selfcausation of God, 175
   on self-mastery, 48
   on soul, 41–42
   taxonomy of passions, 46

theory of self-esteem, 44, 48, 61
   on tranquility, 44
   on virtue and happiness, 36
   on wonder, 46, 47
Detlefsen, Karen, 9, 12, 193, 196, 197, 202, 204
Dewes, Ann Granville, 110n29
domestic power structures, 111–12. *See also* power
dominance
   mechanisms of, 152n4
   of men, 136
Drake, Judith, 5, 106
Duran, Jane, 6
duty
   ethics of, 20
   to God, 90, 200–201

education
   custom and, 78
   inequality in, 132, 134
   power and, 132, 133–34
   rational capacity and, 191
   in religious retreat, 79
   women's need for, 135, 191
Elisabeth, Princess of Bohemia, 53, 55n6
Elizabeth I, Queen of England, 154
Ellenzweig, Sarah, 6
Elstob, Elizabeth, 4, 105, 167
embodiment. *See* Astell, and embodiment
Enloe, Cynthia, 151, 152
equality and inequality, 49, 53, 75, 81, 82, 90, 91, 92n5, 94, 96, 103, 104, 108n2, 130, 132–34, 136–38, 140, 141, 142, 144, 147, 149, 150, 151, 170, 196–97
esteem. *See* Astell, and esteem
eternal damnation, 182
ethos, 163
evil, nature of, 182–83
Ezell, Margaret, 100

Fall, biblical, 22, 58, 59, 62, 63, 67, 71n12, 71n14, 80, 81, 96, 103, 107, 109n8, 190, 191, 194, 198. *See also* prelapsarian
female academy. *See* Religious Retirement
feme covert (married woman), 99, 104, 109n7
feminism
   account of freedom, 87. *See also* will
   Astell and, 201–5
   concept of autonomy, 86
   concept of power, 129
   Descartes's philosophy and, 201–2
   on eradication of fascism, 126n2

feminism (*continued*)
  evolution of, 74–75
  history of theory of, 128–29
  in seventeenth century, 74
  studies of, 2, 91n1
  on subordination of women, 30–31
  theory of freedom in, 85–86
Foucault fatigue, 10, 130
Freedom. *See also* will
  definition of, 22
  feminist theory of, 85–86, 87
  rationality and, 197, 198
  women and, 22, 92n16
Fricker, Miranda, 10, 115–16, 145, 204
Friedan, Betty, 136
Friedman, Marilyn, 32, 86, 204
friendship, 7, 9, 13–15, 18, 19, 21, 24, 27–29,
  31, 32, 33n16, 39, 51–53, 79, 87–90, 121,
  190–96, 199–201

Garrett, Don, 168
General Human Nature Question, 59, 61, 67,
  68, 70
generosity
  acquisition of, 32
  Astell's view of, 45–46, 63–68, 71n14,
  72–73n22
  Cartesian, 33n12, 33n13, 55n8, 70n3, 71n17,
  46, 47, 53
  components of, 66
  concept of, 25, 55n8
  corruption of, 64, 66
  Descartes and, 72n17
  as desire, 65–66
  esteem and, 32, 36, 48
  knowledge and, 70, 71n14
  ontological status of, 65
  and pride, 48, 68
  as principle of understanding, 65
  and submission to status quo, 30
  as a virtue, 21, 24, 31, 45
Gill, Michael, 58
Glover, Susan, 8, 197
God
  arguments for existence of, 169, 170–71,
  174–75, 186, 186n2, 187n13
  attributes of, 177–78, 179–83
  debates on nature of, 12, 169, 178, 186
  duty to, 90, 200–201
  evil as offensive to, 181
  extension of, 185
  glory of, 66, 181
  goodness of, 50, 179–80

  justice of, 182
  kindness of, 51
  knowledge of nature of, 177–79
  notion of self-existence of, 169, 171, 172–73,
  175
  omnipotence of, 183, 184
  as origin of rationality, 198
  people's relationships with, 40, 63, 71n10–11,
  71n13
  perfections of, 174, 176
  power of, 175–76, 184–85
  tripartite nature of, 183–84
  will of, 62
Goldie, Mark, 55n10
Goldman, Emma, 1
Granville, Bernard, 109n13
Granville, George, 109n13
Green, Karen, 16, 110n24
Green, V. H. H., 99
Greenberg, Lynne A., 97
grief, cause of, 39

Halifax, George Savile, Marquis of, 5
happiness, 21, 37, 198
Hastings, Lady Elizabeth, 4
Hedrick Moser, Elisabeth, 10, 192, 195, 202, 203
Herman, Judith
  on desire for total control, 114
  on dialectic of trauma, 127n8
  on effects of trauma, 120–21
  on living in two simultaneous realities,
  127n10
  on psychological trauma, 116–17
  on recreation of ideal self, 124
  on recurring trauma, 113, 120
  on symptoms of trauma, 118
  theory of recovery, 121, 123–24
Hickes, George, 110n31
Hill, Bridget, 5
Hirschmann, Nancy, 86
Hoagland, Sarah Lucia, 126n6
Hobbes, Thomas, 5, 6, 58, 104, 114, 115
Hopkins, Anna, 106, 109n14
human nature
  Calvinists' view of, 58
  claim about goodness of, 67–68
  discussions of, 13, 14
  general question of, 61–62, 70
  Hobbes's view of, 58
  in philosophical studies of, 57
  unsexed, 78. *See also* General Human Nature
  Question
  Woman's Human Nature Question

Human Nature Question, 58–59
humble person, 67
Hursthouse, Rosalind, 27

ignorance, 64, 71n7, 143, 144

Jaggar, Alison, 30, 204
Johns, Alessa, 124
Johnson, Allan, 139
Jones, Catherine, 4

Kinnaird, Joan K., 92n9, 92n12
Kirkham, Damaris, 98
Kirkham, Sarah, 98
knowledge
    criticism of advantage of, 146
    generosity and, 70, 71n14
    of God's nature, 177–79
    of good and evil, 45
    power and, 177
    women and practical, 28

LaCapra, Dominick, 122
Lamy, Bernard, 7, 155, 160
Lascano, Marcy, 8, 12, 193, 197, 200, 202
Laws Resolutions of Womens Rights, The, 97,
    109n10
legacies, 3
Leibniz, G. W., 8
Letters Concerning the Love of God (Astell), 155
liberty. *See* will
Lister, Andrew, 90, 92n12
Littleton, Thomas, 97
locations, 3
Locke, John
    casual principle of, 171, 187n3
    on existence of God, 171, 187n5
    on extension of God, 185
    on human freedom, 49
    impact of ideas of, 5, 8, 55n10, 138, 155
    Two Treatises, 11
logic
    instruction in, 162
    vs. rhetoric, 155–56
    rules of, 156–58
Love, 9, 23, 27, 29, 36–40, 46–48, 53, 55n1, 68,
    72n9, 72n19, 72n22, 85, 87, 88, 94, 119,
    120, 153, 160, 169, 170, 178, 193, 196, 199

Mainardi, Pat, 137
Malebranche, Nicholas
    on infinite perfection, 187n4
    influence of, 5, 7, 8, 21, 38

Search After Truth, 22
    on self-existence of God, 41
    on women's brain, 55n9
marriage
    Astell's writing on, 104–5, 109n6
    behaviour in, 82, 84
    characteristic of good, 88–89
    characteristic of happy, 82, 89–90, 195–6
    characteristic of unhappy, 195–96
    covenants in, 147
    cruelty of husbands, 101–2
    custom and, 82
    deprivation of women in, 119–20
    as divine institution, 81–82, 83–84, 92n12,
        194, 195
    duties in, 194
    as female slavery, 114
    husband's role in, 81
    power structure of, 82, 111, 112, 137, 194
    tyranny in, 114
    wife's role in, 81, 82–83
    women's education prior, 84
    women's status in, 92n11, 96
Masham, Damaris, 3, 4, 55n4, 166
Mazarin, Hortense Mancini, duchesse de, 94,
    112
McCrystal, John, 91n7
McFarlane, 121
men
    attitude to women, 119, 144–45
    domination of, 136
    power of, 138, 139
    pseudo competence of, 144
    self-promotion of, 163
    true interests of, 134
    tyrannical, 123
Meyers, Diana Tietjens, 86
Mintz, Samuel, 38
misogyny, 139
Montagu, Mary Wortley, Lady, 4
More, Henry
    An Antidote Against Atheism, 55n2
    on existence of God, 55n2
    on generosity, 25
    The Immortality of the Soul, 40
    influence of, 7, 9, 38, 59
    on interaction of minds and bodies, 40
Morgan-Curtis, Samantha, 140
Mulso, Hester, 106, 107

New, Melvyn, 94
Nicole, Pierre, 98, 155, 170
Normore, Calvin, 41

Norris, John
    correspondence with Astell, 3, 35, 37–38,
        165–66
    criticism of Astell's reasoning, 40–41
    dualism of, 38
    on human freedom, 21–22
    on infinite perfection, 187n4
    influence of, 7, 8, 9, 94, 98, 155
    Practical Discourses, 22, 34n19, 94
    as religious enthusiast, 55n4
    Treatise Concerning Christian Prudence, 28,
        34n19

Oakley, Justin, 16
occasionalism, theory of, 38, 55n3
O'Neill, Eileen, 6
Owen, James, 4

Passions. *See also* admiration, courage, generos-
        ity, love, wonder
    conception of, 41–42, 68, 200
    effect on will, 29, 44
    management of, 36, 42–8, 55n7, 62, 63, 64,
        77, 80, 85, 89, 90, 102–3, 109n17
    and moral action, 21, 31
    taxonomy of, 46
    types of, 200
    as virtue, 23–24, 72n17, 200
patriarchy
    Astell's critique of, 13, 140
    concept of, 137–38
    cruelty of, 138
    distribution of power in, 138–39
    misogyny as part of, 139
    resistance to, 147
    sexual inequality in, 142
    status of women in, 139, 143
    study of, 14
    as tyranny, 138
    as unjust social system, 138
Paul, the Apostle, Saint, 103, 165, 197
perfection
    of creatures, 172
    dispersion of, 174–75
    of God, 172
    idea of, 172, 176–77
    infinite, 187n4
    of rational human being, 177, 181, 183
    of universe, 180
Perry, Ruth, 4, 98, 108n2, 109n14, 164
philosophy
    history of, 189
    moral traditions in, 20

Pickard, Claire, 72n20, 92n15
Plato, 6, 8, 20, 154, 164, 180
Poullain de la Barre, François, 108n2, 155, 164
power
    Astell's analysis of, 131, 132–33, 137, 151–52
    causes and effects of unequal, 143, 150
    characteristics of, 143
    civility and, 135–36
    credibility and, 146
    effects of unequal, 132, 136, 140
    in feminist theory, concept of, 129, 130
    Foucault on, 130
    knowledge and, 146
    in marriage, structure of, 82, 111, 137, 194
    of men, 138, 139
    in patriarchy, distribution of, 138–39
    resistance to, 151
    systems of political, 143
    of the weak, 133. *See also* domestic power
        structures
prejudice, 26, 32, 36, 37, 116, 145, 150, 156, 204.
        See also Woman's Defective Nature Preju-
        dice
pre- and postlapsarian state of human beings,
        59, 62–65, 67, 68, 70, 71n11, 96, 104 71n9.
        See also biblical Fall
pride
    in courtship, 68
    Descartes on, 48
    moral decline into, 64
    origin of, 66
    rhetoric and, 160
    vs. virtue of humility, 66
proud person, 67
prudence and imprudence, 17, 18, 28–30,
        34n19, 60, 69
PTSD (Post-Traumatic Stress Disorder), 112,
        127nn8–9. *See also* trauma

Quintilian, 154, 160

Rabieh, Linda R., 31
Ramus, Petrus, 155
Rand, Ayn, 1
rationality, 64–65, 77, 78, 198–99
Rawlins, Thomas, 106
recovery
    safety as goal, 121–22
    stages of, 121–23
    theory of, 121
    from trauma, 123, 124
Reflections. See Some Reflections upon Marriage
        (Astell)

Reiss, Timothy, 53
Religious Retirement retreat, 79, 124, 133, 192, 193–94, 199
resistance
limits of, 150
to male authority, 147, 148
objects of, 150
to oppression, 203
to patriarchy, 147
to power, 151
requirements for, 149
tactics of, 147–48
as work, 150
rhetoric
classical and Christian views on, 160
ethos in, 163
forms of, 158–59
instruction in, 161
letter-writing and women's, 162
vs. logic, 155–56
love as guiding principle of, 160
origin of tradition of, 154
pride and, 160
sermon as form of, 158, 159
training in, 153, 192–93
women exclusion from, 154
Rich, Adrienne, 152n2
Richardson, Leslie, 109n5
Richardson, Samuel, 95, 96, 106, 107
ruel, definition of, 152n1

salvation, 63–64, 71n13, 71n14, 93, 121
Scaltsas, Patricia Ward, 92n9
Schmaltz, Tad, 168
Schurman, Anna Maria, 5
science
vs. faith, 77
vs. opinion, 76
Scudéry, Madeleine de, 155
self, 204
self-esteem
account of, 35–36, 41, 43, 46, 48, 50, 53, 51, 61, 67, 68, 73n22, 192
cultivation of, 50–53
vs. self-love, 36
of women, 73n22, 49
wonder and, 47
self-love, 36, 48, 55n1. See also love
self-possession, 49
Serious Proposal to the Ladies, A (Astell)
on concept of authority, 142
on exclusion of women from speaking in Parliament, 162

on idea of Religious Retirement, 79, 133, 124, 192, 193
on nature and existence of God, 170, 171, 178–79, 186
optimistic tone of, 54
on physical appearance of women, 140
on primary task of life, 95
psychological theory of women's behavior, 59
publication of, 16, 35, 149
refrains against custom, 78
on resistance, 148
on societal prejudices against women, 126n4
on tripartite nature of God, 183–84
on will and passion, 102
on women's education, 21, 124, 155
on women's strive to perfection, 67, 72n21
on women's virtue, 25
sermo (conversation), 159
Shaftesbury, Earl of. See Cooper, Anthony Ashley
Shapiro, Lisa, 32, 45, 46, 47
Smith, Florence, 4, 11
Smith, Hilda, 110n25
Smith, John, 59
Snow, Nancy, 48, 51
Some Reflections upon Marriage (Astell)
characteristics of, 108, 111
on condition of ill-married woman, 114
critique of marriage, 11
on difference between friend and enemy, 147
on distinction between women and wives, 165
on healing from trauma, 125
on instruction in rhetoric, 161
intended audience of, 166
optimistic tone of, 54, 80
on origin of men's authority, 165
publication of, 35, 94, 97, 98
on resistance, 148
as response to scandal with duchess of Mazarin, 112
on tyrannized woman, 116
on women's rationality, 164
soul, 41–42, 185
Sowaal, Alice
on Astell's legacy, 13
on Astell's theory of mind, 91n2
on Astell's view of human nature, 7
on Astell's view of prejudice, 126n5
on Astell's view of customs and women's will, 92n14
on Astell's view of judgement, 198
on women's nature, 49

228   Index

Sparrow, Rob, 16
speech
    power of, 158
    relationship with, 160
Spender, Dale, 137–38
Springborg, Patricia, 4, 5, 11, 17, 55n9, 92n10
Squadrito, Kathleen M., 92n10
Stanton, Elizabeth Cady, 149
Stimpson, Catharine, 23
Stoljar, Natalie, 86
suffering, benefits of, 181–82
Sutherland, Christine Mason, 6, 97, 192–93,
    202
swearing the peace against another, 109n15
Syfers, Judy, 137

Taylor, E. Derek, 94, 109n5
Tenures (Littleton), 97
testimonial injustice, 10, 115–16, 204
Thaddeus, Janice, 109n14
Thomas Aquinas, 8, 41, 180
Three Guineas (Wolfe), 126n2
Tindal, Matthew, 104
Toland, John, 104
"To the Ladies" (Chudleigh), 99–100
tranquility, 44
trauma
    characteristic of, 127n8
    definition of, 113
    effects of, 119, 120–21, 192
    experience of, 112
    healing process from, 127n11
    occurrence of repeated, 113
    psychological, 116–17
    recovery from, 121–23, 125–26
    reflections of, 116–20
    structure of, 113–15
    symptoms of, 117, 118, 127n8, 127n9. See also
        PTSD (Post-Traumatic Stress Disorder)
Trauma: Explorations in Memory (Caruth), 113
Treatise of Feme Coverts: Or, The Lady's Law,
    97
tyranny, 114, 143

understanding, 62, 64, 198
unhappiness, 136–37

Van der Kolk, Bessel A., 121, 125, 126, 127n8
vanity, 64, 66
vice, 64, 68–69, 71n12, 200
violence, 112–13, 114
virtue

development of, 200
    in early modern period, 20
    of friendship, 27–28
    of generosity and courage, 25–27
    origin of tradition of, 21, 200
    return from vice to, 71n12
    theory of, 19
    of women, 140–41
virtue ethics, 20, 21, 33n5
Voss, Stephen, 47

Weiss, Penny
    analysis of Astell's ideas, 6, 10, 114
    on Astell's legacy, 13, 16
    on male superiority, 115
    on resistance to oppression, 203
    on women's deception, 192
Wesley, Charles, 96
Wesley, John, 96, 98
Whichcote, Benjamin, 59
Whiston, William, 103
Wigelsworth, Jeffrey R., 110n22
will, human
    in Astell's philosophy, 22, 24, 28, 29, 37, 39,
        40, 41, 43, 44, 46, 47, 51, 53, 55n11, 59, 60,
        61–67, 80, 81, 85, 92n14, 109n17, 198,
    in Chapone, 102–3, 106–7
    in Descartes's philosophy, 32, 42–43, 44,
        70n5, 72n17
    in Norris's philosophy, 22, 55n1
wives
    disadvantage of estate of, 99–100
    freedom and lack of freedom of, 81, 110n24.
        See also will
    image of ideal, 117
    injustices toward, 96, 99, 100, 101, 117, 161,
        194
    self-esteem of, 37
    social status of, 75, 83, 100–101, 194
    submission of, 81, 96, 105, 107, 112, 139, 165,
        194, 196
    vs. women, 82, 165, 194
Wollstonecraft, Mary, 1, 129
Woman's Defective Nature Prejudice, 49, 50,
    53, 60, 61, 116, 126n5, 192, 200
Woman's Human Nature Question, 13, 59,
    60–61, 68, 70
women
    acquisition of knowledge by, 45, 146
    affliction of, 122
    assumption of ignorance of, 144, 145
    in courtship, 68–69

danger of relationships outside friendship, 52
defective nature of, 49
duties of, 20, 91–92n8
early studies on issues of, 97
emergence in public sphere, 105
escape from tyranny, 125–27n6
exclusion from public debate, 154, 162
feeling of indebtedness, 68–69
feeling of love, 24
feeling of thought, 93
friendship and, 27, 32, 193
as God's Workmanship, 37, 49–50
guilt of vanity, 123
happiness of, 21, 37
idea of intellectual community of, 124–25
identity, 50
inconstancy and lasciviousness of, 33n1
insecurity of, 114, 115, 117
intellectual sacrifice of, 144
internalization of, 140
legal independence of, 109n16
limits of capacities of, 17, 192
in marriage, 101, 109n6, 114–15, 119–20, 125,
   126n6
men's domination over, 119, 144–45
obedience of, 50–51
obligations to God, 103
passion of admiration, 23
in patriarchy, 139, 143
as potential scholars, 162
preparation for adulthood, 94
prudent conduct of, 17–18, 28–30

rationality of, 83, 164, 165, 199
resistance to male authority, 147
role in children's education, 78, 101
in sectarian movements, 110n25
self-care, 51
self-esteem, 35–36, 53
social status of, 100, 118–19, 192
strive for perfection, 67, 72n21
subordination of, 30–31, 136, 149, 152n3
suffering of, 203
training in rhetoric, 153, 161, 162
traumatic experience of, 120, 121–23, 125,
   192
unhappiness of, 136–37
vices of, 48, 68–69, 126n5
virtues of, 25, 26, 29–30, 141–42
weakness of ethos of, 163–64
women's education
   learning style, 53–54
   mistakes of, 17
   moral improvement and, 191
   need of special kind of, 191
   prior to marriage, 84
   religious retirement and, 79, 96, 124
   social inequality and, 135, 152n2
   Virginia Woolf on, 133
wonder, 33n10, 36, 46, 47
Woolf, Virginia, 126n2, 133, 141
Woolley, Hannah, 5
writing
   in form of letters, 162
   relationship with speech, 160